Agenda Setting in the U.S. Senate

This book proposes a new theory of Senate agenda setting that reconciles a divide in the literature between the conventional wisdom – according to which party power is mostly, if not completely, undermined by Senate procedures and norms – and the apparent partisan bias in Senate decisions noted in recent empirical studies. Chris Den Hartog and Nathan W. Monroe's theory revolves around a "costly-consideration" framework for thinking about agenda setting, where moving proposals forward through the legislative process is seen as requiring scarce resources. To establish that the majority party pays lower agenda consideration costs as a result of various procedural advantages, a number of the chapters in this volume examine partisan influence at several stages of the legislative process, including committee reports, filibusters and cloture, floor scheduling, and floor amendments. Not only do the results strongly support the book's theoretical assumption and key hypotheses, but they shed new light on virtually every major step in the Senate's legislative process.

Chris Den Hartog is an assistant professor of political science at California Polytechnic State University. He has published articles and chapters about the legislative process in Congress, its evolution, and its effects on congressional policy making. Professor Den Hartog's work includes studies of the 19th-century House of Representatives and the contemporary House and Senate.

Nathan W. Monroe is an assistant professor of political science at the University of California, Merced. His work has appeared in journals such as the *Journal of Politics, Legislative Studies Quarterly, Political Research Quarterly, Public Choice,* and *State Politics and Policy Quarterly*. Professor Monroe previously held faculty positions at Michigan State University and the University of the Pacific.

Agenda Setting in the U.S. Senate

Costly Consideration and Majority Party Advantage

CHRIS DEN HARTOG
California Polytechnic State University

and

NATHAN W. MONROE
University of California, Merced

CAMBRIDGE
UNIVERSITY PRESS

CAMBRIDGE UNIVERSITY PRESS
Cambridge, New York, Melbourne, Madrid, Cape Town,
Singapore, São Paulo, Delhi, Tokyo, Mexico City

Cambridge University Press
32 Avenue of the Americas, New York, NY 10013-2473, USA

www.cambridge.org
Information on this title: www.cambridge.org/9781107006461

First published 2011

Printed in the United States of America

A catalog record for this publication is available from the British Library.

Library of Congress Cataloging in Publication data
Den Hartog, Chris.
  Agenda setting in the U.S. Senate : costly consideration and majority
  party advantage / Chris Den Hartog and Nathan W. Monroe.
     p. cm.
  ISBN 978-1-107-00646-1 (hardback)
  1. United States. Congress. Senate.   2. United States. Congress.
  Senate – Rules and practice.   3. Legislative calendars – United States.
  I. Monroe, Nathan W.   II. Title.
  JK1161.D46   2011
  328.73'077–dc22   2010048888

ISBN 978-1-107-00646-1 Hardback

Contents

Tables and Figures

Tables

Figures

Preface

Discourse regarding the contemporary U.S. Senate bemoans the legislative paralysis that is perceived to be endemic to the chamber and the adverse effects of the paralysis on national policy making. The sources of this perception are plain to see. News coverage of the Senate is rife with stories of hostile speeches, petty bickering, and partisan warfare, and often emphasizes the role of filibusters and holds in facilitating deadlock. From another perspective, however, this characterization is puzzling; the current Congress (the 111th) has enacted several major, controversial policies, including a massive economic stimulus, a far-reaching health care overhaul, and a sweeping reform of the financial system. How could a Congress producing such major changes be seen as gridlocked? One goal of this book is to reconcile these disparate views by explaining how obstruction and policy making exist side by side in the Senate.

Another goal is to address a similar and closely related puzzle that exists among Senate scholars: we all know how easy it is for an individual senator or a small group of senators to tie the chamber in knots, and we all know that the majority wins divisive policy battles. But we do not know how to square these seemingly contradictory beliefs, which are at the heart of many debates about the Senate.

In a sense, our involvement in this debate began on May 24, 2001, when Senator Jim Jeffords announced that he was leaving the Republican Party to become an independent and would side with Senate Democrats on organizational votes. In early 2003 we began writing a paper about the Jeffords switch, which we saw as a golden opportunity to test two competing theories of legislative decision making. One theory is Cox and McCubbins's (2005) cartel model, in which the majority party strongly influences legislative decisions; the other is Krehbiel's (1998) pivot model, in which legislators' preferences determine outcomes and parties have no impact. During our first round of journal reviews, an anonymous reviewer wrote, "The spatial model presented in [the paper] does not present a case for strong parties or one that conforms to the contemporary Senate. The author(s) have adapted Cox and McCubbins's House party cartel model to fit the Senate floor.... Given that the Senate has no germaneness and amendment restrictions (and only a right of first recognition for the majority leader), does this negative proposal power exist? Second, unlike the pivot model, the majority party cartel model suggests that the leadership would propose bills when the status quo is in the F and R interval. While they may propose those bills, can they pass them with 60 votes? In short, the party cartel model applied to the Senate suggests only a weak (and questionable) negative agenda control."

The reviewer expanded on this critique elsewhere in the review and in another review that followed revisions, making clear that, although our results seemed to show party effects in the Senate, it was simply implausible that the majority party was able to overcome the Senate's legislative obstacles. In short, according to the reviewer, there was no theory that satisfactorily incorporated the procedures and norms of the modern Senate that *also* predicted a majority party advantage.

The reviewer's comments, as well as audience reactions to presentations of the Jeffords paper, made two things clear. First, we realized that the anonymous reviewer was not alone. Despite the results we presented (as well as a growing number of other papers with findings of majority party advantage in the Senate), many congressional scholars had difficulty believing that the majority party influences outcomes given the chamber's procedures. In the years since, as we have presented various results from this book as stand-alone papers, we have continued to encounter objections based on the same skeptical question: *how could* the majority party achieve a policy advantage in the face of unanimous consent agreements, holds, filibusters, nongermane amendments, and a general lack of party discipline?

Second, it became clear that if we were going to make serious strides toward addressing these issues, we were going to need a lot more space than could be allocated to a journal article. Over time, we came to see our task as threefold. First, we needed a new theory, parsimonious enough to test and compare with other theories of lawmaking, but also with enough verisimilitude to Senate practices that people would see it as a reasonable analogy to the chamber. Second, we needed to carefully consider Senate procedures and practices with an eye toward better understanding the sources of the majority party advantage. An abstract theory, we knew, would still be unsatisfactory if its assumptions were not grounded in the Senate's legislative process. Third, we needed to test the theory on its own merits. Like any new theory, it had to explain what we already knew but also correctly predict something new. As the reader will find, this threefold thinking ultimately informed the three-part organization of the book; each part revolves around one of these tasks.

During a series of phone calls in late 2005 and early 2006, we finally settled on a way to think about Senate agenda setting that we believe bridges the gap between the strong-party theories developed in the context of the House of Representatives and the complex legislative process in the Senate. Rather than thinking of the Senate game as one focused on blocking, we turned the notion on its head and instead chose to think of it as a bargaining environment in which proposals do not move forward unless someone makes an effort to move them forward. This "costly-consideration" framework became the heart of our solution to the problem posed by the reviewer.

Having a solution in our heads was one thing; turning it into an end product was quite another. It has required the support, advice, and effort of many people and organizations, whom we gratefully acknowledge.

It is impossible to overstate our appreciation for all that Mat McCubbins has done for each of us. He offered invaluable substantive feedback on this project and provided an opportunity to present the theory to a very thoughtful group of scholars at the University of Southern California Law School. More fundamentally, as our graduate school adviser, he ingrained in us the appreciation for theory and scientific method that sits at the core of this project; he pushed us to refine our thinking and our research designs; he devoted countless hours to our intellectual and professional development; he showed patience as we worked to make use of all the guidance he offered. Time and again he has gone above and beyond what can be expected of an adviser, supporting us explicitly and tacitly as we have tried to make our way in the profession and providing good humor and sage advice. Mat has been a great mentor and is a great friend.

Gary Cox also deserves special thanks for both his input on this project and his mentorship. He participated in the earliest conversations about the Jeffords paper and offered a number of extremely useful suggestions as the book progressed. Moreover, we both benefited immensely from observing and assisting him in his research. Gary is a remarkably clear, efficient thinker, and we have tried to mimic those qualities whenever possible. In particular, his approach to creating and testing theories and his conceptualization of parties have had a substantial impact on our scholarship; we are truly fortunate to have had him as a mentor.

Larry Evans was the editor of *Legislative Studies Quarterly* when we submitted the Jeffords paper. Not only did Larry improve that paper through his investment of time and attention, but his arguments and suggestions helped plant the seeds for many of the central ideas in this book. Since then, in addition to offering detailed comments on drafts of a number of papers that became chapters here, Larry has given us advice on a variety of data issues, has answered many of our questions, and has provided encouragement at every turn. He also went well above and beyond in the final stages of the project, helping us to secure interviews with top-level Senate staff members and guiding us in preparing for those interviews. We are very grateful to him for all he has done.

Similarly, we thank Dave Rohde, who has also gone out of his way to support this project on a number of occasions. In addition to offering countless insightful conversations and helpful suggestions, Dave funded a conference on party effects in the Senate that provided a chance to present the earliest version of the theoretical argument and hosted a book seminar at Duke University once the first full draft was complete, where we got excellent, essential feedback. Through the Political Institutions and Public Choice (PIPC) program, he also provided support for research assistance.

The book is much better than it would otherwise have been due to the input of many individuals. Andrea Campbell, Chuck Finocchiaro, Sean Gailmard, Jeff Jenkins, Greg Koger, Jason Roberts, and Greg Robinson offered repeated help and attention and deserve special recognition for their efforts. Bob Dove, Walter Oleszek, Marty Paone, and Lee Rawls were all wonderfully generous in allowing us to interview them; we are deeply appreciative of their time and insights, which substantially improved our understanding of the Senate. Robi Ragan and Jacob Montgomery deserve thanks for a number of helpful comments, but we are particularly indebted to them for guiding us in extending the formal model beyond one dimension, as presented at the end of Chapter 3. We also thank Scott Adler, Sarah Anderson, Nathan Batto, Matt Beckman, Lauren Bell, Rick Beth, Sarah Binder, Jon Bond, Jamie Carson, Mike Colaresi, Mike Crespin, Erik Engstrom, Garrett Glasgow, David Karol, Ira Katznelson, Frances Lee, Beth Lowham, Michael Lynch, Tony Madonna, Neil Malhotra, Forrest Maltzman, Bruce Oppenheimer, David C. W. Parker, Brian Sala, Eric Schickler, Wendy Schiller, Scot Schraufnagel, Barbara Sinclair, Eric Smith, Steve Smith, Melanie Springer, Michiko Ueda, Rick Valelly, Rob

Van Houweling, Greg Wawro, Nick Weller, John Wooley, various participants at meetings of the American Political Science Association and the Midwest Political Science Association, and a number of anonymous reviewers for feedback and questions on various parts of the book.

We also owe thanks to a number of students who provided excellent research assistance: Minghang Cai, Feilong Chen, Randall Collett, Mike Crespin, Ben Goodhue, Linda Mamula, Selene Marcum, Colleen O'Driscoll, Amanda Robinson, Greg Robinson, Lauren Schneider, Maggie Stockel, Charles Szafir, W. Bryce Underwood, and Matthew Wray. Even with their help in collecting data, however, many of the analyses in the book would not have been possible without the generosity of other scholars. Scott Adler, Andrea Campbell, Gary Cox, Nolan McCarty, Mat McCubbins, Burt Monroe, Garrison Nelson, Keith Poole, Howard Rosenthal, Charles Stewart, John Wilkerson, and Jonathan Woon all provided data, either specifically for us or by posting it on their Web sites. Each deserves commendation for this service. During the final stages of this project, we benefited from the efforts of Eric Crahan and Jason Przybylski at Cambridge University Press, and from editorial assistance by Ana Shaw.

We received generous financial support from a number of sources, without which it would have taken twice as long to do half the job. For their support, we gratefully acknowledge the Intramural Grants Program at Michigan State University; California State University State Faculty Support Grant SL001-108400-SF0105; the Political Science Departments at Cal Poly, Michigan State University, Northwestern University, UC San Diego, and the University of the Pacific; the deans' offices at the University of the Pacific's College of the Pacific and UC Merced's School of Social Sciences, Humanities, and Arts; and Linda Halisky, the dean of Cal Poly's College of Liberal Arts. For graciously granting us opportunities to present parts of the book, we additionally thank the Political Institutions and Public Choice Program at Duke University, the Miller Center of Public Affairs at the University of Virginia (twice), the Institute for Governmental Studies at UC Berkeley, the Department of Political Science at UC Santa Barbara, and the University of Southern California Gould School of Law.

Our rich work environments have helped us to think more clearly and to maintain motivation over the long course of this project. For many forms of intellectual stimulation and other support and encouragement over the years, we thank Paul Abramson, Craig Arceneaux, Valentina Bali, Neal Beck, Jeff Becker, Eric Chang, Dennis Chong, Belinda Davis, Ron Den Otter, Jamie Druckman, Elif Erisen, Liz Gerber, Tom Hammond, Tom Hansford, Cullen Hendrix, Rick Hula, Gary Jacobson, Ken Janda, Shawn Kantor, Sam Kernell, Mike Latner, Anika Leithner, Arend Lijphart, Skip

Lupia, Victor Magagna, Burt Monroe, Matt Moore, Steve Nicholson, Chuck Ostrom, Phil Roeder, Hendrik Spruyt, Dari Sylvester, Jessica Trounstine, Alex Whalley, Jean Williams, Katie Winder, and Ning Zhang.

Finally, no project of this magnitude would be sustainable without the support of our friends and family, to whom we offer individual thanks:

Chris

I thank all of my family and friends, who always have meant so much to me, for all they have done for me. I also thank Nate's family for being such wonderful hosts the many times I visited during this project. Finally, I thank the late Lee Rawls for his extraordinary help with this book. I knew Lee far too briefly but consider myself exceptionally fortunate to have known him at all. He had a remarkable effect on my thinking about the Senate, for which I will always be grateful. More importantly, his generous, unassuming, good-humored manner made him a joy to be around, and I will always remember him very fondly.

Nate

Brad Franca, Chris Hudelson, and C. W. Smith, friends for 27 years and counting, have provided unending (and quite welcome) distractions; they have each been there when I needed them most, and I am truly grateful. Arjuna Farnsworth has been a constant source of intellectual stimulation and support and has proved to be as good a friend as anyone could hope for; I consider myself lucky to know him. My sister Amy is one of my favorite people to laugh with, and after I've spent hours staring at a computer screen, a good laugh goes a long way. I hope she knows how much I love and appreciate her for it. My parents, Keith and Mary, cheered us on at every step of this project, no matter how small the step, which is a microcosm of the love and support they have offered my whole life. I can only hope that my kids someday feel about me the way that I feel about them. Liz, my wife, has shown incredible patience and understanding, even as this project has at times robbed her of my presence and attention. Her love and belief in me are always felt and deeply appreciated. Finally, this book might have been done months sooner if not for all the hide-and-seeking, pony riding, playing "bad," and golf-carting that Will and Abby (who never did finish Chapter 4) suckered me into ... and I loved every minute.

For Liz, Abby, and Will – NWM
For my family, Lee Rawls, and Tommy L. – CFD

PART I

COSTLY CONSIDERATION

I

Costly Consideration and the Majority's Advantage

During 1997 and 1998, the United States Congress wrestled with H.R. 2646, the Education Savings Act for Public and Private Schools, a bill that proposed the creation of tax-free education savings accounts. Most Republicans favored the bill, while most Democrats opposed it (Hosansky 1997; Kirchhoff 1998). Republicans held 52 percent of the House seats (227 of 434 seats at the time the bill passed) and 55 of the 100 Senate seats.

The bill passed through the House quickly. It was introduced on October 9, 1997, reported from the Ways and Means Committee on October 21, and brought up, debated, and passed (without any amendments having been offered) on October 23. On the final passage vote, Republicans voted 215–8 in favor; Democrats voted 190–15 against.

In the Senate, however, the fight over the bill was much different. The chamber took up the bill on the floor by unanimous consent on October 29; but on October 31 and November 4, the Senate voted against invoking cloture, each time with 56 votes for cloture and a nearly perfect partisan split.

The bill was then set aside until the following March, when majority leader Trent Lott made a motion to bring the bill up on the floor. Republican Senate Finance Committee chair William Roth proposed an amendment – a bundle of changes designed to lure Democratic votes (Kirchhoff 1998) – and on March 17 the Senate voted 74–24 to invoke cloture on the motion to proceed, with all 55 Republicans and 19 of 43 Democrats voting in favor. The Senate then considered the bill and adopted Roth's amendment by voice vote on March 18, but it quickly became apparent that Democrats would continue to obstruct the bill unless they got additional concessions. On March 19 and again on March 26, the Senate refused to invoke cloture (with 54 and 58 votes in favor, respectively). On March 27, Lott and Democratic leader Tom Daschle agreed on a unanimous consent agreement in which Republicans conceded to Democrats the right to offer several amendments on the floor.

Up to this point, the story of H.R. 2646 illustrates many widely accepted claims about the role of parties in Congress. Congressional scholars frequently characterize the House as a chamber in which the majority tends to steamroll the minority party, and characterize the Senate as a chamber in which the minority has broad powers to thwart the efforts of the majority. Conventional wisdom holds that the Senate's extensive reliance on unanimous consent agreements for conducting its business, as well as the need for 60 votes to overcome the threat of a filibuster, presents daunting obstacles that the majority struggles to overcome.

Senate scholars also argue that the Senate's amendment process, which places few restrictions on senators' ability to offer amendments on the floor, creates significant problems for the majority. The process gives minority senators a way to present amendments that they hope will divide the majority party and prevent majority leaders from pushing through their legislative agenda. As we see in the case of H.R. 2646, the minority party has substantial tools for protecting its ability to offer amendments.

The Senate took up H.R. 2646, under the terms of the unanimous consent agreement, on April 20. Over the next few days, the chamber considered and disposed of various Democratic and Republican amendments. But there is a curious pattern to the disposition of these amendments: the chamber tabled, ruled out of order, or voted down almost all the Democrats' amendments, adopting only a few Democratic amendments that had the support of a majority of Republicans. On the other hand, the Senate adopted several Republican-sponsored amendments, some of which had Democratic support but some of which faced strong Democratic opposition. Once it finished with amendments, the chamber passed the bill as amended on a 56–43 vote; Republicans voted 51–3 in favor, and Democrats voted 40–5 against.

The perceived role of the majority party from the conventional viewpoint is somewhat ambiguous. Some authors seem to assert that the Senate's procedures keep the majority party from having any more influence over legislative decisions than do individual senators, or groups of senators other than the majority party; others appear to be more agnostic about the role of the majority party, seemingly open to the possibility that the majority party has some advantages. But claims that the majority plays a predominant role and has significant advantages elicit widespread skepticism.

However, this traditional thinking sits uncomfortably alongside some of the particulars of the H.R. 2646 example – especially once the bill reached the floor. For instance, why did no controversial Democratic amendments succeed, while controversial Republican amendments did? Since minority party members offered several amendments, how did they end up with a bill they overwhelmingly opposed? Also, given that more than 40 senators voted against the bill on final passage, as well as on several early cloture motions, how did it ultimately overcome the filibuster and pass? For that matter, even some of the pre-floor facts of the case raise questions. Why did a number of senators who strongly opposed the bill allow it to be scheduled more than once by unanimous consent? And why was it the committee chair and the majority leader who got to make the first proposals, against which subsequent bargaining occurred, regarding amendments and unanimous consent terms? Why did the minority leader not follow a similar strategy, offering a proposal and then making incremental concessions and side-payments until the minority could pass a bill that was more to its liking? Conventional wisdom offers few answers to such questions. Our take is that the conventional view captures much of what is important about Senate behavior but also misses some crucial elements.

The Senate literature, which is largely atheoretical, tells us that we should not expect to see the majority party systematically passing the legislation it wants. But the literature offers little else in the way of generalizations about which actors, if any, systematically succeed in passing the policies they favor.[1] It tells us that the Senate is complicated and sometimes seems to imply that it is *too* complicated for general theorizing.

Numerous recent empirical studies, however, conclude that the majority party influences Senate decisions (Bargen 2003; Campbell, Cox, and

---

[1] Krehbiel's (1998) pivotal politics model is, in a sense, an exception. It is a formal theory that is quite specific about which actors in the Senate affect policy and how they affect it. But we view it as separate from what we characterize as the Senate literature. The pivot model is a more general theory, aimed at explaining which proposals become laws rather than explaining the related, but different question about the Senate's internal workings that we address. It includes the House and the president as prominently as the Senate, and incorporates legislative procedures only in broad strokes, meaning it says little about the details of Senate procedure.

As we point out in Chapter 3, our model makes some predictions similar to those of the pivot model but makes other predictions at odds with the model. In Chapter 10 we test predictions from both models.

McCubbins 2002; Crespin and Finocchiaro 2008; Den Hartog and Monroe 2008a; Gailmard and Jenkins 2007; Koger 2003; Koger and Fowler 2006; Lee 2009). But such studies frequently elicit skepticism, and not only from the conventional point of view – even many scholars who believe that parties matter, or at least suspect that they do, ask the great unanswered question regarding Senate parties: *how* can the majority influence the agenda, given the way the Senate goes about its business?

Of course, congressional literature prominently features theories of legislative decision making that emphasize parties' influence over legislation. But like the conventional wisdom, these partisan theories have trouble explaining the case of H.R. 2646. They emphasize majority party influence through agenda setting rather than through party discipline on substantive votes (Aldrich and Rohde 2000; Campbell, Cox, and McCubbins 2002; Cox and McCubbins 1993, 2005), but they offer limited explanations for why the majority would be stymied initially, then have to offer concessions to the minority party to push the agenda they wanted.[2] This lack of explanatory power largely reflects the historical focus of the congressional organization literature – including partisan theories – on the House of Representatives. It arises from an approach that takes little account of the Senate's different organizational environment.

The focus on the House has contributed to the widespread conceptualization of agenda setting as a gatekeeping, veto-based process. This thinking fits neatly with the House legislative process, in which the Rules Committee serves as an effective instrument for controlling the floor; but the Senate has no equivalent control mechanism. Such veto-based models seem less applicable to the upper chamber, where the majority party scraps, battles, and bargains its way to final passage. The example of H.R. 2646 illustrates why House-based partisan theories do not transfer comfortably to the Senate – they do not explain how a Senate majority manipulates the agenda.

The Costly-Consideration Theory

We offer a theory of legislative decision making that bridges the gap between these two schools and helps us better understand the Senate. In spirit, our take is similar to that of Rawls (2009), who characterizes the

---

[2] The House literature does, however, provide insights into how procedural majorities might allow the majority party in the Senate to influence the agenda (Rohde 1991; Van Houweling 2003). For an explicit treatment of the Senate, see Rohde (1992).

majority caucus as the team that plays offense and the minority caucus as the team that plays defense. Extending Rawls's analogy slightly, imagine a football game in which one team always plays offense: the majority is in a much better position than the minority to score; this does not mean that the majority scores on every drive or that the minority never scores off a turnover, but overall we expect the majority to score decidedly more often than the minority.

An aspect of agenda setting prominently highlighted in recent years is the distinction between "positive agenda control," the power to ensure a final vote on a proposal, and "negative agenda control," the power to prevent a final vote on a proposal (Cox and McCubbins 2005). Most Senate literature focuses on negative agenda power, whereas, in a sense, ours is a theory of positive agenda power; that is, we are most interested not in who can block bills, but rather in who can pass them.

However, we diverge from previous treatments of agenda setting in three important respects. First, we emphasize that agenda setting in the Senate requires getting a proposal to a final passage vote – which we refer to as *final consideration*, or just *consideration*[3] – as opposed to merely offering a proposal on the floor. In many legislatures, offering a proposal and final consideration are tantamount, and this distinction is not necessarily useful. In the Senate, however, the difference between offering a proposal on the floor and having the chamber vote on that proposal can be enormous.

Second, we conceptualize agenda setting as a costly process. For a bill's proponents, navigating the various procedural minefields that can kill a bill on the floor sometimes requires great effort and substantial resources. Such resources are scarce.

Third, we treat influence over the agenda as continuous rather than dichotomous. Existing literature conceptualizes negative and positive agenda influence largely as a matter of absolute agenda power; that is, an actor has either complete negative agenda control or zero negative agenda control, and has either complete positive agenda control or zero positive agenda control. In our theory, though, both the majority and its opponents hold partial agenda influence. One way of characterizing our thinking is that partial negative agenda influence is distributed widely

---

[3] This usage of the word *consideration* is at odds with the usual usage, which refers to any type of floor activity on a bill. We use various other terms, such as *offering* or *proposal of amendments*, *floor time*, *floor action*, or *floor activity*, to refer to forms of consideration other than final consideration.

in the Senate, and positive agenda influence is a matter of being able to overcome opponents' negative agenda influence – and the majority is in a better position than its opponents to do this, giving it an agenda-setting advantage.[4]

Our theory's logic is similar to the logic of bargaining games (Rubinstein 1982), in which actors make proposals about how to divide a fixed benefit, and the actor who makes the first proposal is able to claim a bigger share of that benefit by making a strategic proposal that the other actor will accept because a counteroffer would be too costly to be worthwhile. In our model, the majority party's first-proposal power combines with costs the minority must bear to make counterproposals to give it a similar advantage. It uses this advantage to claim a bigger share of the benefit (which in our model is the policy space).[5]

One of the strengths of our theory is that it incorporates assumptions that are central to the conventional wisdom, such as the possibility of filibusters and the broad right of senators to propose policies via amendments. But because we include additional assumptions that we believe are quite plausible in light of Senate practice, the theory leads to the *unconventional* conclusion that the majority party can often manipulate Senate decisions in its favor. The three main additional assumptions that underpin our theory are, first, that agenda setting is costly; second, that it is less costly for the majority party than for others; and, third, that the majority party has a first-proposal advantage.

We formalize our theory in a game-theoretic model that is similar in nature to many previous legislative agenda-setting models. The model provides a link between formal spatial models – a staple of congressional theory – and the heavily empirical Senate literature that often portrays Senate agenda setting as a matter of bargaining between the majority and the minority but rarely offers specific theories about the structure or consequences of this bargaining.

We anticipate that some readers will be skeptical about our spatial modeling approach. One likely critique is that our assumptions oversimplify

---

[4] In this regard, we have misgivings about applying the distinction between positive and negative agenda power to our theory. Whereas the distinction frames negative and positive powers as discrete (i.e., it is possible to have one without having the other), they are flip sides of the same coin from our point of view. The size of the costs that a proposal's supporters must bear to get it to a final passage vote is a function of others' negative agenda influence.

[5] A difference between our model and bargaining games is that, in our model, the chamber's final decision about what division of the benefit to accept is made by the floor median rather than by agreement between the two parties.

the Senate's complex procedures; another is that a one-dimensional model is too crude to capture the rich context of Senate politics. We agree that we dramatically simplify an institution that is extraordinarily complex, with the upshot that our model neither captures every interesting aspect of Senate decision making nor explains every legislative battle in the Senate. Moreover, we do not claim that our model is the "correct" way to think about the Senate (from our point of view, there is no such thing). But our goal is not to explain everything or to present an unassailable model. Rather, it is to advance understanding of Senate policy making by providing a better theory than exists at present; to us, this means a theory that explains behavior not explained by other theories and that does so in a relatively parsimonious way. Simplification comes with the territory. We agree that the Senate's complexity is fascinating, and as readers will see, our theory is thoroughly grounded in Senate procedures.

The contribution of our costly-consideration theory is evident in the case of H.R. 2646. The majority party ultimately succeeded in advancing the bill to final consideration against strong minority opposition, but doing so was difficult and costly. The majority *proposed* the bill on the floor without much difficulty. But to move the bill from initial proposal to final passage, it paid significant costs to overcome filibusters, used its first-mover bargaining advantage to schedule minority amendments in return for getting final consideration of the bill, and employed a variety of procedural tools to keep its initial proposal more or less intact. As we see it, the story of H.R. 2646 is a highlight reel of consideration costs and majority party procedural advantage.

Consideration Costs, Parties, and Legislative Process

Throughout the book we use a few concepts that are central to our thinking but that can easily be understood to mean a variety of things. In this section we therefore clarify what we mean when we use the terms *consideration costs*, *majority party*, and *minority party*.

Consideration Costs
We assume that legislators are rational utility maximizers. But when we refer to costs, we especially want to avoid giving the impression that we believe there is some point in the legislative process that is analogous to a market exchange in which there is a buyer and a seller who first agree to a mutually acceptable selling price, then explicitly trade payment for a good. Rather, as in basic economics, we mean opportunity costs – that

is, the utility that would follow from the next-best use of whatever scarce resources one sacrifices by taking a particular course of action.[6]

Given the intended audience for this book, a perhaps useful illustration is the sort of costs entailed in obtaining a graduate degree. During grad school, one pays opportunity costs by sacrificing time, energy, potential earnings, and other things that could be put to good alternative uses, in the hope of obtaining a better outcome down the road than would occur if one did not go to grad school. Similarly, in the Senate, policies' proponents must sacrifice things they value in order to push their proposals through the chamber's complex legislative process to a final vote, but nonetheless often do so in the hope of passing legislation that they value. Such sacrifices are what we mean when we use the term *consideration costs*.

The universe of costly sacrifices that senators make to gain consideration of proposals presumably comprises a virtually unlimited number of resources, including things as obscure as five minutes not spent on a photo-op with constituents or not enjoying dinner with one's family because of stress induced by legislative bargaining. We make no attempt at a definitive accounting of all consideration costs, but there are some that we see as most significant:

- Legislators' time, attention, and energy
- Staffers' time, attention, and energy
- Side-payments used to build a winning coalition[7]
- Legislators' votes
- Political chips or favors that a legislator can call in from, or offer to, another legislator
- Campaign resources

Until this point, we have discussed legislators' goals only as a matter of utility calculations that follow from policy outcomes and the sacrifices made to shape policy outcomes. But, of course, *any* outcome that increases a legislator's utility is a potential goal of that legislator. Moreover, the Congress literature emphasizes goals other than policy outcomes, especially electoral goals. Clearly, electoral outcomes not only are a major source of utility, but are affected by policy-making decisions. Hence, a

---

[6] Note that our notion of costly action has roots in transaction cost economics literature (Alchian and Demsetz 1972; Coase 1937; Demsetz 1968; North 1981; Williamson 1985). For other recent work explicitly considering the implications of legislative transaction costs in the Senate, see Koger (2004) and Wawro and Schickler (2004, 2006).

[7] By *side-payments*, we mean concessions on unrelated policy dimensions, often in the form of support for pet programs or district projects.

theory of policy making such as ours should incorporate the effects of electoral goals (Smith 2007).

Obviously, legislators value some of the items on our list because they sometimes translate into electoral benefits. In this respect, our discussion already includes electoral considerations. But two other factors that can fundamentally affect a legislator's chances of winning reelection are the reputations, or brand names, of the legislator's party and of the other party. We expand our discussion of consideration costs to include such effects later in this section. Partly in order to lay the foundation for that discussion, however, we turn first to our conception of parties.

The Majority and Minority Parties

Scholars use the word *party* in different ways, referring to such diverse entities as voters registered to a given party, national or state party organizations, or co-partisans holding government offices. Occasionally, this gives rise to arguments that stem more from definitional differences than from substantive disagreement. In the congressional policy-making literature there is less disagreement about terminology; the term is commonly understood to refer to a party caucus in a particular legislative chamber and that caucus's efforts to act collectively.

However, even among Congress scholars there is no consensus about exactly what *collective efforts* means. There is broad agreement that parties create institutional structures to try to achieve goals that they pursue, but disagreement about what counts as part of these institutional structures. For example, though party leaders are clearly part of this structure, committee chairs are sometimes treated as part of the organization and sometimes not. Similarly, there is broad agreement that it entails attempts to overcome collective action problems in pursuit of shared goals, such as managing the party's brand name, passing policies desired by most caucus members, holding a majority of the chamber's seats, and claiming a disproportionate piece of the distributional pie. But there is disagreement about which of these goals matters, how much each matters, and how they interact. Finally, there is disagreement about what tools parties use to solve collective action problems and how successful these tools are.

Such differences, though often subtle, can have significant consequences for our understanding. Consider the hypothetical example of a Democratic committee chair using the chair's power to push through an alternative-energy bill loaded with pork. If the chair is seen as an agent of the majority party, the bill could be interpreted as evidence that the chair worked to foster the Democrat's reputation; or it could be interpreted as evidence that the chair worked to achieve a policy goal shared by many caucus members; or it could be interpreted as evidence that the chair worked to distribute district projects across the caucus membership; or it could be interpreted as evidence of some combination of these things. And if the chair is seen not as an agent of the caucus, but instead as a rival power, the chair's actions might be interpreted as having nothing to do with party organization. Therefore, though our goal in this book is to articulate a theory of policy making, and *not* to articulate a theory of party organization or of partisanship more broadly conceived (i.e., partisan actions aside from policy making), we spell out our thinking about what counts as part of party institutions and what purposes they serve.

We use the term *majority party* to refer to the majority party caucus and the institutional structure it creates to influence the legislative process. We construe *institutional structure* to mean more than just party leadership and organizations; it also includes the shared expectation that caucus members will exhibit some level of fealty to a set of commonly agreed-upon behavioral norms. Members are generally expected to support the party on key procedural votes; committee chairs are expected to use their powers to promote party goals when relevant and to avoid harming the party's collective interests; party leaders are expected to do the same and to use their powers to foster collective action. This, of course, is hardly a novel take on party institutions. It is similar to, if not the same as, those of both the cartel and conditional party government theories (Aldrich and Rohde 1998, 2000, 2001, 2005; Cox and McCubbins 1993, 2005; Kiewiet and McCubbins 1991; Rohde 1991).

Like others, we believe that, in addition to having multiple individual goals, caucus members have multiple collective goals, including those already mentioned. But our view is closely aligned with Lee's (2009) insightful assertion that one collective goal stands out as paramount: influence over the legislative process. Lee argues that influence over the legislative process is the collective good from which others flow; it underpins the party's efforts to manage the brand name, pursue policy goals, claim the lion's share of distributive benefits, and achieve other goals. With apologies to David Mayhew (1974: 16), for the caucus, influence over the legislative process "has to be the *proximate* goal."

We also agree with Lee's (2009: 13) claim that "collective action problems have been exaggerated in the study of congressional party politics." Her argument is not that such problems are nonexistent, but that their magnitude has been overstated. She dissects the application of free-riding logic to congressional parties and finds it wanting in various ways. For instance, individual members' contributions to the group effort often *do* affect whether the public good is supplied; moreover, such contributions are easily monitored, and small-group dynamics alone might induce cooperation. Also, unlike much of the literature, she emphasizes that when selective incentives are used to maintain cooperation, they are often positive incentives that more than offset the cost of cooperation. Finally, she notes that, contrary to common supposition, senators often do not perceive voting with the party as entailing a sacrifice.

Throughout the book we tend to frame the Senate in terms of "the majority party" battling "the minority party." When we use the term *minority party*, we typically have in mind the minority caucus and its institutional structure, but *minority* can also be construed as referring to any coalition that opposes efforts of the majority caucus and leaders, including cross-party coalitions and individual senators of either party. We emphasize the minority caucus because its organization – which is similar to the majority's in many respects, though with fewer resources – is generally the most potent opponent for the majority.

The legislative process is the linchpin between this notion of parties and our costly-consideration theory. In most legislatures, floor time for dealing with legislative proposals is scarce, and some form of rationing must therefore be used to decide which proposals the chamber works on (i.e., there is not enough time for every proposal – or every proposal that a member would like to make – to get a full hearing before the entire chamber). Such rationing mechanisms take many forms, but each legislature's process for passing legislation creates one or more points at which rationing occurs. Moving a proposal beyond these key points entails opportunity costs (at a minimum, there are opportunity costs that follow from spending scarce floor time on some bills rather than on others).

At each rationing point, the legislative process grants some privileged group of legislators greater influence than other legislators over decisions about which proposals go forward (e.g., committees have disproportionate influence within their jurisdictions). Put differently, the privileged group can move things forward at lower cost than can other (groups of) legislators. The distribution of costs across various actors in the chamber may be *relatively* even or uneven. The Senate falls closer than most legislatures to the relatively even end of the spectrum, but even in the Senate, costs are unequally distributed.

This brings us back to our central claim that the majority faces lower consideration costs than the minority. This is a generalization that we think is usually the case and thus serves as a useful simplifying assumption.

To some extent these lower consideration costs are grounded in Senate procedures. For example, the right of first recognition allows the majority leader to fill the amendment tree, and thus imposes high consideration costs on others' amendments. Overwhelmingly, however, the majority's lower consideration costs are a function of its ability to maintain enough cooperation to control committee memberships and to win many procedural votes that have the effect of lowering majority consideration costs or raising minority consideration costs.

We sometimes hear the objection that "the majority wins just because it has more votes." The implication is that members might be voting together and winning procedural votes because they agree on policy, rather than out of any sense of loyalty or responsibility to the party. This misses the key point: what matters is that the majority *wins procedural votes*, not that it wins *by inducing cooperation*. We do not claim that it wins only because it induces cooperation from party members. In fact, quite the opposite, we assume that it sometimes wins procedural votes just by letting members vote the way they want to vote and that leaders are only too happy to let things unfold this way, since it requires no extra effort, inducements, or arm twisting. But when that will not suffice, leaders have tools for garnering cooperation. The main significance of the majority's numerical superiority is that, all else constant, it does not have to work as hard to get enough votes to win many procedural decisions.[8]

We do not argue that the Senate majority always wins procedural votes or achieves all its goals, any more than does an economic cartel like OPEC. We reiterate, our claim is not that it has the kind of absolute control often associated with the Westminster-style ideal, or even the kind of strong agenda influence sometimes associated with House majorities. But even the Senate's comparatively weak majority has the wherewithal to successfully manipulate the legislative process more often than not.

Other Factors Related to Consideration Costs

We now return to the topic of how electoral goals interact with consideration costs to affect policy making. Given that many voters decide how to vote much more on the basis of candidates' partisan affiliations than on policy positions or individual attributes, parties' reputations matter a great deal to members of Congress, and things that happen during the policy-making process can affect those reputations.

---

[8] Most procedural questions are decided by majority vote. This claim may not hold on supermajority votes, such as cloture.

The idea that parties promote policy platforms aimed in part to improve the party's reputation is common. This suggests that a party's electoral goals are embedded in the party's policy preferences. When we model policy preferences, we are also modeling electoral incentives to some extent.

But electoral incentives are more complicated than that. Lee (2009: 9) notes that "[t]he grim logic of two-party competition is that a party can potentially gain as much electoral mileage from damaging its opposition's reputation as from building a positive record of policy achievement of its own." Blocking the majority party's efforts to achieve its promised policy objectives can be a source of electoral advantage for the minority party, in two ways. First, if supporters and independent voters expect the majority party to deliver results and will punish it for not doing so, which often seems to be the case, then the minority party can damage the majority's reputation among those groups by being obstructive. Second, evaluations of the minority party might improve among the party's supporters if they credit it for blocking unwanted policies.

There is a relatively simple way to incorporate these electoral effects into our model. Assuming that parties' policy preferences account for the effects of electoral motivations generally, we need only account for electoral effects that deviate from the norm.

Short-term or issue-specific considerations sometimes create opportunities for one or both parties to score reputational points by acting more or less aggressively in the legislative arena. For the minority party, expected electoral gains from blocking make the party more determined to oppose the majority's efforts, which has the effect of increasing *majority* consideration costs. On the other hand, expected electoral *losses* from blocking make the party less determined to oppose the majority's efforts, which has the effect of lowering *majority* consideration costs.

The flip side is that, for the majority party, expected electoral losses from failing to deliver on promises might make the party willing to absorb greater consideration costs in order to pass a proposal; and expected electoral gains from painting the other party as the party blocking popular policies might make the party less willing to absorb consideration costs.[9]

Events surrounding the majority Democrats' financial overhaul bill in the spring of 2008 illustrate our points. Republicans obstructed efforts to schedule the bill, as they had done with many Democratic legislative

[9] If, on a particular issue, the minority's expected electoral losses/gains are of the same size as the majority's expected gains/losses, then the electoral effects might be a wash. But the effects are based on the reactions of different groups of voters, and there is no guarantee that different groups' attribution of electoral credit or blame will be so well ordered.

policy priorities during the 111th Congress. Majority leader Harry Reid then staged an unusual series of votes on which he forced Republicans to repeatedly block the bill. The stunt drew attention to Republican obstruction, which Democrats portrayed, with apparent success, as "the party of 'no'" protecting Wall Street fat cats. Not wanting to be seen as protectors of Wall Street at a time when it was deeply unpopular, Republicans relented and dropped their opposition to scheduling the bill (Sloan and Schatz 2010).

Aside from electoral costs, majority party homogeneity also affects consideration costs. The idea that higher levels of policy agreement among caucus members lead to stronger party leaders (and lower levels of policy agreement among caucus members lead to weaker party leaders) is most closely associated with conditional party government (Aldrich and Rohde 1998, 2000, 2001, 2005; Rohde 1991) but is also part of other studies of parties (Cooper and Brady 1981; Cox and McCubbins 1993, 2005). A common thread is that, as the caucus becomes more unified, it gives party leaders more power to push proposals through to passage. In so doing, it makes it easier to move a majority proposal through the system – that is, it lowers majority consideration costs. It also strengthens the leader's hand procedurally, which often raises minority consideration costs.

Another factor related to consideration costs is the size of the majority, which Smith (2007) emphasizes as having an important effect on Senate policy making. Majority size is not an explicit parameter of our model, but our model captures its impact in the parties' consideration costs. Often, part of the majority's cost of moving a proposal forward consists of things, such as support for a project, that a party leader trades to other senators in exchange for those senators' votes on a key matter. Since majority party senators are more predisposed than minority party senators to vote with the majority party, they should generally demand less in return than minority senators; all else constant, the cost of buying enough votes will increase as the majority size decreases.

People tend to think of the Senate as requiring 60 votes and of the majority party as needing to buy some votes in order to win. This is obviously true of many votes on which a filibuster is possible; in such cases, consideration costs increase as majority size decreases. But many procedural motions, such as tabling motions, cannot be filibustered, meaning the majority needs only 51 votes to win. In many such cases, the leader has a majority without needing to buy votes, in which case majority size does not clearly matter. In short, majority size is one aspect of consideration costs, but the relationship between the two is not straightforward.

Senate Procedures, First-Proposal Power, and Consideration Costs

In later chapters, especially in Part II, we delve into details of various Senate procedures. In this section, we briefly sketch some of the points we make about the chamber's legislative process.

One can think of agenda setting as occurring at three different stages of the Senate's legislative process: the committee stage, the scheduling stage, and the floor stage. In this section we briefly survey some of the procedural mechanisms that give the majority party agenda-setting advantages at each stage (we examine these mechanisms in greater detail in Part II). We focus especially on how procedures shape both consideration costs and the right to make a first proposal. Table 1.1 summarizes several key procedural mechanisms and legislative strategies, and indicates in each case whether it affords the majority party first-proposer power, decreases majority party consideration costs, or increases minority consideration costs.[10]

Committees

In the Senate, as in the House, committees significantly influence the legislative agenda. Most of the work of legislating occurs in committees, and committees also decide the fate of most legislation (Endersby and McCurdy 1996; Evans 1991). At this stage, committee chairs – members of the majority party – wield substantial power to either move proposals forward to the floor or keep them bottled up in committee (Evans 1991). In addition, the chair's mark represents an important source of agenda influence over committee decisions, giving the chair almost complete control of the base bill – namely the first proposal – that is made open to amendment and roll call votes in committee. Opponents of provisions included in the mark need to have the support of a majority within the committee to strike these provisions, which requires securing the support of one or more members of the majority party on the committee. The alternative is to vote against the motion to report the entire bill to the floor, which would mean giving up other items in the measure that the minority wishes to see enacted. Thus, the bargaining advantages of the majority party begin at the earliest stages of the legislative process in the Senate.

Moreover, in the event that a committee or its chair is not amenable to a bill that the majority leaders favor, a tactic of increasing importance

---

[10] Note that this table is not intended to be exhaustive. Rather, it is meant to highlight some of the key features of the majority party's agenda-setting advantage and to identify the ways in which they affect proposal power and consideration costs.

TABLE 1.1. *Key Senate Procedures and Strategies That Affect First-Mover Advantage and Consideration Costs*

Tool	Description	First-Mover Advantage?	Decrease Majority Consideration Cost?	Increase Minority Consideration Cost?	Literature
Rule XIV	Under Rule XIV, a measure is placed directly on the Senate calendar, bypassing committee, if the measure is objected to after the second reading.	Yes	Yes		Oleszek (2004: 249–50), Sinclair (1997: 34–6) Tiefer (1989: 594)
Committee gatekeeping	With a numerical advantage and control of the position of committee chair, the majority party can bottle up bills it wants to kill but open the gate for bills it prefers. Chair's mark in large part determines the initial form of legislation.	Yes	Yes	Yes	Evans (1991: 45–72)
Majority special recognition rights	When several senators seek recognition from the presiding officer, the majority leader is recognized first and the minority leader second. Bill managers, usually committee chairs and thus majority party members, are recognized after the leaders but before other senators.	Yes	Yes	Yes	Oleszek (2004: 222, 225), Sinclair (1997: 38)
Early cloture petition, limits on post-cloture floor activity	A cloture petition can be filed as soon as a bill is brought up on the floor (but not before). Rule changes in 1979 and at subsequent times have limited post-cloture floor activity to 30 hours, which includes time for debate and the time taken up by votes on procedural motions. Only germane amendments are in order after cloture has been invoked.		Yes		Binder and Smith (1997: 8, 142), Oleszek (2004: 244–5), Sinclair (1989: 129), Tiefer 1989: 721–9)

"Filling the amendment tree"	Because only certain degrees, forms, and types of amendments can be in order at a given time, the majority leader or the bill manager can use his or her recognition advantage to preclude other senators (particularly members of the minority) from offering their amendments.	Yes	Campbell (2004), Oleszek (2004: 232), Palmer and Bach (2003), Schiller (2000)
Motions to table and points of order on amendments	A bill manager can move to table an amendment, thus ending debate on the amendment and, with a majority vote in favor of the motion, killing the amendment. In reference to motions to table, Oleszek (2004: 236) writes, "[S]enators generally support the party leadership on procedural votes." Points of order can be used in similar fashion on budget-relevant measures.	Yes	Oleszek (2004: 222, 236), Sinclair (1997: 45–46), Tiefer (1989: 658–671)
Budget reconciliation	The majority party can use the reconciliation process – which is immune to filibusters and requires only 51 votes for passage – to advance some substantive policies that are controversial and would thus be susceptible to delay or blockage by a minority coalition under normal procedures.	Yes	Keith (2008a), Rawls 2009

in recent years is the use of Rule XIV to place measures directly on the Senate calendar – from which the majority leader can call them up – without first referring them to committee (Evans and Oleszek 2001). This procedure has often been used for high-priority items on the majority party's legislative agenda (Oleszek 2004), and can both speed the process by which a measure reaches the floor and avoid potential committee bottlenecks. Any senator can use this tactic to place a bill directly on the calendar, but the majority leader's scheduling prerogatives make the tactic all but useless for any senator who lacks the majority leader's support (Sinclair 1997).

Scheduling

These scheduling prerogatives flow largely from the majority leader's "right of first recognition." That is, when the floor is open and the majority leader stands to be recognized, the chair recognizes the majority leader, regardless of whether others also stand to be recognized. This gives the leader the ability to propose a course of action before anyone else. An upshot is that the majority leader effectively monopolizes the power to make scheduling proposals (i.e., unanimous consent requests and motions to proceed) (Tiefer 1989).

The combination of Rule XIV and the effective right to make unanimous consent requests guarantees the leader the ability to propose scheduling whatever version of a bill the leader wants to propose and to do so before anyone else can make a proposal. In spatial terms, one might think of this as the ability to make a proposal at a specific point in the policy space, which is one of our model's assumptions.

Of course, the ease with which one or more senators can obstruct approval of these proposals is central to conventional accounts of the Senate. We agree that the majority party has no sure defense against such attacks; indeed, many majority proposals linger and die for want of unanimous consent or 60 votes. But the majority is not defenseless against such attacks; it often successfully overcomes attempts at obstruction.

An aspect of the Senate with important ramifications that are not fully appreciated in the literature is that *all* senators have proposals that they want the Senate to act on, and this gives them a reason to avoid unnecessary conflict with the majority leader. Lee Rawls, majority leader Bill Frist's chief of staff, emphasizes the point: "The members can't stand to know that they're not going to do anything. It just drives them crazy. They are genetically coded to get in, achieve, get back home. So if they showed up – and let's say the country was at four percent unemployment,

six percent real growth – and they only passed two bills for the year,
they'd be devastated."[11] Current and former minority staffers cite the
desire for achievement as a reason all-out minority obstruction is not a
viable option; a senator considering obstruction must weigh the benefits
against the possibility of retaliation. And no one would be happy with a
war of all against all, in which everything were obstructed. This sometimes causes senators to refrain from obstruction even when they oppose
a measure; at other times, it prompts minority senators to accept proposals that disproportionately favor the majority but that include elements
minority senators want enacted.

The majority leader is well positioned to take advantage of this desire,
because the leader can use individual senators' goals as carrots and sticks
with which to garner support for unanimous consent requests, motions
to proceed, and cloture motions. For example, the leader can offer to
include a senator's pet projects or programs in a bill, or the leader can
threaten to block pet projects. Others can also make such offers, but the
right of first recognition makes the majority leader's offers more credible than other senators' offers.[12] Such "buying" of votes often allows the
majority leader to eliminate objections to consent requests or to pick
up 60 votes.[13] To be sure, minority senators sometimes maintain high
cohesion, prevent cloture, and thwart the majority. Likewise, in some
instances a minority coalition hijacks the agenda and forces the majority party to accept unwanted legislation. But this implies only that the
majority party does not get its way all the time; it does not imply that the
majority party *never* gets its way.

Floor Amendments

Majority party advantages at the committee and scheduling stages of
the legislative process are not always sufficient to prevent proposals the
majority opposes from showing up on the floor, given the open amendment process and the lack of a germaneness requirement in the Senate.
But the majority party also enjoys various advantages that empower it to
effectively combat hostile amendments in many instances.

---

[11] Interview with the authors (September 6, 2010).

[12] Ainsworth and Flathman (1995) make a similar, albeit nonpartisan, argument that the
majority leader's first-proposal power creates a bargaining advantage in negotiations
over unanimous consent agreements.

[13] *Roll Call* notes that majority leader Harry Reid's filibuster-killing success rate for the
111th Congress (as of April 2010) was 90%, putting him on pace to eclipse the previous
mark (63%) set by Mike Mansfield in the 94th Congress and matched by Bill Frist in the
109th Congress (Pierce 2010).

First, there are various circumstances under which floor amendment proposals *are* restricted. For instance, the majority leader sometimes uses the right of first recognition to "fill the amendment tree," preempting others from offering amendments (Campbell 2004; Oleszek 2004; Schiller 2000). In addition, all amendments to a measure must be germane once cloture is invoked, sometimes giving the majority leader an incentive to file for cloture as early as possible during floor action on a measure in order to limit amendments (Oleszek 2004; Sinclair 1997; Tiefer 1989). Also, the budget resolution and reconciliation process allows the majority to enact some policies with a bare majority, and the Byrd rule creates a point of order against "extraneous matter" in budget reconciliation bills, which limits the set of amendments that can be offered (we return to the topic of budget reconciliation in Chapter 10). Finally, the majority leader's bargaining advantage over consent requests enables the leader to negotiate at least marginally greater restrictions on amendments than the minority would otherwise accept (Ainsworth and Flathman 1995).

When the minority offers a hostile amendment, the majority leader or the floor manager can offer a motion to table any such amendment. If approved by a simple majority, this nondebatable motion has the effect of killing the amendment in question. Various Senate procedural experts describe votes on motions to table as instances in which senators are strongly predisposed to vote the party line, making tabling motions a tool primarily of majority leaders (Gold 2004; Marshall, Prins, and Rohde 1999; Oleszek 2004; Tiefer 1989). Thus, the much touted ability of individual (minority) senators to *offer* amendments may not actually undermine the majority party's ability to influence the agenda, because offering an amendment is not necessarily equivalent to getting a vote on the substance of the amendment (Den Hartog and Monroe 2008b).

Our interpretation of the aforementioned majority procedural advantages is that, in a variety of ways, they make it easier – that is, less costly – for the majority party to propose measures and push them toward final passage than for the minority party. In particular, the majority party enjoys the ability to make the first proposal at both the committee and scheduling stages. The majority faces costs in pushing proposals toward final passage, but the minority party faces the same costs, plus additional costs, in trying to do the same.

Plan of the Book

The book is divided into three main parts. The first situates our work within congressional literature and presents our model, the second provides evidence supporting our premises about the majority party's agenda-setting advantages in the Senate, and the third tests predictions of our model.

In Chapter 2 we review literature relevant to Senate decisions. We identify what we see as the conventional wisdom – namely, that Senate procedures undermine majority party agenda-setting efforts – and discuss the limited extent to which House-generated theories of party influence have gained currency as explanations of the Senate. But we also note that a substantial amount of recent work indicates that the Senate majority does influence chamber decisions, creating the puzzle that motivates this book – how could that be the case?

We present our model in detail in Chapter 3. It is a complete-information, extensive-form, one-dimensional game in which the majority party has the first opportunity to propose a change to the status quo policy, the minority party then has the option of making a counterproposal, and the floor median then decides whether the outcome is the adoption of the majority proposal (if any), the adoption of the minority proposal (if any), or a continuation of the status quo policy. If either party makes a proposal, it also pays a cost to have the proposal considered – and the cost is higher for the minority party than for the majority party. The main implication of the model is that, for status quos in many regions of the policy space, the majority party can make a proposal that is to the majority side of the floor median, that the floor median prefers the status quo, and that the minority will not counter because there is no counterproposal that the floor median would prefer to the majority proposal *and* that would produce a large enough gain for the minority to justify its paying the associated consideration costs. A key implication of the model is that status quos in most regions of the policy space either will be replaced by new policies on the majority side of the space or will be located on the majority side to begin with and will be unchanged.

The second part of the book provides evidence supporting our premises about the majority party's advantages in the Senate. In this part, we examine the nature and extent of the majority party's agenda-setting advantage at successive stages of the Senate's legislative process.

We begin in Chapter 4 with the committee stage. The chapter first reviews literature on Senate committees, noting the general agreement that the majority party dominates committee decision making (though conventional wisdom holds that this advantage is undone later in the legislative process). We discuss the nature of this domination and present data for each standing committee, showing that majority-sponsored bills are more likely to be reported from committee than are minority-sponsored bills.

Chapters 5 and 6 deal with scheduling of bills – that is, deciding which calendar bills are taken up on the Senate floor after having been reported from committee (or, in some cases, without having gone to a committee). The first of these chapters deals with scheduling broadly. The majority party's advantage in advancing bills beyond the committee stage is often thought to be undone partly at the scheduling phase of the legislative process. Filibusters and the Senate's reliance on unanimous consent seem to empower the minority party to block majority efforts. We present various scheduling data we have gathered and show that, although the majority party does not gain an additional advantage at this stage, its committee advantage is perpetuated during scheduling. That is, the proportion of majority bills on the calendar that are scheduled roughly equals the proportion of minority bills on the calendar that are scheduled; but in absolute terms, far more majority bills are scheduled because far more majority bills make it to the calendar in the first place.

In Chapter 6 we narrow our focus on the most frequently discussed aspect of scheduling, filibusters, arguing that the adverse impact of filibusters on the majority party's ability to manipulate outcomes is smaller than one might gather from the literature's preoccupation with filibusters. Though filibusters sometimes stymie the majority, in many circumstances – which are largely overlooked – the filibuster either does not thwart the majority at all or only partially thwarts the majority but does not keep it from getting much of what it wants. We emphasize that, when the majority wants to pursue a bill that the minority opposes, there are various possible outcomes. First, the majority might take no action at all because it knows the bill would be successfully filibustered if pursued. Second, the majority might pursue passage, fight to overcome a filibuster, and lose the fight. Third, the majority might pursue passage, fight to overcome the filibuster, and win the fight. And fourth, the majority might pursue passage, and there might be no filibuster because the minority knows it would lose the fight. We emphasize the point that the literature focuses largely on the first two categories, in which the majority loses. We agree that plenty of cases fall into these two categories. But we argue against what we see as congressional scholars' fairly common tendency to use such cases as a basis for inferring (or at least for strongly suspecting) that the minority party wields something like an absolute veto in the Senate. We advocate a more balanced view that also takes into account the third and fourth categories, in which the majority wins and the minority is unable to stop it. We end the chapter with Senate legislative case studies illustrating each of the four categories, as well as data showing how often the majority wins cloture fights dealing with the scheduling of bills.

In the thinking of many scholars, the Senate's amendment process plays the role of Scylla to the filibuster's Charybdis, with majority legislative endeavors almost surely doomed to founder on one or the other. We thus examine various aspects of the amendment process in Chapters 7, 8, and 9. Chapter 7 deals with how the Senate disposes of amendments. Using data we have collected on all amendments offered during several Congresses, we show that minority-offered amendments are much more likely than majority-offered amendments to be killed by procedural means without ever being voted on directly – suggesting that, for the minority party, gaining consideration of its proposals is more costly than the literature often seems to suppose. This in turn suggests that the amendment process is a less powerful tool for the minority party than is widely believed.

In Chapter 8 we take a closer look at two procedures used to kill many amendments: tabling motions and points of order. Using data on tabling motions and amendments, we show that the bulk of tabling motions are made by majority party senators, that the Senate is more likely to agree to tabling motions made by majority party senators than to tabling motions made by minority party senators, and that tabling motions are used to kill far more minority- than majority-offered amendments. Similarly, we find evidence that points of order disproportionately kill minority-sponsored amendments.

Part II ends with Chapter 9, which examines the effect of successful amendments on policy outcomes. We show an asymmetry in the effects of amendments. Adoption of an amendment that "rolls" the minority party makes it more likely that the minority party will be rolled on final passage of the bill.[14] However, adoption of an amendment that rolls the majority party *does not* make it more likely that the majority party will be rolled on final passage of the bill. This suggests that the minority party does not use the amendment process to fundamentally undermine the majority's efforts and that the majority party does use the amendment process to push bills opposed by the minority.

In Part III we turn to tests of predictions from our theory. In Chapter 10 we first test our model's predictions about the proportion of passing

---

[14] When we say a party is rolled, we mean that a majority of the party's voting members vote against something but it is approved nonetheless.

bills that will move policy in the direction wanted by the majority party, using roll call data from each Congress in the postwar era. We show that, contrary to conventional wisdom, it is consistently the case that most passing bills move policy in the direction of the majority party. We also conduct a more nuanced test of the effects of changes in consideration costs. Our model predicts that, all else constant, as it becomes less costly for the majority party to garner consideration of bills, Senate outcomes should be more to the majority's liking. Using data on bill outcomes, we test this prediction by taking advantage of the fact that Senate procedures create lower majority costs for budget bills than for regular bills. We find that, as predicted, the majority party gets more of what it wants on budget bills than on regular bills. This finding is particularly salient given the centrality of budgeting to public policy.

In Chapter 11 we summarize our results and discuss our conclusions regarding our theory and the role of parties in the Senate. We end by suggesting directions for future research, noting especially the potential for applications of our theory in comparative contexts.

2

The Textbook Senate and Partisan Policy Influence

Like many scholarly enterprises, ours revolves around a puzzle: how do we reconcile the Senate majority party's presumed inability to bias outcomes in its favor with empirical findings that the Senate majority party *does* bias outcomes in its favor? In this chapter we present our take on literature related to this question. We draw insights from traditional Senate scholarship and from the literature on House parties.

Conventional Views of the Senate

A long line of Senate scholarship either explicitly or implicitly assigns little significant policy-making influence to parties. Going back to the earliest and most influential postwar studies of the Senate, the literature focuses on questions regarding how the Senate makes decisions and how power is distributed within the chamber, but at least in passing, such works tend to minimize the role of parties. Though rich in contextual scholarship, this literature offers little in the way of general explanations of Senate behavior.

Matthews (1960: 8), for example, explicitly raises the question of power within the chamber: "Officially, all senators are equal. Yet if the Senate is similar to other groups, some have far more influence than others. What are the patterns of influence in the Senate? Who is influential and why?" He goes on to argue that Senate "folkways" create power inequalities, but he is clear that these folkways do not include much in the way of party influence: "With rare exceptions the senators are not beholden to the party leaders; they had little to do with the senators' nomination or election. The tradition of localism and popular reverence

for legislative 'independence' largely frustrate any efforts by ... Senate
leaders of a party to 'purge' unfaithful members. As a result, the political
parties in the Senate are, when compared with the parties in most parliamentary democracies and a number of American states, rather disunited
organizations" (Matthews 1960: 119–121).

According to subsequent literature, the individualism that Matthews
saw as a defining feature of the distribution of Senate power became *more*
pronounced over the decades that followed (Huitt 1961; Lehnen 1967;
Ripley 1969; Sinclair 1989; Smith 1989). The 1950s Senate observed by
Matthews came to be seen as a collegial, clubby organization in which
senators typically refrained from exercising procedural prerogatives
when using them would impinge upon the chamber's ability to operate
effectively. Ripley (1969) argues that during the two decades following
World War II, the Senate changed from a decentralized, committee-based
power structure to an even more decentralized, increasingly individualistic power structure. In considering the role of party leaders, he enumer-
ates their duties as a threefold set of expectations (and limitations): to
state party positions; to appeal for unity on important bills (though coer-
cion is "illegitimate"); and to collect and distribute information about
scheduling. Ripley's (1969: 106) conclusion that "parties in the present
Senate play a limited role in restricting the options and choices of individual members" seems, if anything, a generous characterization of the
general view of party strength at the time.

With few exceptions (Brady, Brody, and Epstein 1989; Patterson
1989), this sense of strong individualism at the expense of party influence
continued among Senate scholars through the 1970s and 1980s (Bullock
and Brady 1983; Clausen and Cheney 1970; Davidson 1985, 1989a;
Oppenheimer 1985; Sinclair 1989; Smith 1989; Walker 1977). By the
late 1980s, the transformation toward individualism observed by Ripley
(1969) had apparently reached full maturity. According to Davidson
(1985: 250), "[T]he hard core of Senate leadership today is its steward-
ship – some would say subservience – to the scattered goals and schedules
of the Senate's 100 members and to the Senate as an institution." Indeed,
"the term Senate leadership, for many observers, is an oxymoron: a pure
contradiction, like military intelligence" (Davidson 1989a: 275).

According to Sinclair (1989), an influx of new members with different
policy views in the late 1960s and early 1970s, coupled with changes in
the media environment and the introduction of newly contentious issues
to the Senate agenda, transformed the Senate into an institution dominated by individual senators using their institutional power to pursue

national reputations on the Senate stage. Moreover, the policy-making arena of choice increasingly was not Senate committees, but the Senate floor – where amendment activity, lengthy speeches, and dilatory tactics were becoming mainstays of life in the upper chamber (Smith 1989). According to Smith (1989: 348), "[E]xcessive individualism and chaos on the floor appear to be as much of an equilibrium as the Senate can achieve." Thus, the best that Senate floor leaders could hope to do was accommodate and manage these varied individual interests with creative procedural scheduling, as evidenced by the rise in complex unanimous consent agreements (Smith and Flathman 1989).[1]

We suspect that the relative inattention to parties and the repudiation of the notion that parties substantially influence decisions are in part a product of how political scientists tended to conceptualize parties for much of the postwar era. That is, through at least the late 1980s, "party influence" was largely equated with the Westminster-style responsible-party model, in which party leaders dictate party positions to party backbenchers and then pursue these positions primarily via strong party discipline on substantive votes.[2] With this as the standard, it is not surprising that Senate parties seemed to have negligible power.

Another factor that no doubt contributed to the prevailing view of Senate parties is the congressional literature's limited attention to partisan agenda setting. By the early 1990s, however, there was a well-established line of scholarship in which agenda setting featured prominently. Congressional scholarship began to incorporate formal models of legislatures that highlighted the significance of agenda setting (Gilligan and Krehbiel 1990; Plott and Levine 1977; McKelvey 1976; Shepsle 1979; Shepsle and Weingast 1987; Weingast and Marshall 1988). At the same time, following an increasingly apparent rise in congressional partisanship in the post–reform era, these scholars began to focus their theoretical and empirical efforts on the question of whether – and to what end – parties manipulate the congressional agenda (Cox and McCubbins 1993, 1994; Kiewiet and McCubbins 1991; Krehbiel 1993; Rohde 1991).

This literature, however, focused almost entirely on the House of Representatives; Senate scholarship did not follow suit. Instead, the

---

[1] On unanimous consent agreements and the logic of their use, see also Keith (1977) and Krehbiel (1986), respectively.

[2] Consider, for example, the sentiment in the last sentence of the earlier Matthews (1960: 119–121) quote: "As a result, the political parties in the Senate are, when compared with the parties in most parliamentary democracies and a number of American states, rather disunited organizations."

procedural realities of the modern Senate, paired with a continuing sense of strong individual prerogatives, created a growing disjuncture between the House and Senate literatures on the question of party influence. Over the past two decades, the claim that the House majority party enjoys a consistent, pronounced advantage in setting the legislative agenda has become widely accepted by congressional scholars (Smith 2007). The same cannot be said regarding the Senate majority party.

In fact, as the role of parties in House decision making has grown, so too has the resistance of many scholars to claims of Senate majority party power. This resistance is particularly stark in the face of attempts to export agenda-setting theories directly from the House to the Senate (Smith 2007). In one concise statement, Smith (2005: 256–257) sums up a chorus of opinions on the role of parties in shaping policy in the Senate:

> The absence of general limits on debate and amendments limits the value of majority status and having a strong majority leader. Under precedent established in the 1930s, the majority leader is recognized to speak or make a motion before other senators seeking recognition. This privilege gives the majority leader the opportunity to move that the Senate take up certain legislation, offer an amendment, propose a unanimous-consent agreement, or address a subject of the leader's choice. The right of first recognition does not guarantee that the Senate will vote on the majority leader's proposals. The minority party, if cohesive, may block legislation by filibuster, even by refusing to allow a vote on the motion to proceed to the consideration of a measure.

> Preventing Senate consideration of a policy proposal, even if opposed by a majority, is generally not possible. Any senator may offer an amendment on any subject to most legislation. That is, non-germane amendments are allowed on most measures. As a general rule, therefore, the majority leader is unable to prevent certain subjects from receiving floor consideration. The leader can filibuster an amendment or take the underlying bill off the floor (by unanimous consent), which produces a stalemate.

This characterization succinctly captures the main conclusion, as well as the underlying reasoning, of the mainstream view of Senate parties. The basic majority party agenda-setting challenge is as follows. If the party has controversial policy items it wishes to have considered, it will be faced with holds, filibusters, and the need for unanimous consent. However, if the party wishes to keep unwanted bills from being considered, it will have to battle these proposals as they bubble up onto the floor through the Senate's open amendment process.

Ironically, the sharp rise in partisan conflict over the past two decades might have *strengthened* this viewpoint. Many scholars see the Senate of the 1990s and 2000s as one in which partisanship merely exacerbates the gridlock and dysfunction caused by individualism. That is, though the literature now broadly acknowledges rising partisanship in the Senate, many scholars still view the chamber as fundamentally individualistic. From this viewpoint, partisan and individual goals act as competing interests, putting enormous pressure on Senate leadership to deliver partisan advantage in a chamber set up to empower individual interests (Sinclair 2001a). Instead of resulting in partisan advantage, however, this has, according to the conventional view, resulted in either gridlock (Binder 1999, 2003; Smith 2005) or compromise (Oppenheimer and Hetherington 2008).

Along these lines, the filibuster is now a subject of substantial scholarship, including studies of the procedure's history (Wawro and Schickler 2004, 2006), the sources and consequences of attempts to reform the procedure (Binder 1997; Binder and Smith 1997; Koger 2006, 2007; Swift 1996), and the question of how to measure filibusters (Beth 1995, Beth and Bach 2003). Filibuster activity increased sharply from the 1960s through the 1980s (Binder and Smith 1997; Davidson 1985; Smith 1989) and has become even more common over the past two decades (Evans and Lipinski 2005; Koger 2010; Sinclair 2002, 2005).[3] Moreover, while filibustering in the middle of the 20th century was focused primarily on killing legislation, the modern version of this tactic has been expanded and used as leverage for other ends, such as policy concessions on unrelated matters (Sinclair 2002).

One way of gauging the current state of the discipline is to look at how American politics textbooks present Senate agenda setting:

The rules of the Senate ... reflect an egalitarian, individualistic outlook. The right of individuals to debate at length, and to offer amendments on any subject, is generally protected. Only extraordinary majorities can limit debate or amendments. And for reasons of practicality, most scheduling is done by unanimous consent. The majority party usually must negotiate with minority party members to schedule floor action and to bring important measures to a vote. (Smith, Roberts, and Vander Wielen 2006: 112)

Increasingly, it has been the party leadership in the Senate that has tried to direct the traffic. The Senate's rules do not allow the centralization of power in the party leadership that has been seen in the House.... So the Senate's majority and minority party leaders consult extensively with their party colleagues, rather than

---

[3] Filibustering of judicial nominations, in particular, has drawn much attention from scholars (Bell 2002, Beth 2002, Binder and Maltzman 2002, Koger 2008, Wawro and Schickler 2006). Moreover, a wave of Republican filibusters of legislation being pushed by Democrats gained a great deal of publicity during the 110th Congress.

command them, to build the unanimous consent agreements that allow bills to
be brought to a vote without risking a filibuster by an unhappy senator. (Hershey
2007: 254)

[T]he Senate's rules emphasize individual prerogatives (unlimited freedom to
debate and to offer amendments, including nonrelevant amendments) and minority rights (those of the minority party, a faction, or even a single senator). "The
Senate," said one member, "is run for the convenience of one Senator to the incon-
venience of 99." (Davidson, Oleszek, and Lee 2008: 259)

Thus, despite the acknowledged rise in partisanship, the textbook view
of the Senate remains. It emphasizes the plight of party leaders, who are
seen as constrained, impotent, and beholden to the power of individual
senators exercising their institutionally supported prerogatives.

Do We Present a Straw Man?

One potential critique is that our characterization of the conventional
view (i.e., the majority does not influence outcomes because its opponents, whether the minority party or individual senators, thwart its legislative efforts) is a straw man. While we admit that our characterization
omits some nuances of various scholars' takes on the Senate, we think it
is entirely defensible.

We see three possible forms of the straw man allegation. First, one
might read us as saying the conventional view implies that majority party
opponents dominate the majority party. This is not our take on the conventional literature (and we agree it would be a straw man if it were).

The second form of the allegation is that the Senate literature *does*
offer examples of the majority party using procedural tools and caucus
cohesion to win legislative battles, contrary to our partyless characterization. We acknowledge that the literature features many anecdotes wherein
the majority party wins a procedural fight at some point in the legislative
process during the battle over a particular bill, but works featuring such
anecdotes typically also feature many examples of opponents thwarting
majority efforts. Some authors offer no explicit conclusions about the
balance of influence between the majority and it opponents, leaving readers to guess whether the author thinks the majority has any systematic
advantage. In a sense, we think it fair for authors in this category to
claim that we mischaracterize them, inasmuch as they do not say the
majority has no advantages; but we think it would be unreasonable for
such authors to claim that we have seriously mischaracterized their work,
given that they give readers little or no impression that they think the
majority systematically wins legislative battles.

In other instances, authors explicitly address the question of majority influence but conclude that no broad generalization is justified. A common variant of this take is that the Senate is such a complex mix of individualism, fluid coalitions, flexible rules, easy amendments, and supermajoritarianism that no generalization can possibly capture enough Senate behavior to be worthwhile.

We emphasize that an important point of agreement among all these variants is that each either suggests, asserts, or implies that there is insufficient reason to accept propositions along the lines of our main contention – that is, that the Senate majority party's advantages allow it to systematically bias policy in its favor. Thus, although in some cases our characterization of the conventional wisdom is something of a simplification, we feel that it is still a reasonable portrayal of the conventional view.

The third form of the straw man allegation is that, although many people in the field still buy into one of the lines of thinking we have described, many others have come to suspect, if not outright believe, that the majority party has systematic advantages. Observation of recent Senate scholarship and conference interactions convinces us that a fair number of people fall into this category. Even these scholars, however, remain troubled by the literature's inability to explain how the majority party *could* have an advantage; common thinking seems to be, "My gut tells me the majority party matters, but no one has yet provided a way to reconcile my gut instinct with the things that the conventional view has taught me about the Senate." Scholars who think this way do not buy the *conclusion* that we characterize as the conventional view (i.e., that there is no majority party advantage) but do buy the major *premises* that we characterize as the underpinnings of the conventional view (the Senate's amendment process makes it easy for any senator to offer an amendment, etc.).

Even from this perspective, our characterization is not a straw man inasmuch as most scholars think the premises seem to support the conclusion that the majority party cannot systematically manipulate decisions. Given that our theory shares the basic premises of the conventional view, however, another way of thinking about it is that we build on conventional thinking to address a serious conundrum in the literature. What differ are the conclusions that we draw about party influence. Indeed, this is how we see our work – not as a wholesale refutation of conventional literature, but as a work that uses the insights of previous literature to draw new conclusions about the Senate.

Party Effects in the Senate

As previously noted, works dissenting from the conventional view have become more common in the past decade.⁴ A collection of essays entitled *The Contentious Senate*, edited by Rae and Campbell (2001), made a cautious but clear case for reconsidering the role of parties in the Senate. In the introductory chapter, Campbell and Rae (2001: 2) set the stage for a break from the conventional wisdom: "We join a small but growing set of congressional scholars who focus on the impact of mounting partisanship on party leaders and party caucuses in the Senate.... We conclude that party affiliation is indeed playing a wider role in the contemporary Senate."

Several chapters in the volume reinforce this claim. Sinclair (2001b), for example, acknowledges the continuing need for the majority leadership to consult with the minority party but outlines a number of scheduling strategies that increasingly provide for majority party agenda-setting advantages. Similarly, Evans and Oleszek (2001) point to a growing arsenal of procedural devices – such as filling the amendment tree and bypassing committees by means of Rule XIV – that Senate majority leaders use to promote the party's "message" items. In analyzing three major Senate floor battles from the 106th Congress, Davidson (2001: 41) argues that these fights "dispel this impression of muted partisanship. In all three cases, party leaders planned and orchestrated the proceedings, and party lines remained relatively firm in voting." He goes on to conclude, "On the evidence of these three cases, at least, one must say that the Senate, like the House of Representatives, has become a pervasively partisan institution" (42).⁵

In a series of underappreciated conference papers, Schiller (1995, 2000, 2001) also began to lay the groundwork for thinking about partisan agenda setting in the Senate, making a somewhat restrained argument for majority party procedural advantage on the Senate floor. In her earliest work on the topic, investigating the use of floor procedural tactics

---

⁴ Ornstein, Peabody, and Rohde (1993: 18) had previously noted possible party effects: "If the increased partisanship between the parties and the increased homogeneity within them continues, the patterns of policymaking in the Senate will be significantly different from the pattern of the postwar period."

⁵ Evans (2001), using a similar "three bill" approach, draws similar conclusions. In particular, he shows that party leadership is very active and effective at setting and managing the floor agenda on two of the three bills he looks at, and largely inactive on the third.

by party leaders, Schiller (1995: 25) concludes, "Whatever emphasis has been placed on the impact of rules in the Senate has focused on how the filibuster prevents successful leadership and thwarts a party majority from enacting preferred policies. However, this is too narrow a window from which to view Senate procedure. There are means by which leaders can circumvent the need to invoke cloture to enact legislation and the cases presented here reveal attempts to do just that."

Schiller investigates the effectiveness of various floor management tactics – especially "filling the amendment tree" – showing some evidence of success on high-priority majority agenda items, but is careful to also point out the limitations of leaders' powers, based partly on the power of individual senators (Schiller 2000, 2001).

Quantitative Evidence of Partisan Agenda Setting

Following these largely qualitative analyses of Senate partisanship, a variety of quantitative studies of party effects – some specific to agenda setting and some more general – pointed toward similar conclusions. Campbell, Cox, and McCubbins's (2002) investigation of party roll rates in the Senate shows a huge disparity between majority and minority party roll rates, with the majority consistently achieving low roll rates and the minority suffering rolls more than a quarter of the time. The results, which they take as indicators of a majority (negative) agenda-setting advantage, are even more pronounced for post–World War II Congresses. Gailmard and Jenkins (2007) extend this analysis, demonstrating that majority roll rates are similar in the House and Senate but vary in an important way depending on the agenda-setting capacity of the majority party over a particular type of agenda item (e.g., on nominations the Senate shares agenda-setting power with the president). It is interesting, however, that the minority party's major weapon for affecting the agenda, the filibuster, is not particularly relevant in predicting the minority party's roll rate in the Senate (Gailmard and Jenkins 2008a).

Beyond roll rates, which serve as a summary measure of negative agenda-setting advantage, there is also evidence of majority party influence at specific stages of the agenda process. Campbell's (2001) work reveals that, like their counterparts in the House, Senate majority party contingents on committees – especially the most powerful committees – are representative of the party as a whole, leaving Senate committees well positioned to act as agents of the party. Krutz (2005) shows that the Senate majority party structures committee processes and thereby increases the likelihood of committees working on majority-sponsored bills. Koger and Fowler (2006) demonstrate that majority party members are more likely than their minority party counterparts to have their bills advance out of committee.[6]

Recent results also indicate a majority party agenda-setting advantage on the floor. Yakee (2003) shows that Senate (and House) leaders strategically schedule controversial votes on major legislation right before long recesses, adding time pressure and giving themselves extra bargaining leverage. This strategic scheduling context is further demonstrated by Evans and Lapinski (2005), who argue that holds are actually an informational tool used by the leadership. Moreover, they show that the average number of holds per party member drops significantly as that party gains majority status, suggesting that the majority party is better able to schedule bills favored by its own membership. And evidence presented by Campbell (2004) suggests that, at least in some cases, the majority leader uses his or her own version of "fighting fire with fire" by counter-amending and by filling the amendment tree to fight off attacks and secure the majority party floor agenda.

Perhaps the most comprehensive assessment of the Senate's agenda content is Lee's (2009) analysis of partisanship and agenda politics. Her study aims to understand why "fellow partisans in Congress agree across so many diverse issues while simultaneously disagreeing with members of the opposing party" (Lee 2009: 18). She argues compellingly that this behavior goes beyond common ideology and is the result of heavily institutionalized partisan "teams" that seek to manipulate the Senate's agenda for both policy and public perception benefits. Lee's results suggest meaningful majority party influence over the composition of the Senate's agenda.

Evidence of a Partisan Policy Advantage

Several recent studies have demonstrated a majority party bias in Senate policy outcomes. Bargen (2004: 25) looks at the direction of policy movement on final passage and finds that "when Democrats are in the majority they pass a generally liberal policy agenda.... Republican majorities behave just the opposite." Chiou and Rothenberg (2003, 2006) find support for their "party plus pivots" agenda-setting model by showing that "gridlock scores" are best explained by the gridlock intervals associated

---

[6] Moore and Thomas (1991) foreshadow this result.

with key party actors.[7] Combining interest group scorecard and Senate roll call data, Roberts and Bell (2008) find that, when casting votes, individual senators do not defect from their party's preferred position more frequently than do their counterparts in the House of Representatives.

Beyond the roll call record, evidence suggests that the distribution of benefits, as doled out by the Senate, also tends to be biased toward the constituents of the majority party. According to Crespin and Finocchiaro (2008), distribution of earmark dollars significantly favors the majority party.[8] More abstractly, in earlier work (Den Hartog and Monroe 2008a), we found that the 2001 change in majority party control of the Senate following Jim Jeffords's party switch increased the value of Democratic "constituent firms," while devaluing their Republican counterparts.

Notwithstanding these findings, the big question remains unanswered: *how* could the majority party have an advantage? Like many other scholars, we assume that any majority party policy influence in the Senate stems predominantly from an agenda-setting advantage rather than from party discipline on substantive votes and that the debate turns largely on the question of whether such an advantage exists. We address this topic from both theoretical and empirical perspectives in the rest of the book.

Summary

Scholarship on the post–World War II Senate mostly characterizes the chamber as dominated by the prerogatives of individual senators and minority coalitions, often at the expense of party leaders. This conventional view has evolved to account for the rising partisanship of the past two decades but largely concludes that increased partisanship has led to increased Senate stalemate or compromise, but not to a majority party advantage.

Yet over the past decade, a growing number of studies have found evidence of party effects. Some of this evidence points directly to times in the legislative process when the majority party has an agenda-setting advantage; some simply points to broad patterns of majority party bias over legislative outcomes. However, this new evidence of partisan

---

[7] Note, however, that there is some debate as to the proper calculation and interpretation of gridlock intervals and scores (Binder 2008; Chiou and Rothenberg 2008a,b).

[8] See also Shepsle et al. (2009) on the distribution of pork in the Senate.

advantage comes largely without a satisfying theoretical framework. In the next chapter, we present a theory aimed at answering that question in a theoretical sense. Then, in the chapters that follow, we investigate empirically the plausibility of this theoretical approach by looking systematically at the crucial stages of the legislative process in the Senate. It is to these tasks that we now turn.

3

The Costly-Consideration Agenda-Setting Theory

Congressional scholars widely believe that the majority party's influence over the agenda in the U.S. Senate is limited, due mainly to the chamber's supermajoritarian procedures and open amendment process. In this chapter, we present a spatial theory of agenda setting that incorporates these aspects of Senate procedure, yet leads to the conclusion that, although it is unable to dictate the agenda unilaterally, the majority party nonetheless influences the agenda to an extent largely unappreciated by prior scholarship.

One of the contributions of this model is to resolve the apparent contradiction in Senate scholarship discussed in the preceding chapter: recent studies conclude that the majority enjoys greater legislative success than the minority, but there is little understanding of how this could be the case. A strength of our model is that it incorporates conventional beliefs about Senate procedures and provides a clear analogy to Senate procedure.

The model's assumptions reflect the broad theoretical premises we discussed in the first chapter: first, agenda setting is costly; second, it is less costly for the majority party than for others; and, third, the majority party has a first-proposal advantage.

In a sense, our model is a one-dimensional spatial version of nonspatial bargaining models (Rubinstein 1982). One advantage of our model, however, is that it incorporates the effect of the status quo on bargaining outcomes (in bargaining models, the reversion in the absence of a deal is that each actor gets nothing, which is clearly not the case in the Senate).

In the remainder of the chapter, we first lay out the assumptions and structure of our model and then discuss how the game plays out under various circumstances. In Appendix A, we also consider the implication of relaxing some of our simplifying assumptions. In Chapter 10, we return to the model to derive and test several hypotheses.

Consideration and Agenda Setting

Before presenting our model, we remind the reader of a key aspect of our terminology and our conceptualization of agenda setting – discussed in some detail in Chapter 1 – that together provide important underpinnings for our model. We use the term *consideration* prominently, but our definition is different from that in common usage; for us, it means getting a final passage vote on a proposal rather than making a proposal – or even making a proposal and having it debated, amended, or otherwise acted upon by the floor. Similarly, we believe *agenda setting* in the Senate should be defined as getting a final passage vote on a proposal. Thus, when we refer to proposals being considered, what we mean is getting a final vote on passage.

The reason is straightforward. In many cases, the power of agenda setting stems from the ability to affect things such as a group's choice set or the order in which a group votes on alternatives (McKelvey 1976; Riker 1982; Schofield 1978; Shepsle 1979; Shepsle and Weingast 1984). In such cases, it is usually assumed that a proposal offered by an agenda setter will be voted upon. If, however, making a proposal does not carry with it a guarantee that the proposal will be voted upon, then simply being able to offer a proposal, or to garner floor actions that fall short of a vote on acceptance of a proposal, does not necessarily grant any agenda-setting power.[1]

Most studies of congressional agenda setting implicitly equate proposal and consideration of a proposal, but most such studies focus on the House of Representatives. The assumption is quite sensible in the context of the House, since most significant bills reach the floor via a special rule that structures the amendment process and stipulates that there will be a final vote on the bill.

In the Senate, however, it is quite plausible that there is a disjuncture between the ability to propose a measure and the ability to guarantee that it will be voted upon. Filibusters, tabling motions, and many other procedural tactics often prevent proposals, whether bills or amendments, from

---

[1] Obviously, legislators benefit in various ways from proposing items on the floor, offering debate and amendments, and engaging in other floor actions. For present purposes, however, the utility derived from these activities is beyond the scope of our theory and, moreover, is generally not considered in most theories of agenda setting.

being voted on directly. In other words, much of the shaping of choices that senators vote upon – that is, much of the agenda setting – occurs on the floor (Smith 1989). Defining agenda setting as getting something *to* the floor, or as getting at least some type of floor activity, thus runs the risk of missing much of the important action in the Senate. What is important from an agenda-setting perspective is getting the floor to vote on passing the proposal.

The Costly-Consideration Agenda-Setting Game

Actors
As noted, the model is a one-dimensional, complete information game. It features three players: the majority party proposer, M; the minority party proposer, Mi; and the floor median, F; all are assumed to have linear, symmetric, single-peaked utility functions. The utility functions for each of the three actors are

$$u_M(x) = -|x - M| - c$$
$$u_{Mi}(x) = -|x - Mi| - k$$
$$u_F(x) = -|x - F|$$

In these functions, x represents the location of policy on a given dimension; M, Mi, and F, respectively,[2] represent the actors' ideal point on that dimension; c is the unique consideration cost paid by the majority proposer; and k is the unique consideration cost paid by the minority proposer. Note that c and k will be zero if the associated actor chooses not to make a proposal and that each actor's utility decreases on a given dimension as policy moves away from the actor's ideal point. Table 3.1 summarizes our model's notation and definitions.

Intuitively, the majority party proposer (M) represents a delegate of the majority party caucus, such as a party leader or a floor manager, who enjoys procedural advantages that follow from the standing rules, precedents, chamber norms, caucus rules, or majority party cohesion on procedural votes.[3] The minority party proposer (Mi) represents a coalition of senators with preferences at odds with those of M. We label

---

[2] We distinguish between players and their ideal points by italicizing references to their ideal points.
[3] Unlike some models (e.g., Cox and McCubbins 2005), we do not assume that the majority party proposer represents the caucus's ideological median voter.

TABLE 3.1. *Model Notation and Definitions*

Notation	Definition
Actors	
M (*M*)	Majority proposer (majority proposer's ideal point)
Mi (*Mi*)	Minority proposer (majority proposer's ideal point)
F (*F*)	Floor median (floor median's ideal point)
Costs	
c	Majority consideration cost
k	Minority consideration cost
Proposals	
a	Majority proposal
b	Minority proposal

this actor the "minority party" proposer because we think the minority party caucus is typically the most formidable opposition coalition. Given the Senate's individualistic character, however, a wide range of coalitions – including single senators, sometimes from the majority caucus – oppose the majority party on different occasions. Accordingly, some readers might prefer to think of Mi as the "opposition proposer," without specifying that the actor represents the minority party. A crucial distinction between M and Mi is that M wields the majority party's procedural advantages and Mi does not. Finally, the move by the floor median at the end of the game represents the chamber making final decisions by majority vote. (We assume there is no party discipline on final votes – not because we think such discipline never occurs, but because we emphasize that the majority party can manipulate outcomes even in the absence of discipline of final passage votes; to the extent that such discipline exists, our model understates the majority party's advantage.)[4]

Sequence, Actions, and Additional Assumptions

The sequence of the game, shown in Figure 3.1, is as follows. First, M moves for consideration of a proposal, *a*, or does not; if moving for consideration, M pays a consideration cost, *c*, to have the proposal considered by the chamber.[5] Second, Mi either moves for consideration of a

---

[4] One might ask, "Why doesn't the floor median simply make counterproposals at her ideal point?" The short answer is that in our model the costs of gaining consideration for the bill deter the floor median from doing so. In fact, all else constant, the majority party proposer does *better* as the opposition proposer's ideal point moves closer to the floor median. We expand upon this in Appendix A.

[5] For simplicity, we show outcomes rather than payoffs at each end node in Figure 3.1.

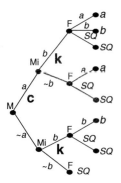

FIGURE 3.1. Extensive Form of the Costly-Consideration Agenda-Setting Game.

counteroffer, *b*, or does not; if moving for consideration, Mi pays a consideration cost, *k*, to have the proposal considered by the chamber. Third, F chooses between the status quo and whatever proposals M and Mi have offered.[6] The outcome of the game (i.e., the chamber policy decision) is whichever alternative F chooses.[7]

We also assume that $c < k$. That is, we assume that the majority party actor pays a lower consideration cost than his counterpart. This assumption is, perhaps, both the most crucial and most controversial of the model. Accordingly, we spend the whole of Part II of the book – Chapters 4 through 9 – presenting arguments and empirical tests to establish the plausibility of this assumption. Thus, we hope skeptical readers will set their concerns aside for the moment, focus on the model, and reengage

[6] Note that if both M and Mi propose bills, F chooses simultaneously among the three alternatives (*a*, *b*, or *SQ*). A more literal representation of actual legislative practice would be to treat a minority proposal as an amendment to a majority proposal and to have F first choose between *a* and *b*, then choose between the winner and the status quo. Modeling F's decision as a simultaneous choice yields the same result as the more nuanced but less parsimonious two-stage choice.

[7] In some cases, such as when the majority leader fills the amendment tree, the minority does not have the right to make a counterproposal. In other cases, the majority uses second-degree amendments to opponents' first-degree amendments to modify the opponents' proposal (see Wilkerson 1999 on various permutations of amendment strategies and their effectiveness). Our model essentially excludes each possibility, since it specifies that each side gets exactly one proposal opportunity. This choice is defensible inasmuch as each of those situations biases outcomes farther in the majority's favor than does the situation we model (i.e., the minority getting the final proposal). In other words, we model the toughest case for the majority party. Our model can easily accommodate each situation; however, the minority being unable to make a proposal is a special case in which the minority consideration cost is prohibitively high. When the majority uses second-degree amendments against minority amendments, it is essentially raising new barriers to passage of the proposal (i.e., raising consideration costs).

the question of asymmetric consideration costs in later chapters. For now, we note merely that consideration costs c and k represent the scarce resources, such as time, that legislators devote to pushing a bill to the point of final consideration.

We make a number of additional assumptions to simplify the model. The first two are innocuous: we assume that neither M nor Mi makes a proposal if indifferent between making a proposal and not making a proposal, and that F accepts a proposed bill (i.e., a or b) over the status quo if indifferent between a proposal and the status quo. We also assume that $M < F < Mi$ (i.e., we assume a leftward majority party).

The next two simplifying assumptions do have substantive significance for the outcomes of our game. These assumptions are plausible but clearly will not hold all the time. The first is that the ideal points of M and Mi are equidistant from the floor median's ideal point. Though clearly an oversimplification, this premise makes sense inasmuch as it holds constant one of the possible sources of (dis)advantage for each party and thereby helps to underscore the impact of costs and first-proposal power. If, for example, M were closer to F than Mi, M would be in a better position, relative to Mi, to offer bills that F likes on pure policy grounds. The second assumption is that k (and thus c) is smaller than the distance between the ideal points of M and Mi. In Appendix A, we relax each of these assumptions in turn and discuss some of the implications; in short, the basic results of the model – most important, the advantage to the majority actor – remain largely unaltered, and in some cases become even more pronounced under the relaxed assumptions.

Backward Induction

We now consider what the outcomes of the game will be for status quos in different regions. We do not provide a formal proof; we instead sketch the logic of the game, which is fairly straightforward. Given the nature of the game, we can use backward induction to find a subgame perfect equilibrium. In this section, we describe the backward induction in the hope of giving the reader an intuitive sense of how the game plays out and why it plays out the way it does. In the section that follows, we offer a series of examples to help illuminate the dynamics of the model.

We begin with the last move, in which the floor median, F, chooses an alternative, and that alternative is the outcome of the game. This stage is fairly trivial: F will consider the locations of the status quo, as well as whichever of the possible alternatives, a and b, have been proposed, and will choose the one that is closest to F. This creates an important constraint that affects decisions of the majority and minority players: to be successful (i.e., passed by the chamber), any proposed alternative to the status quo must be at least as close to F as the status quo.

In the preceding step of the game, Mi considers whether there is a proposal, b, that (1) is an improvement of at least k over the outcome that will occur if Mi does not make a proposal (i.e., will offset the consideration costs of the offer) and (2) will be preferred by F to both the status quo and a (if M has made a proposal). If so, then Mi proposes the b that meets these conditions and is closest to Mi; if not, then Mi makes no proposal. Since, at the time of this decision, Mi knows the status quo, whether M has made a proposal, and (if so) the location of a, this is a straightforward choice for Mi. An important effect of the cost, k, is to create an interval the width of k, centered around F, which we call the *minority no-offer zone*. In essence, if either the status quo or a majority proposal is in this zone, then the largest possible policy gain that the minority could achieve by making a proposal (that F would accept over the status quo and the majority proposal) is outweighed by the consideration cost of such a proposal, so the minority's best course of action is to make no (counter) proposal.

Since this zone plays a significant part in the solution to the game, we label the leftward (i.e., the majority-side) end of the interval NO_L and the rightward (minority-side) end of the interval NO_R, as shown in a number of the figures that follow.[8] If either the status quo or a is in this zone, then it is not possible for Mi to make a proposal that meets both the conditions above. Since there is at least one alternative in this interval (the status quo and/or a), F will not accept any b that is outside the interval and thus farther from F than at least one alternative; but there is no potential b in the interval that is enough of an improvement for Mi over the alternative to offset the cost, k (since the no-offer zone has width k).

In the first move of the game, M considers what offer (if any) Mi will make, as well as what the outcome of the game will be, in the absence of an offer from M. M looks for a proposal, a, that (1) improves on that outcome by more than the consideration cost, c, that M must pay to propose a and (2) is preferred by F to both the status quo and the best counterproposal (if any) that Mi can make. If there is such an a, the optimal proposal, a^*, for M will be the point that meets this condition and is

---

[8] Note that, under our standard model, $NO_L = F - k/2$ and $NO_R = F + k/2$. However, in Appendix A, where we relax some of the assumptions, this does not always hold true.

closest to *M*. Note that the majority's cost, *c*, creates a majority no-offer zone, similar to the minority no-offer zone. We explain the effect of this zone in the next section.

Illustrations of the Game's Dynamics

Before discussing outcomes of the game, we examine examples that illustrate the logic of the model. We can unpack the dynamics of the minority no-offer zone by viewing the game from the perspective of the minority proposer Mi. Note that Mi will make decisions about whether or not to make a proposal based on simple utility calculations, and recall that there are two components of Mi's utility function: policy distance and consideration costs. Mi's utility decreases as policy moves away from her ideal point and also as she pays costs to gain consideration of a proposal.

With that in mind, Figure 3.2a represents the hypothetical scenario in which the status quo is at the minority proposer's ideal point, *Mi*, and the majority proposer, M, has made a proposal, *a*, on his side of the floor median, *F*. This is not the equilibrium proposal (we discuss equilibrium majority proposals later). It does, however, represent a quintessential example of a large majority policy advantage and a real legislative pickle for the minority actor.

The gray bar in Figure 3.2a shows the size of the utility loss – based purely on increased policy distance between the new proposal and the status quo – that Mi will suffer if she decides not to make a counter-proposal. Because *F* is closer to M's proposal than the status quo, the proposal will pass, and Mi will suffer a large utility loss.

In a costless world, the minority actor could minimize this loss by making a counterproposal. Of course, Mi's proposal would have to be closer to *F* than was M's proposal, *a*, in order to ensure that it would win out. This has the effect of constraining how far in her direction the minority proposer can move policy. But continuing our hypothetical example into Figure 3.2b, we see a counterproposal, *b*, made by Mi that significantly reduces her policy utility loss. Mi's proposal brings policy back to the minority side of the floor median's ideal point, *F* prefers that proposal to both the majority proposal and the status quo, and thus it would pass.

However, it is not in Mi's best interest to make this counterproposal, and Figure 3.2c shows why. In order to have proposal *b* considered, Mi must pay a consideration cost, *k*, which adds to her utility loss. We convert the size of this cost into the same metric as policy utility in Figure 3.2c, as represented by the textured bar. If Mi does make counterproposal

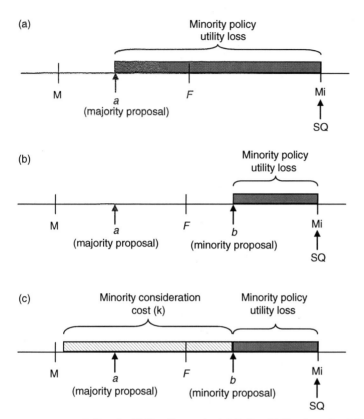

FIGURE 3.2. Minority Utility Example: (a) Policy Utility Loss for Minority Actor from Majority Proposal, (b) Minority Utility Example: Policy Utility Loss from Minority Counterproposal, and (c) Policy Utility Loss Plus Consideration Cost for Minority from Minority Counterproposal.

b, then she still suffers some policy utility loss, plus the cost of consideration. If we compare the pure policy loss from Figure 3.2a with the summed utility loss in Figure 3.2c, we see that Mi is actually better off simply allowing the majority proposal to go without a counter.

If we tweak our example just a little, it is easy to understand the logic of the minority no-offer zone. Figures 3.3a and 3.3b present a counterfactual scenario that leaves Mi perfectly indifferent between making a counterproposal, *b*, in response to M's proposal, *a*, which is at the left edge of the minority no-offer zone, NO_L. The policy loss from M's proposal (the gray bar in Figure 3.3a) is equal to the sum of the policy loss from Mi's proposal (gray bar in Figure 3.3b) plus the consideration cost (the textured bar in Figure 3.3b).

(a)

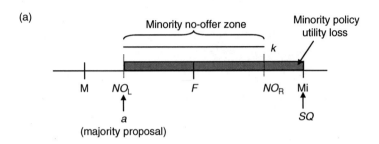

(b)

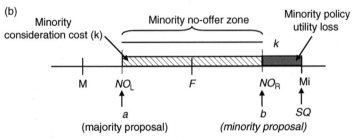

FIGURE 3.3. Minority Proposer Indifference Example: (a) Utility Loss without a Counterproposal and (b) Summed Utility Loss with a Counterproposal.

By assumption, Mi would not make a proposal in this knife edge case. But this misses the point. The key is that M can constrain Mi by making a proposal on the majority side of the space that is just close enough to F to prevent a viable, utility-improving counteroffer. If, for example, we hold the rest of our Figure 3.3 example constant and imagine different locations of M's proposal, it is easy to see how any proposal by M between NO_L and NO_R would prevent a utility-improving counteroffer from Mi. More generally, there is no utility-improving counterproposal for any majority proposal or status quo that falls in the minority no-offer zone, because no passing minority proposal would represent a policy utility improvement large enough to offset the consideration cost, k. This is precisely why the minority no-offer zone is the size of k and centered on F.

Shifting our example again, we can see that the dynamics underlying the majority advantage shown earlier are not dependent on having a status quo at the minority proposer's ideal point. Figures 3.4a and 3.4b make the same type of counterfactual utility comparisons as Figures 3.2a–3.2c and 3.3a–3.3b, but in this case the status quo is inside the minority no-offer zone, between F and NO_R. We can see that the majority proposal, a,

(a)

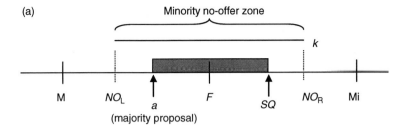

(b)

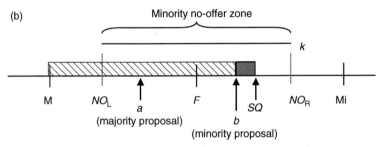

FIGURE 3.4. (a) Minority Utility Loss for a Status Quo in the Minority No-offer Zone without a Counterproposal and (b) Minority Utility Loss for a Status Quo in the Minority No-offer Zone with a Counterproposal.

which brings policy as far to the majority side of the space as F will allow (i.e., as F will prefer to the status quo), creates a sizable policy loss for Mi (represented by the gray bar in Figure 3.4a). But just as in our previous examples, her prospects are even worse if she pays the consideration cost to make a proposal, b, because although the policy loss is minimized, the summed utility loss (gray bar plus textured bar in Figure 3.4b) is much larger than the pure policy loss from the majority proposal.

To this point, however, we have not considered the majority proposer's consideration cost in any of our examples. Like that for Mi, the utility function for M consists of both policy distance *and* consideration costs, and this combined calculation will be central in determining whether M makes a proposal. For instance, if we simply add the majority's consideration cost, c, to the preceding example, as shown in Figures 3.5a and 3.5b, we can see that the outcome is very different.

Similar to the minority no-offer zone, M's consideration cost creates a majority no-offer zone of size c, centered on F. In the present example, we have assumed that c is large enough that the status quo from our

(a)

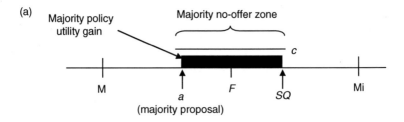

(b)

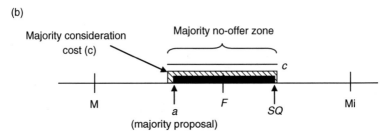

FIGURE 3.5a AND b. Majority Consideration Cost Example: Policy Utility Gain.

previous example falls just inside the right edge of the majority no-offer zone. In Figure 3.5a, the black bar represents a policy utility *gain* for M, since his proposal, *a*, moves policy closer to his ideal point. However, to get that proposal considered, M must pay cost *c*, which reduces his utility more than enough to offset his policy gain from proposal *a*, as shown in Figure 3.5b by comparison of the black (policy gain) and textured (consideration cost) boxes. Thus, despite an opportunity for policy gain, the consideration cost is simply too high and the majority actor will not make a proposal.[9]

Keeping the dynamics of the examples in mind, we can now more comfortably turn to a comprehensive discussion of equilibrium outcomes.

Outcome of the Game

The outcome of the game depends on which of four key intervals includes the status quo. Moving from left to right across the policy space, the first of these intervals runs from the left end of the space to NO_L. As shown in Figure 3.6a, the equilibrium outcome for status quos in this interval is that M proposes $a^* = NO_L$, Mi makes no offer, and F accepts the majority offer over the status quo. To see why this is so, consider what would

[9] Mi would also have the option to then make a proposal after M passes, but because the status quo is between her ideal point and *F*, there is no proposal that will move policy closer to her ideal and be preferred by F to the status quo (not to mention consideration costs).

happen if M made a proposal even slightly to the left of NO_L: Mi would be able to make a counteroffer of NO_R that would be worth the cost, k, and that F would prefer to a. If $a = NO_L$, however, the best offer Mi could make that F would prefer to a would be slightly to the left of NO_R – and thus not enough of an improvement over a to warrant paying the cost, k, of making a counteroffer.

The second key interval runs from NO_L to the point that is half the size of c to the right of F (i.e., $F + c/2$ – what we might also call the right edge of the majority no-offer zone), as shown in Figure 3.6b. The equilibrium for status quos in this region is that the majority makes no offer, the minority makes no offer, and the status quo remains intact. All points in this region are in the minority no-offer zone, meaning the game boils down to M trying to find a proposal that F will prefer to the status quo and that will improve on the status quo by more than c, but there are no such proposals. For status quos between NO_L and F, any proposal that M prefers to SQ will be rejected by F. For status quos between F and $F +c/2$, there are alternatives that would be closer to both M and F, but none of these would improve on the status quo enough to warrant paying the consideration cost, c, of the proposal. Note that for status quos in this interval, we observe an effect similar to the one typically attributed to a filibuster veto player (Brady and Volden 2006; Chiou and Rothenberg 2003; Krehbiel 1998).

The third key interval runs from $F + c/2$ to NO_R, shown in Figure 3.6c. The equilibrium for status quos in this region is that the majority proposes a^* that is exactly as far to the left of F as SQ is to the right of F, the minority makes no offer, and F accepts a^* over SQ. Status quos in this interval are still within the minority no-offer zone, so the game again boils down to M trying to find a proposal that F will prefer to the status quo and that will improve on the status quo by more than c. In this case, however, such proposals exist, and M will propose a that makes F indifferent between the status quo and a (recall that we assume F will choose a in such cases).

The last interval runs from NO_R to the right end of the space, shown in Figure 3.6d. As with the leftmost interval – and for essentially the same reasons – the equilibrium outcome for status quos in this interval is that M proposes $a^* = NO_L$, Mi makes no offer, and F accepts the majority offer over the status quo. As before, if M made a proposal to the left of NO_L, Mi would be able to make a counteroffer of NO_R that would be worth the cost, k, and that F would prefer to a. But if $a = NO_L$, Mi's best

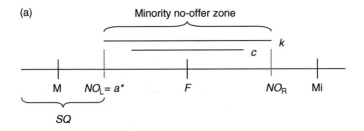

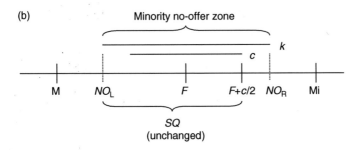

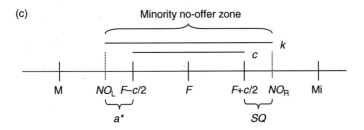

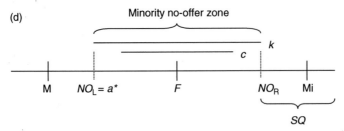

FIGURE 3.6. (a) $SQ < NO_L$, (b) $NO_L < SQ < F + c/2$, (c) $F + c/2 < SQ < NO_R$, and (d) $NO_R < SQ$.

offer that F would prefer to *a* would be slightly to the left of NO_R and not worth making given the cost, k, that it would entail. Of course, the outcomes in this interval differ markedly from those in the first interval in terms of the benefit to M. In the leftmost interval, in at least some cases (status quos closer to M), M makes proposals that result in net utility decreases, in the hope of minimizing losses. For the rightmost interval, all outcomes represent net utility gains for M.

The Model's Implications

Our model generates various predictions. We discuss some of them in broad terms here but derive and test more specific hypotheses in Chapter 10. Perhaps most significantly given conventional thinking, it implies that, with a uniform initial distribution of status quos, most policies will wind up on the majority party side of the floor median. Indeed, the only interval from which status quos do not wind up on the majority side of the floor median is $[F, F + c /2]$. In addition, increasing majority costs serves mainly to increase the size of the zone on the minority side of the floor median in which status quos are protected against majority proposals, while decreasing majority costs decrease the size of this zone. Substantively, one might think of this result in terms of the varying effectiveness of minority-side filibusters. We test these predictions in Chapter 10.

Also, for many status quos, increasing minority costs allow the majority to move policy closer to its ideal point, while decreasing minority costs force the majority to accept policy closer to the floor median, all else constant. Another implication of our model is that, in some instances when the status quo is to the left of NO_L, the majority may have to suffer a loss in utility (i.e., act to move policy away from its ideal point) in order to forestall the even greater loss that would occur in the absence of a majority offer.[10] This type of scenario – in which the majority cannot prevent itself from becoming worse off than it is to begin with, yet can manipulate outcomes to minimize its losses – underscores a critical departure in the way that we conceptualize agenda setting. Our framework implies that agenda power is more fruitfully conceptualized as being continuous rather than dichotomous (hence our preference for the phrase "agenda influence" instead of the more common "agenda control"). Actors in the Senate rarely dictate the agenda without any constraints; rather, they use whatever advantages they can to influence the

---

[10] See Jenkins and Nokken (2008) for instances of this type of behavior in lame-duck sessions.

agenda to whatever extent they can. Sometimes they have tremendous influence, and sometimes they do not.

Is the Model Generalizable Beyond a Single Dimension?

To this point, we have restricted the model to a single-dimension policy space. What happens if we go beyond one dimension?[11] Assuming we maintain (as closely as possible) all of the other assumptions, the short answer is that the basic results hold.

To see this, consider a two-dimensional version of the model, where M, F, and Mi weight policy utility on each dimension equally, and F is the median on both dimensions. For purposes of the immediate discussion, also assume that the three actors' ideal points are arrayed along a straight line in the two-dimensional space (we relax this assumption later). Figure 3.7a depicts the model in two-dimensional space. Note that the circles in this figure are *not* indifference curves of the actors; rather, they help demarcate relevant intervals of status quos. Of particular importance are the concentric circles centered on F. The larger circle is the two-dimensional equivalent of the minority no-offer zone, and the smaller shaded circle is equivalent to the majority no-offer zone.

There are four distinct intervals of status quos, which are roughly analogous to the intervals discussed in relation to Figures 3.6a–3.6d. First, consider all status quos that fall outside of the circles centered on M and F. Much like the outcomes shown for status quos identified in Figure 3.6d, here M will propose a^*, Mi will find it too costly to make a counterproposal, and F will prefer the new proposal to the status quo.

To understand this result, notice that a^* is located at the edge of a circle, centered on F, with a radius of $k/2$; note also that this is the point on that circle farthest from Mi. In other words, a^* is located at the two-dimensional equivalent of NO_L. The best alternative proposal that Mi could make would be at the mirror point on the circle, which is the other end of a line that constitutes the circle's diameter and begins at a^*. But since the diameter of the circle equals k, the policy gain from making the counterproposal will be perfectly offset by the consideration cost.

Next, consider all status quos that fall within the circle centered on M (equivalent to status quos identified in Figure 3.6a).[12] As in the single-

---

[11] We are indebted to Robi Ragan and Jacob Montgomery for their instrumental role in solving the multidimensional equilibrium and helping to produce the figures in this section.

[12] More precisely, the interval is defined by a circle with radius $|M - F| - k/2$, centered on M.

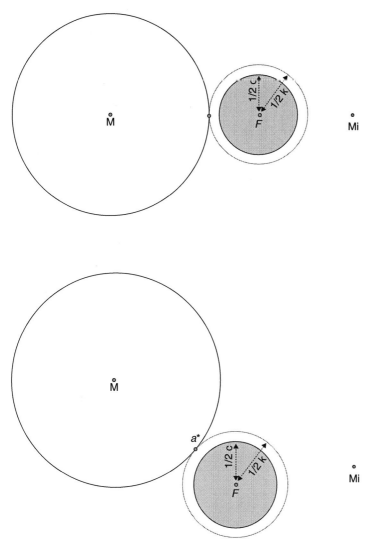

FIGURE 3.7. Costly-Consideration Model in Two Dimensions: (a) Actor Preferences on a Line and (b) Actor Preferences Not on a Line.

dimensional case, here M again proposes a^*, Mi does not counter, and F accepts the proposal. As in the one-dimensional case, this interval is interesting in that it represents a case where M will make a proposal to move policy *away* from his ideal point. By failing to make a proposal to address any of the status quos inside the circle, M would incur a greater utility loss because Mi would then have an incentive to make a counterproposal that moves policy to (or near) her ideal point. This is the case because, as we can easily see from the figure, the distance between any point in the circle and *Mi* is far larger than *k* (the diameter of the outer circle centered on *F*).

The third relevant interval is analogous to the set of status quos identified in Figure 3.6b. This interval, represented by the shaded areas of the figure, includes the area inside the smaller circle centered on *F* (with radius *c/2*) and the line segment that runs between *a** and the closest point on that circle. All of these status quos will remain unchanged. Because all of the shaded status quos are within both the minority and majority no-offer zones (i.e., the circles centered on *F*), neither actor can make a proposal that F will accept and achieve a policy improvement large enough to offset his or her own consideration cost. The line-segment status quos remain in place for exactly the same reason as do the status quos between the left edges of the minority and majority no-offer zones in one dimension: they are in perfect tension between *M* and *F*, and are also inside the minority no-offer zone.[13]

The final interval is the "donut"-shaped area that includes all of the space between the smaller and larger circles centered on *F* (except the shaded line segment just discussed). As with the status quos discussed in reference to Figure 3.6c, M will make proposals as close to his ideal point as *F* will accept. In this two-dimensional context, this means M makes proposals along the shaded line segment, such that the distance from *F* to the status quo is the same as the distance between *F* and the proposal. Another way to think about this, for any status quo in the donut, would be to draw a circle centered on *F* where the status quo was a point on the circle; M's proposal would be the point where that circle intersected the shaded line segment.

Stepping back to take stock of the general pattern of results, we see that they are quite similar to the one-dimensional case. All policy either (1) moves to *a**, (2) moves to the line segment just right of *a**, or (3) remains unchanged. As in the one-dimensional case, there are some policies, to the right of *F* (and slightly above and below), that M would like to move but cannot because of consideration costs. However, the vast majority of the two-dimensional space includes status quos that will be moved toward M's ideal point, improving his net utility.

---

[13] This result becomes straightforward when you consider that this line segment is a portion of the larger line segment that connects *F* and *M*, meaning that (1) any proposal that M would want to make would be along this line, and (2) any movement along that line necessarily constitutes a *policy* loss for either F or M.

Briefly, consider what happens if we relax the assumption that the three actors are arrayed along a straight line. Figure 3.7b shows this slight deviation. It would be tedious to retrace our steps through each status quo interval, as this assumption causes virtually no change in the basic intuition or results. It simply changes the point of tangency between the *F*- and *M*-centered circles, and thus changes the location of a^* and of the shaded line segment. However, the basic flow of policy movement is the same: disproportionately, policy moves toward the majority party actor.

Summary

In this chapter, we have presented a new theory of agenda setting in which the ability to make the first proposal and the differential costs associated with gaining consideration of proposals give the majority party more influence than the minority party over the agenda. This in turn gives the majority substantial power to affect legislative outcomes and, in particular, to ensure that most outcomes will be more favorable to the majority than to the minority. One strength of our model is that it incorporates widely shared beliefs about aspects of Senate procedures that are usually thought to undermine, if not negate, the majority party's ability to manipulate the Senate agenda. Another strength is that, although our interest in the Senate drove the design of our model, we designed it to provide a flexible framework that will make it suitable for the study of a broad array of legislatures. We discuss this at greater length in Chapter 11.

We believe that one of the key insights of our approach is a move away from thinking about proposal (and, for that matter, veto) powers as absolute rights that various actors either have or do not have. Instead, by modeling such powers as widely shared but costly to use, we move toward a conception of agenda setting in which some level of agenda influence is enjoyed by many (perhaps all) legislators, but that this influence is distributed unevenly.

PART II

SENATE PROCEDURE AND
CONSIDERATION COSTS

Introduction to Part II

The purpose of Part II is to provide empirical support for our claims
about consideration costs. To this end, we examine Senate decisions at
the committee stage (Chapter 4), the scheduling stage (Chapters 5 and 6),
and on the floor (Chapters 7, 8, and 9). We show that, at each stage except
scheduling, majority proposals are disproportionately likely to move forward in the legislative process; that is, a majority-sponsored proposal
that reaches a particular stage is more likely than a minority-sponsored
proposal that reaches the same stage to move forward in the process.

We want to emphasize four points about the data analyses in this part
of the book. First, the results are *not* meant to be taken as a series of independent tests demonstrating party effects. Second, the results *are* meant
to establish that the majority party has a systematic (but not absolute)
advantage when it comes to moving proposals to final consideration.
Third, we do not argue that the majority wins at each stage on every
bill that it gets to final consideration or that it needs to do so to pass its
proposals. Senate agenda influence does not follow from repeated applications of the same approach, as with the House and special rules. Senate
agenda influence is a more ad hoc affair. It tends to be cobbled together
on the fly, in response to fluid and ever-changing circumstances. Finally,
we remind readers of our earlier point that we are not trying to demonstrate that the majority wins procedural votes *only* by inducing members
to vote with the party; we assume they sometimes win because of leaders'
manipulation of selective incentives and sometimes win without leaders

doing anything to influence anyone's vote. What matters most for our purposes is that the majority disproportionately wins procedural votes.

Research Design

We use the same basic research design repeatedly in the chapters that follow. In this research design, we assess the "treatment" of majority status across periods where party control of the Senate changes hands. In most cases, we draw inferences by identifying how Democratic and Republican proposals (either bills or amendments) fare differently when they get the treatment and when they do not. Thus, each party's set of proposals is a "group," and our tests ask whether individual proposals in the treatment group (1) do better than the control group and (2) do worse when they switch from being the treatment group to the control group (i.e., lose majority status), and vice versa.

In quasi-experimental terms, this is a standard "switching replications" setup.[1] Generally, these sorts of designs have very strong internal validity (Trochim and Donnelly 2007); the multiple-group, multiple-observation structure is generically desirable, from a causal inference standpoint, in any design. But beyond that, by switching the treatment between groups across time periods, we can test more than one prediction within the design.

Because we have multiple observations before and after the "switches" (i.e., for virtually all of our tests, we observe each party for multiple consecutive Congresses as the majority and minority before and after changes in majority status), we can assess the cross-group pattern, across multiple observations, during the initial treatment and control assignments, and then again for the period after they switch. In other words, for both periods, we expect the majority (whoever that is) to do better than the minority.

But note that these cross-group tests are conceptually distinct, from a causal inference standpoint, from *within*-group tests across the switch. Hypothetically, it is possible for one party to benefit significantly from the majority-status treatment, while the other does equally well in the minority and in the majority. If this were true, then the cross-group tests might look as expected – the group in the majority would do better in each case – but this would be true only because of the treatment response of *one of the groups*. If this were the case, however, we would find a glaring

---

[1] In Chapter 9, the design is a slightly different hybrid in that it includes a "factorial design" element. We discuss this slight deviation before the relevant analysis.

lack of support for our assertions when we compared within-group changes across the switch, since for both Democrats and Republicans we expect the application (or removal) of the majority-status treatment to increase (decrease) the success of their proposals. In this sense, the design places a high burden of proof on our claims.

A Brief Note on Our Data

In the empirical analyses that run through the rest of the book, we use different time series in different analyses. With the exception of the post–World War II time series used for one analysis in Chapter 10, our time series all begin with the 101st Congress (1989–1991). Our initial goal was for each analysis to stretch from the 101st Congress through at least the 106th Congress (1989–2001), which would allow us to compare three Democratic-majority Congresses (101 through 103) with three Republican-majority Congresses (104 through 106). Our analyses of committees and scheduling, however, include only Congresses 101 through 105, because we use data – gathered, and shared generously, by others – that include observations on relevant variables only through the 105th Congress. Also, our analysis of amendments in Chapter 9 uses the 101st through 109th Congresses. When we gathered data for that chapter, we hoped to extend all time series throughout the book to the 109th Congress; in the end this proved prohibitively costly, but we included the already-gathered additional data in Chapter 9.

4

Committees and Senate Agenda Setting

Congressional scholars often emphasize procedural and agenda-setting differences between the House and Senate. The chambers' committee systems, however, are broadly similar. Moreover, the Senate majority party advantage at the committee stage is recognized – though not emphasized – as part of the conventional view of the Senate.[1]

This chapter thus differs from those that follow inasmuch as it is not about presenting evidence contesting the conventional view. Rather, we provide an overview of Senate committee procedures and literature related to various aspects of committee behavior, then present data illustrating the legislative results of committee action. It is like the other chapters, however, in that it is focused on presenting the sources of the majority party's consideration cost advantage.

We begin by briefly summarizing the processes for making committee appointments and selecting committee chairs. The next section examines bill introduction and referral, and is followed by a section about committee action on bills, with particular emphasis on the powers of chairs. In the final section, we present data comparing the proportion of each committee's referred bills sponsored by senators of each party with the proportion of each committee's reported bills sponsored by senators of each party. We show not only that the majority party repeatedly sponsors proportions of referred bills greater than its share of Senate seats, but also that

---

[1] The conventional view breaks sharply with the partisan perspective inasmuch as it views committee action as easily undone or undermined at later stages of the Senate process. As Smith and Lawrence (1997: 164) put it, "Senate committees have long had less influence over policy choices because of the ease with which policy alternatives are proposed and opposed on the Senate floor." We address this issue in detail in Chapters 7, 8, and 9.

the proportion of majority-sponsored bills reported from committee is even more disproportionate to the majority's share of the chamber's seats.

Selection of Committee Members and Chairs

Committee sizes, ratios, membership, chair and ranking member designations, and funding ratios are all set by resolutions (submitted separately for the majority and minority parties) adopted by majority vote of the chamber at the beginning of each new Congress (Gold 2004). However, the majority party advantage on Senate committees depends on chairs acting as faithful agents of the party caucus to a greater extent than is the case in the House. This is because the Senate majority party does not enjoy the disproportionate seat advantage on some committees (Sinclair 2007), nor does it have as much success creating committees that are representative of the party caucus (Kloha 2006).

In the Senate, unlike the House, committee ratios, even in the most powerful committees, typically reflect party ratios in the chamber (Kloha 2006; Schneider 2003; Sinclair 2007). Thus, whereas the House has disproportionately large majority party contingents in high-externality committees, ensuring a stronger hold on committee voting decisions, Senate committee seat shares are more uniform. Still, given that virtually all committee voting decisions are based on majority rule, this is not a fundamental problem for majority party agenda setting.

The process of making committee assignments in the Senate is similar to that of the House, with firm party control of the process. Each party has a panel that makes assignments, which must be approved by the party caucus (Campbell 2001; Schneider 2003). In the House, this tends to translate into committees with party contingents that roughly match the preferences of their respective caucuses. These representative committees are thought to be likely to produce committee outcomes in line with caucus preferences, at least for externality-producing committees (Cox and McCubbins 1993). In the Senate, however, there is mixed evidence regarding whether committees are generally representative of the parties' caucuses. Campbell (2001: 68–69), in a study of Senate committee representativeness from 1877 to 1989, concludes that "with the exception of a few committees, the majority party contingent on most committees was not significantly different from their party."[2] Kloha (2006), however, finds

---

[2] Frisch and Kelly (2004) find that leaders play a more important role than previously appreciated in doling out committee assignments within their party. Assuming leaders act

a bigger discrepancy between House and Senate committees. Using committee assignment and seat share data from 1975 to 2001, he finds little evidence of majority party ideological stacking or disproportionate seat shares on Senate committees, arguing that this is the case because leaders have little incentive to stack committees if committee action can easily be undone on the floor. An important caveat, however, is that his time series ends before the 2004 adoption of a Senate Republican Conference rule that gave the majority leader the power to unilaterally fill at least half of the majority party slots in major committees such as the Appropriations, Armed Services, and Finance panels (Preston 2004).

Despite proportionate committee ratios and questionable committee representativeness, we see two essential features of the Senate committee system as the basis for majority party domination of committee actions. First, committee chairs are always majority party members (Oleszek 2007). Given the powers of chairs (outlined in the section after next), this is of central significance. Assuming chairs use their powers to advance party goals – giving the majority party the potential for substantial agenda power in committee – and given the selection procedures in the modern Senate, there is at least some incentive for chairs to act as agents of the caucus, at least on key party issues.

In the contemporary Senate, all chairs are chosen by secret ballot within the majority caucus. Thus, theoretically at least, chairs are accountable to at least a majority of the party caucus. Still, long-serving members have historically been able to accrue some autonomy over time, and in some instances the party has found it difficult to remove them because of Senate norms (Evans and Oleszek 1997). After a particularly troubling incident in which Appropriations Committee chair Mark Hatfield blocked a balanced-budget amendment in the 104th Congress against the wishes of the newly minted Republican majority, the Senate Republicans strengthened their control of chairs (Evans and Oleszek 1997). In 1997 Senate committee chairs became subject to six-year term limits (Oleszek 2007), a party rule that was employed by Republicans during their time as the majority party over most of the past decade. More generally, both parties have been more aggressive about ensuring that good party agents occupy key chair positions.

Two examples illustrate this point. Following the 2004 elections, Senate Republicans faced their first round of termed-out chairs. On

in the interests of the party, their results suggest an additional mechanism by which Senate committees would be made representative.

the Judiciary Committee, this meant that Arlen Specter was in line to become chair, a prospect that deeply concerned many within the party. Specter, a well-known supporter of abortion rights, had "celebrated his reelection victory by issuing a thinly veiled warning to Bush that any judicial nominees opposed to abortion rights would have a hard time getting confirmed" (Eisele 2004). After initial backlash from the party and the Bush administration, which generated major uncertainty over whether Specter would become chair, the Pennsylvania Republican began an unusually public campaign to assure fellow Republicans that he would not block judicial appointments on grounds of abortion politics (Dewar 2004a). After two weeks of direct and indirect assurances to his colleagues, Specter finally secured the chair by issuing a statement "pledging prompt hearings and votes on President Bush's judicial nominees" (Dewar 2004b).

Democrats found themselves in a similarly difficult situation following the 2008 elections. In the weeks leading up to the election, there was increasing speculation that Democrats were considering options to nudge 91-year-old Robert Byrd out of his long-held post as chair of the Appropriations Committee (Pierce 2008). Many party members were reportedly concerned that Byrd's age and poor health might keep him from effectively pursuing policies espoused by many members of the new unified Democratic government (Newmyer 2008). Ultimately, Byrd stepped down as chair of the Appropriations Committee, claiming it was a decision that he came to on his own.

While Byrd's replacement as Appropriations chair was not explicitly an act of discipline by the party, there was speculation that party pressure to resign may have been brought on, in part, because he had strayed from the party on some important issues. And regardless of the reasoning behind it, Byrd's exit illustrates the importance placed on committee chairs by the Senate majority party. Especially for a committee as important as Appropriations, having a strong, able chair is seen as essential for advancing the party agenda, even at the risk of violating seniority and potentially insulting the Senate's longest-serving member.

Majority leaders have reason to be selective in evaluating chairs, since chairs of Senate committees are extensions of the party leadership. Effective chairs must coordinate committee action with caucus preferences and will in turn have a disproportionate influence over the party's policy priorities and strategies. Thus, a general fit with the party may be an important factor.

Bill Introduction and Referral

Bill introduction and referral are, by and large, nonpartisan processes. Bills are introduced on the Senate floor and, under Rule XIV, are to be read twice (by title only) before being referred to committee (Gold 2004). Most bills are simply deemed to have been read twice and are referred to the appropriate committee of jurisdiction by the presiding officer (with the assistance of the parliamentarian) without any notable fanfare or dispute. In some cases, bills are referred to multiple committees. But unlike the speaker of the House, the Senate's presiding officer does not have authority to refer a bill to multiple committees; rather, the Senate handles sequential or joint referrals via unanimous consent (Gold 2004).

There are instances, however, in which majority leaders wish to bypass committee, because of either urgency or the fear that it might not be reported by a committee with jurisdiction (Sinclair 2007). Under Rule XIV, a bill is not referred to committee if any senator objects to the first and seconding readings of the bill; rather, the bill goes directly to the calendar (Gold 2004; Oleszek 2007). Use of this tactic has increased in recent years, especially on high-priority party items (Evans and Oleszek 2001; Oleszek 2007; Sinclair 2007).

The use of Rule XIV in this fashion is not formally reserved for the majority leader; all senators can use this method to send legislation straight to the calendar, and many do so on some occasions. But because of the majority leadership's advantage at the floor scheduling stage (see Chapter 6), this tactic appears to be a tool primarily of the majority leaders. Since moving the bill from the calendar to the floor is nearly impossible without the majority leader's support, there seems to be little advantage in adopting this strategy (Gold 2008; Sinclair 2007). As Gold (2008: 82) describes it, "[S]cheduling the measure ... remains the majority leader's prerogative. The leader's involvement is needed before measures sent to the calendar under Rule XIV are brought to the floor. Use of Rule XIV can be an exercise in futility if the leader refuses to schedule a measure that has reached the calendar by this means." Of course, a senator could offer a bill stranded on the calendar as a floor amendment (see Chapters 7, 8, and 9), but that could be done if the bill were not on the calendar, so there is no clear advantage to having steered the bill around committee.

Figure 4.1 shows, for Congresses 101 through 106, the share of all bills not referred to any committee that was sponsored by Democrats, as well as the share of seats held by Democrats. The data are consistent with

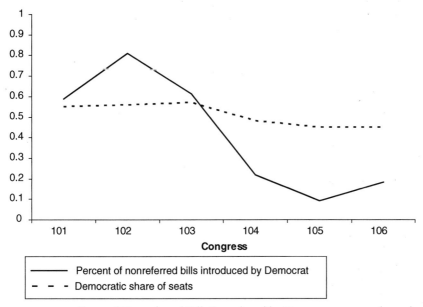

FIGURE 4.1. Share of Nonreferred Bills Introduced by Democrats, 101st through 106th Congresses.

the claim that Rule XIV is not widely used by minority bill sponsors as a tool for circumventing majority influence at the committee level. In each Congress, the share of nonreferred bills sponsored by a majority party member is greater than the share sponsored by a minority party member and is also greater than the majority party's overall seat share.[3]

Committee Scheduling and Chairs' Powers

Evans (1991:13) argues that control over the agenda is "the most significant form of procedural power employed by committee chairs." And as we see it, the power of the chair is the hub of the majority's consideration cost advantage at the committee stage. This power manifests itself in a variety of ways. It begins with decisions about when the committee will meet. Standing committees are required to have regular meeting days but can meet on additional days by call of the chair (Gold 2004). So when there are pressing agenda items awaiting action, the chair can unilaterally

---

[3] The number of nonreferred bills for each of the 101st through 106th Congresses is 68, 132, 93, 73, 65, and 82, respectively.

create more committee time to move those proposals through the early legislative process.

Moreover, once committee hearings begin, chairs have considerable discretion over the timing and substance of those hearings. Not only do they have the authority to decide if and when hearings are scheduled, they also have a disproportionate influence over the lineup of witnesses (Oleszek 2007). Though the minority has some influence over who is called to testify, the chair can stack the witness list (Oleszek 2007). Mechanically speaking, as an agenda-setting device, this is not especially important. That is, theoretically, the chair could skip the hearings stage and move a bill forward to markup. But in terms of advancing the party agenda, hearings are an opportunity to get the public, other external actors, and other senators on board in support of a piece of legislation. In terms of the theory we have laid out, this ability to dictate the terms of the conversation and advance the party message (Evans and Oleszek 2001) can have the effect of lowering the consideration cost at later stages of the legislative process.

A similar argument applies to chairs' control of committee staffs' time and attention (Evans 1991; Oleszek 2007). Much of the work of preparing bills for subsequent chamber action happens at the committee stage and requires enormous effort by committee staff members. This translates into both negative and positive agenda-setting power for the chair. If the chair favors a bill, he or she can direct the staff to give the legislation more time and attention. Alternatively, when the chair prefers to see a bill die, he or she can ensure that the committee staff neglects it, even if there is some support for it on the committee (Oleszek 2007).

Some of this staff attention goes to aiding the chair in developing the chair's mark, the version of the bill that is presented to the committee (Carr 2005). This power to shape the initial proposal represents an important source of agenda influence over committee decisions, giving the chair almost complete control of the base bill that is made open to amendment and roll call votes in committee. Opponents of provisions included in the mark need to have the support of a majority within the committee to strike these provisions, which requires securing the support of one or more members of the majority party on the committee. The alternative is to vote against the motion to report the entire bill to the floor, which would mean giving up other items in the measure that senators might wish to see enacted.

At the very least, offering the initial proposal puts the chair in a favorable bargaining position. In early 1994, after months of discussion with fellow committee members about how to construct a "bipartisan" bill to overhaul health care, Finance Committee chair Daniel Patrick Moynihan surprised his colleagues by outlining a much more liberal proposal than expected, including a provision for universal coverage. Despite disagreeing with some of Moynihan's proposed provisions, Senator John Breaux admitted, "If you start with a compromise, all you can do is compromise the compromise" (Rubin 1994).

Once the initial proposal is set, the chair can push the legislation through committee at a faster than normal rate, if needed. In the Senate, markup and hearings often occur at the full committee level rather than in subcommittee (Oleszek 2007: 99). Thus, the chair can compress the time allotment for these activities – or eliminate hearings all together – if action on a bill is time sensitive. They can also end debate or markup unilaterally, meaning there is no filibuster at the committee level (Gold 2004). Alternatively, the chair can draw these processes out for bills he or she wishes to delay or kill but has some incentive to schedule nonetheless (Evans 1991; Oleszek 2007).

In short, Senate committee chairs have a disproportionate influence over committee agenda setting. They can unilaterally raise or lower the costs of moving a proposal beyond committee.

Partisan Patterns of Bill Introduction, Referral, and Reporting

Work by Koger and Fowler (2006) offers convincing empirical support for the claim that the Senate majority party has a significant agenda-setting advantage at the committee stage. Using a dataset of every bill introduced in the Senate from 1973 to 1998, they find that the committee "report rate" (i.e., the percentage of a member's bills that reported) for majority party members is higher than for their minority party counterparts and that report rates change dramatically with changes in party control of the Senate. They also show that majority sponsorship increases the likelihood of a bill being reported from committee, controlling for a host of variables capturing preference-based, electoral, and institutional factors.

In this section, we examine data bearing on whether majority-sponsored bills are more likely than minority-sponsored bills to be reported from Senate committees. Given that Koger and Fowler's analysis uses the same dataset we use, that their research design is similar to the one we use in subsequent chapters, and that their findings are consistent with our expectations, we conduct no econometric analysis in this chapter. Rather,

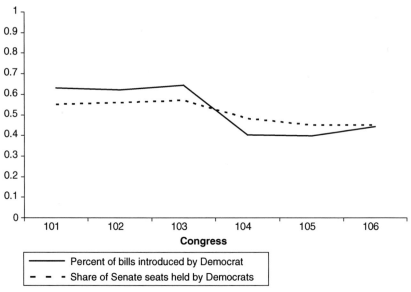

FIGURE 4.2. Share of Introduced Bills Sponsored by Democrats, 101st through 106th Congresses.

we present data that illustrate the pattern Koger and Fowler find. For each standing committee in each Congress from the 101st through the 106th, we graph both the proportion of committee-reported bills that were sponsored by Democrats and the proportion of bills referred to the committee that were sponsored by Democrats.

We use data from the *Congressional Bills Project*,[4] which has an observation for each S. bill and allows us to observe, among other things, which committee(s) each bill was referred to, whether it was reported from committee, and the party of the bill's sponsor. By comparing three Congresses with Democratic majorities (101st through 103rd) with three Congresses with Republican majorities (104th through 106th), we can highlight behavioral patterns that change when the majority party changes.

We see the first of these changes in Figure 4.2, which shows, for each Congress, the share of all introduced bills that were sponsored by

[4] We thank Scott Adler and John Wilkerson for sharing data from their *Congressional Bills Project: 1989–1998*, NSF 00880066 and 00880061, available at http://www. congressionalbills.org/index.html. (The views expressed here are those of the authors and not the National Science Foundation.)

Democrats; it also shows the share of seats held by Democrats in each Congress. We see that, when there is a Democratic majority, Democrats introduce a larger share of bills than do Republicans. This pattern flips when there is a Republican majority, and Republicans introduce a larger share of bills than do Democrats. We also see that, in all cases, the majority party introduces a share of bills that is larger than its share of seats in the chamber. From a partisan perspective, one can easily imagine that this results from majority senators having a higher expectation than minority senators of legislative success, all else constant (though we make no claim to be testing this proposition with the data shown here).

Given the majority party's seeming high degree of control over committee actions, we should see signs of it enjoying success in getting its bills out of committee. This could be taken to mean that we should see more majority- than minority-sponsored bills being reported from each committee; however, since more majority bills go to committee in the first place, such a pattern would be consistent with there being no majority bill-selection advantage within committee. We therefore offer the conjecture that the share of majority-sponsored bills reported from a committee will be greater than the share of majority-sponsored bills referred to that same committee, thus controlling for the greater share of majority-sponsored bills sent to committees in the first place.

The graphs in Figure 4.3 show the pattern of bill referral and bill reporting for each standing committee in each of the six Congresses.[5] Each graph shows two trends. The dashed line in each graph is the share of bills referred to that committee that were sponsored by Democrats; the heavy solid line is the share of bills reported from the committee that were sponsored by Democrats.

The results offer strong support for our conjecture. Across the committees, we see a remarkably consistent pattern: except for a small number of committee–Congress observations, the share of reported bills sponsored by a Democrat is always higher than both the share of referred bills sponsored by a Democrat and the share of reported bills sponsored by a Republican – *when there is a Democratic majority*. In

---

[5] The *Congressional Bills* data include one variable denoting whether a bill was reported from committee. However, this variable is a dummy that shows only whether the bill was reported from *any* Senate committee. For bills referred to more than one committee, the data do not tell us which committee(s) reported the bill. We thus exclude multiply referred bills from data reported in Figure 4.3. Also, we show no graph for the Budget Committee, because it handled too few bills to generate a meaningful graph. For our treatment of majority budgeting advantages, see Chapter 11.

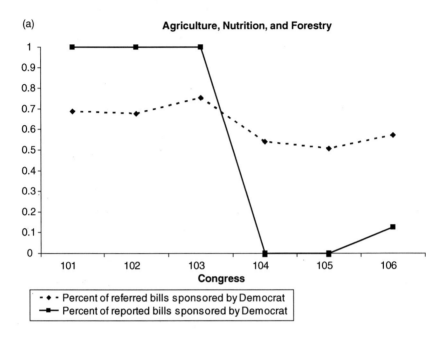

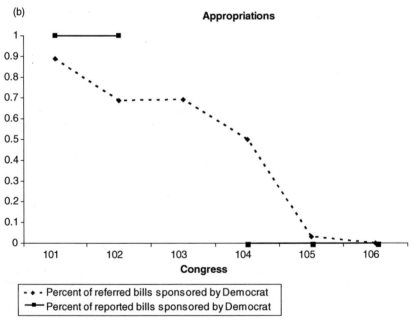

FIGURE 4.3. Bill Referral and Reporting, by Party and Committee, 101st through 106th Congresses.

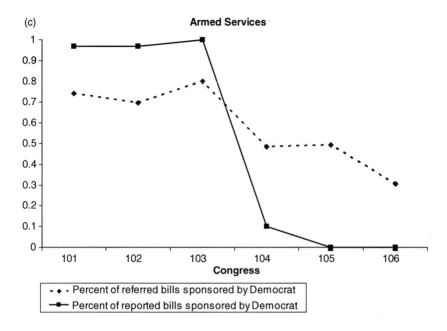

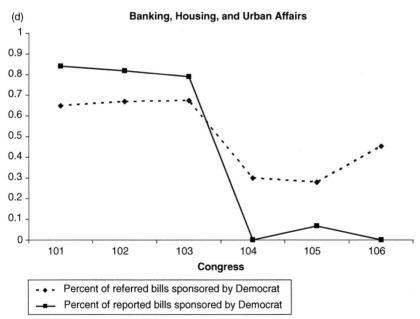

FIGURE 4.3. *(continued)*

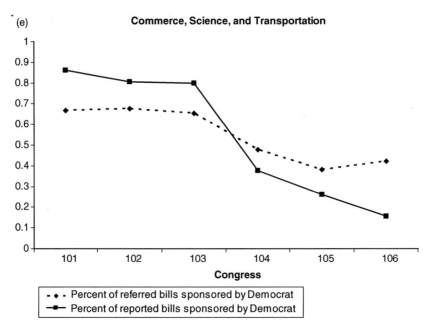

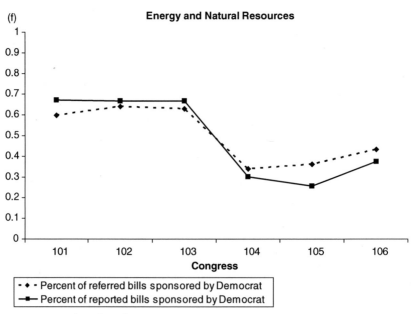

FIGURE 4.3. *(continued)*

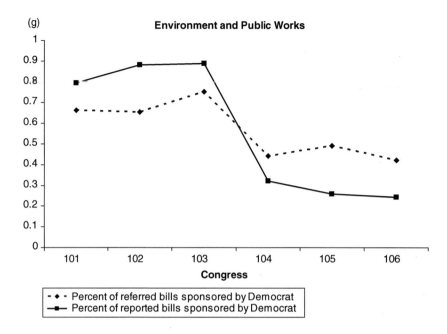

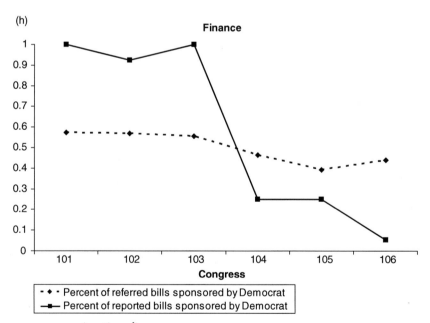

FIGURE 4.3. *(continued)*

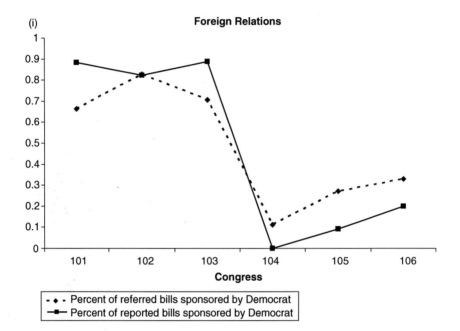

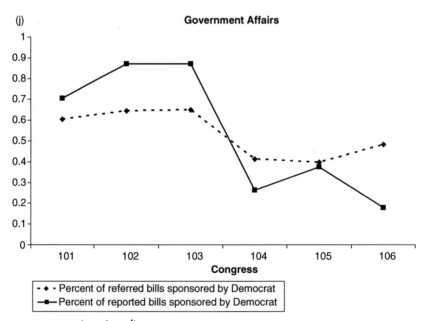

FIGURE 4.3. *(continued)*

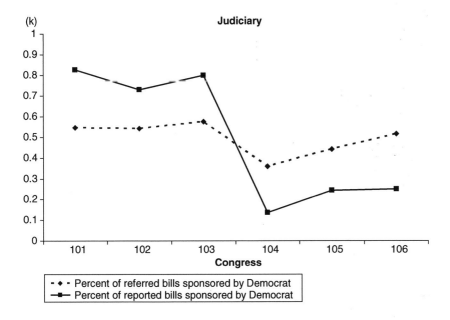

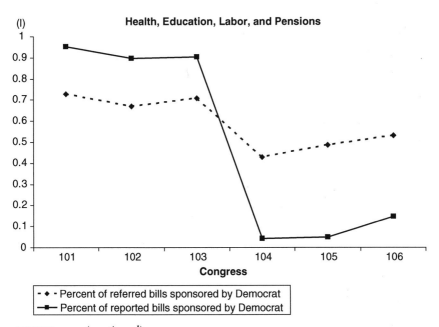

FIGURE 4.3. *(continued)*

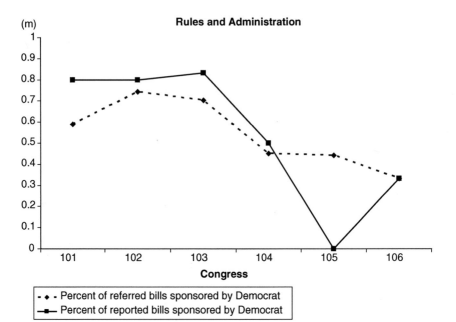

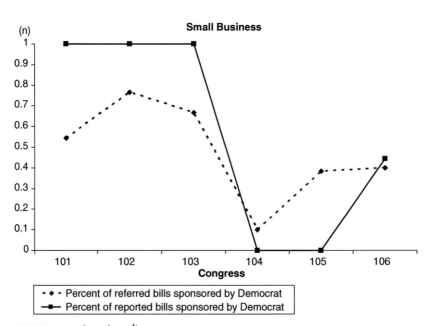

FIGURE 4.3. *(continued)*

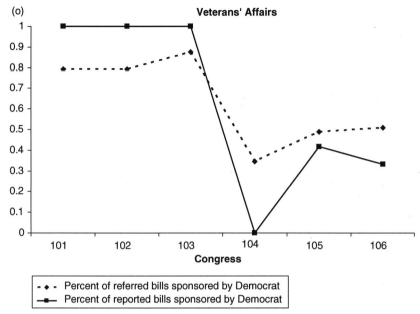

FIGURE 4.3. *(continued)*

the Republican-majority Congresses, however, the opposite is true: the share of Republican-sponsored reported bills outstrips the shares of Republican-sponsored referred bills and of Democrat-sponsored reported bills. In other words, almost every committee in every Congress bears out our conjecture and suggests majority party filtering of bills at the committee stage.

Could the Results Reflect a Difference in Minority-Sponsored Bills?

One potential problem with inferring from the graphs that the majority-sponsored bills are more likely to be reported is that we do not account for possible confounding factors. In other words, minority-sponsored bills could systematically differ from majority-sponsored bills in some respect other than the sponsor's party, and it is possible that the difference, rather than disproportionate majority influence over committees, explains the pattern. Particularly given that we use comparable research designs in subsequent chapters (i.e., we compare majority-sponsored bills with minority-sponsored bills), we briefly discuss two reasons we think it unlikely that such a factor explains our results.

First, when we compare bills by sponsor party in subsequent chapters, we typically use multivariate analysis and control for possible confounding factors such as sponsor ideology. Second, there is one factor that we do not control for and think is the most plausible remaining confounding factor; this is the extent to which the bill sponsor introduces the bill not because he or she hopes to see it pass, but in order to send a favorable signal to voters. Or put another way, minority party members might introduce bills that they know are not viable candidates to become law, in the hope of electoral rather than policy benefits.

If this were the case, however, it would likely be so because minority senators think their bills are less likely to pass than do majority senators. This is more or less our whole point – the majority is systematically advantaged in passing bills it favors, and the minority is systematically disadvantaged. But a bigger flaw in the argument that minority bills might be less viable because they are aimed at constituents is that it relies on the premise that bills introduced in order to change policy will be different from bills introduced to curry constituent favor. There is little reason to believe this. It suggests that senators trying to change policy introduce bills that their constituents find suboptimal; that is, they try to put in place policy changes that are not the ones that would maximize the sponsor's chance of reelection. Clearly, though, senators try to change policy in ways that will make them more electable, so there is little reason to think minority bills are inherently less viable than majority bills.

Summary

The conventional view of Senate committees is relatively consistent with partisan theories of agenda setting. The role of chairs as the central agenda-setting actors in committee is widely (if often tacitly) acknowledged. As we have described in this chapter, chairs have considerable discretion over when committees meet, who testifies at hearings, what version of a bill the committee uses for markup, what staff members pay attention to, how long committee business takes, and when votes are called.

Thus, the power of the chair, inasmuch as he or she acts as an agent of the party, is important in thinking about the earliest stage of majority party agenda setting in the Senate. And as we described earlier, the rules governing the selection of chairs rely on approval of the majority caucus. Combined with the addition of term limits on Senate chairs, it seems that chairs have at least some incentive to toe the party line. Thus, while Senate committee decisions are not typically as partisan as those in the House, Senate committees have been increasingly more partisan in the past two decades (Sinclair 2007: 46), and majority control of committees has tightened in the same period (Aldrich and Rohde 2005).

On the basis of the committee data presented in this chapter, it can be concluded that majority party bills are significantly more likely to be reported than minority party bills. This disparity is even more lopsided than the ratio of majority to minority bills introduced. In short, it seems that, at the committee stage, consideration costs are lower for the majority party than for its opponents.

5

Scheduling Bills in the Senate

In this chapter we turn our attention to the Senate's floor stage and ask whether the majority party has an advantage in influencing which bills reach the floor. Most work on this topic emphasizes hurdles posed by the supermajoritarian nature of Senate scheduling and ways in which these hurdles undercut the majority party's ability to influence the agenda (Beth and Bach 2003; Binder and Smith 1997; Brady and Volden 2006; Krehbiel 1998; Smith 2005; Smith and Flathman 1989). We agree that filibusters, holds, and objections to unanimous consent requests – as well as threats of such tactics – constitute nontrivial consideration costs that limit the majority party by rendering it unable to schedule some bills that it would like to schedule (we consider the role of filibusters in the next chapter). We believe, however, that the emphasis on scheduling obstacles has drawn attention away from equally important questions regarding whether the majority enjoys an advantage among bills that *are* scheduled. The majority's inability to schedule everything it would like to schedule does not imply there is no majority-favoring bias in the set of bills that do reach the floor. Nonetheless, there is little empirical work that sheds light directly on the nature of bills that are scheduled.

We address this gap by bringing various data to bear on the topic of Senate scheduling. In doing so, we focus on whether the majority party enjoys greater success in scheduling its bills than does the minority party – in other words, whether it pays lower consideration costs at the scheduling stage. We find that the set of bills that are scheduled contains a disproportionate number of majority-sponsored bills, though it seems this bias is derivative of the majority's advantage at the committee stage rather than at the scheduling stage. However, we also find evidence that scheduled minority-sponsored bills are likely to be uncontentious, whereas scheduled majority-sponsored bills are more likely to be contentious. This suggests the majority party is better able to schedule bills that face political opposition.

Scheduling Bills in the Senate

There are essentially two options for scheduling bills in the Senate[1] – a motion to proceed or a unanimous consent agreement[2] – each of which is notoriously prone to dilatory tactics. The option of making a motion to proceed is in practice a prerogative of the majority leader, and such motions need only a bare majority to pass; but because they are usually debatable and thus subject to filibusters, agreeing to a motion to proceed often requires at least the implicit agreement of 60 senators. Moreover, since most bills are scheduled by unanimous consent, and a proposed unanimous consent agreement can be blocked by any senator, floor action on most bills is presumed to require the acquiescence of a supermajority. In addition, the Senate's practice of allowing individual senators to place holds on legislation (i.e., to block even a motion to proceed, at least temporarily) augments the widespread ability to forestall floor action on proposals.

Senate scholarship has long emphasized filibusters (Beeman 1968; Binder and Smith 1997; Burdette 1940; Oppenheimer 1985; Wawro and Schickler 2006), unanimous consent agreements (Ainsworth and Flathman 1995; Krehbiel 1986; Smith and Flathman 1989), and their obstructionist consequences – notably the ability of individual senators and the minority party to thwart majority party efforts to shape the floor agenda (Brady and Volden 2006; Krehbiel 1998; Oppenheimer and Hetherington 2008; Smith 1989, 2005; Wawro and Schickler 2006). This has led to a widespread view of the majority leader as a weak, often harried figure, at the mercy of members of both majority and minority parties, whose primary job and motivation is to try to coordinate the schedule and allocate floor time as efficiently as possible – a view encapsulated by Davidson's (1985) labeling of the majority leader as the

---

[1] We use the term "scheduling" strictly to mean bringing bills up for debate or other action on the Senate floor. The term is sometimes also used to refer to proposals (especially by the majority leader) to take up legislation or the offering of a proposed work schedule.
[2] We forgo a detailed discussion of scheduling procedures. For brief overviews of the process, see Beth (2003), Oleszek (2001a), and Saturno (2003); for more detailed discussions, see Gold (2008), Oleszek (2007), and Tiefer (1989).

"janitor for an untidy chamber." Before the 1990s, there was little sense
in the literature that the floor leader was an agent of the majority party
rather than of the chamber as a whole (Davidson 1989a, b; Huitt 1961;
Matthews 1960; Oppenheimer 1985; Ripley 1969). This view has given
way more recently, as partisanship has become more pronounced, to a
view of the majority leader as a partisan agent. But leaders' greater efforts
at partisan agenda setting are nonetheless thought to be countered by
concurrent increases in minority party cohesiveness, which leads to more
effective minority party use of dilatory tactics to block majority efforts
or to force compromises (Oppenheimer and Hetherington 2008; Sinclair
2007; Smith 2005, 2007). One manifestation of this leadership struggle, outlined by Evans (2001), Evans and Oleszek (2001), and Sinclair
(2007), emphasizes the need for both parties to get their central messages
to the public. Such message politics magnify and complicate the procedural struggle, because both passing and preventing the passage of laws
can be effective means of getting a party's message across.

We agree with the conventional view that Senate scheduling procedures deeply shape the chamber's behavior, are fundamentally important to study, and grant some level of blocking/bargaining power to the
minority party and to individual senators (and, for that matter, to majority party senators who are not on the same page as most of the caucus).
Indeed, our theory was built with these majority consideration costs in
mind. But we also believe that the emphasis on actions being blocked and
on the majority being forced to compromise has led to an imbalance in
the literature, in which not enough attention has been given to proposals that actually reach the floor. Too often, from our point of view, the
fact that the majority cannot shape *all* scheduling decisions to its liking
seems to lead to the conclusion that it is unable to shape *any* decisions
to its liking – or at least that it is no more able to do so than is the
minority party.

There is a considerable basis for questioning this view. To be scheduled, most bills must first go through committee and then be brought up
on the floor.[3] And as we showed in Chapter 4, bills sponsored by majority party senators are substantially more likely than are bills sponsored
by minority party senators to be reported from committee. Of course,

[3] As discussed in Chapter 4, Senate Rule XIV makes it relatively easy for a bill sponsor to
ensure that a bill circumvents committee and goes directly to the calendar (Gold 2008).
This process is used for only a small percentage of all bills introduced (Rundquist 2003);
when it is used, it is often used by committee or party leaders to expedite consideration
of a measure (Sinclair 2007).

having an advantage at the committee stage might do the majority party no good if, at the scheduling stage, the possibility of obstructionism allowed the minority party to ensure scheduling of a mix of bills that did not favor either party. (We take this as the most extreme version of the consequences of supermajoritarian procedures; since such procedures can be wielded at least as well by the majority party as by the minority party, it would be odd to claim that they empower the minority to produce a mix of scheduled bills that favors the minority.)

On the other hand, given that the set of bills coming out of committee disproportionately favors the majority party, if their leaders were able to ensure that each majority-sponsored, committee-reported bill merely had the same chance of being scheduled as each minority-sponsored committee-reported bill, then the set of bills that reach the floor would disproportionately favor the majority party. Koger and Fowler (2006), who find that majority-sponsored bills are also more likely to be approved by the whole Senate, essentially claim that the latter scenario prevails in the Senate, with the majority's scheduling advantage stemming primarily from its control over committees. Their study, however, does not include data regarding which bills reported from committee reached the floor, except inasmuch as bills that pass the chamber must necessarily have been scheduled. Our work here thus complements their study by focusing explicitly on which bills that get out of committee are scheduled.

If, moreover, the majority could ensure that its reported bills had a *better* chance of being scheduled, then the majority's committee advantage could be amplified at the scheduling stage. There are reasons to suspect that this is the case. Attention to limits on the majority leader's ability to schedule bills has to some extent obscured advantages held by the leader when it comes to bargaining over scheduling. And as we see it, these advantages are the key to understanding why the majority party enjoys lower consideration costs at the scheduling stage.

First, the use of dilatory tactics is not necessarily an appealing strategy, because it can entail greater expected sacrifices and smaller expected benefits than is often appreciated in the literature – and this is the case, though not in exactly the same ways, both with refusing consent requests and with filibustering. Consider the strategy of refusing consent. This strategy may result in a reduced passage of bills or projects favored by the refusing senator, perhaps in direct retribution for the refusal (Krehbiel 1986; Sinclair 2005). Refusing consent, moreover, does not ensure that the bill in question will be blocked. There is some chance that the majority leader will propose scheduling the bill by motion to proceed, which if successful would eliminate the benefit of refusing consent – and even if unsuccessful might impose an additional burden on the refuser by forcing a filibuster. Once a bill is successfully scheduled by a motion to proceed, senators who might have used the threat of filibuster to negotiate some concessions are no longer in a position to do so.

Now consider filibustering. It requires time, energy, and other resources that are scarce for all senators and have many valuable alternative uses.[4] It may also entail an additional downside if, like refusing consent, it reduces the likelihood that pet projects will be passed. And filibustering does not guarantee that a bill will be killed; it merely increases the chances.

In recent decades, threatened filibusters have outstripped actual filibusters as the dilatory tactic of choice (Oleszek 2007); this is potentially significant, since this tactic seems to entail fewer sacrifices than actual filibustering. However, threatening a filibuster puts a senator in a position in which he or she may be forced to choose between either following through on the threat – which requires sacrifice – or not following through, thereby reducing the credibility and effectiveness of such threats in the future – which is also costly.[5] And as with actual filibusters, the benefit of a threatened filibuster is uncertain, since it does not guarantee that a bill will not be scheduled.

Second, the offering of either a motion to proceed or a consent request to schedule a bill is in practice the prerogative of the leader (Beth 2002; Gold 2008; Saturno 2003).[6] This gives the leader a guaranteed opportunity to propose scheduling a bill as well as credible veto power over scheduling a bill (Evans and Lipinski 2005), which can be used as carrots

---

[4] See Bawn and Koger (2008) and Koger (2007, 2010) on the downsides of filibustering. For a vivid illustration of how scarce time is, see Oleszek (2007: 188–189).

[5] Majority leaders do not always automatically give in to holds and threatened filibusters. Rather, they consider the credibility of the threat in deciding how to react (Sinclair 2005). There is little empirical evidence regarding holds; in one of the few empirical studies, Evans and Lipinski (2005) compare holds from the 95th and 97th Congresses and find that Republican holds were more likely to succeed when Republicans were the majority than when they were the minority.

[6] In an interview with the authors (September 7, 2010), Marty Paone – former chief of staff for Senate majority leader Robert Byrd – remarked, "It is extraordinarily rare for anyone but the majority leader to make a motion to proceed." If an opponent did try to make the motion, he noted, the majority leadership would "squash it like a bug. That's when you tell your members, 'Look, I don't care if it's the Lord's Prayer, you vote against. This is not the majority leader that made the motion, this is not debatable. I don't care what the substance is, I don't care how much this affects your state – you are not voting for this motion if you ever want any committee assignments or anything else down the road from the majority leader. This is an affront to the majority. You are part of the majority; it should be an affront to you too.'"

and sticks in bargaining over the agenda. The leader's right of first recognition, moreover, gives the leader the ability to make the first proposal in bargaining over the agenda. In what we consider a significantly underappreciated article, Ainsworth and Flathman (1995) offer a model in which the majority leader uses these advantages to successfully bargain over scheduling, thereby biasing scheduling decisions in ways the leader favors. In line with much of the literature of the time, Ainsworth and Flathman conceptualize the leader not as an agent of the majority party, but rather as an agent of the Senate as a whole, whose motivation is to make the chamber run as efficiently as possible. If we assume instead that the leader's motivation is to bias outcomes for the benefit of the majority party, then the bargaining advantages should result in a majority bias in the set of bills that is scheduled.

Whose Bills Are Scheduled?

In this section, we examine whether there is a majority advantage in choosing whether bills that come out of committee are brought up on the floor. Except as otherwise noted, data used in this section are drawn from Scott Adler and John Wilkerson's impressive *Congressional Bills Project*,[7] which they graciously share. From their data, we have extracted the subset of Senate bills that they code as having been reported from committee and created a dataset with an observation for each of the 1,902 such bills for the 101st through 105th Congresses.[8] To their data we have added a variable that captures whether the bill was scheduled, allowing us to directly examine the scheduling of bills that come out of committee and whether there is a majority advantage at this stage.[9] We use these data to test the following hypotheses:

> **Hypothesis 5.1.** Majority-sponsored bills that get out of committee are more likely than minority-sponsored bills to be scheduled, ceteris paribus.

[7] E. Scott Adler and John Wilkerson, *Congressional Bills Project: 1989–1998*, available on the project homepage at http://www.congressionalbills.org/index.html.

[8] The data used here include only Senate bills – and not joint, concurrent, or simple resolutions from the Senate or measures of any type that originated in the House. We identified bills reported from committee using Adler and Wilkerson's *ReportS* variable. We have excluded from our analysis a small number of bills that were reported from committee but were referred to another committee without being considered on the floor.

[9] Here we code a bill as scheduled if it is brought up on the floor by any means. The data were collected using the "All Actions" listing on Thomas.loc.gov.

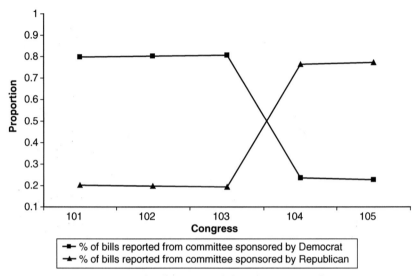

FIGURE 5.1. Proportion of Bills Reported from Committee by Sponsor Party, 101st through 105th Congresses.

> **Hypothesis 5.1**$_{\text{Null}}$. Majority-sponsored bills that get out of committee are not more likely than minority-sponsored bills to be scheduled, ceteris paribus.

The intuition of our research design is to see whether the probability of Democrat-sponsored bills being scheduled is higher when Democrats are the majority party (101st through 103rd Congresses) than when they are the minority party (104th and 105th Congresses) and whether Republican-sponsored bills are more likely to be scheduled when Republicans are the majority than when they are the minority.

Consistent with Koger and Fowler's (2006) findings and with our committee-specific results from Chapter 4, across our time series the set of committee-reported bills includes more majority- than minority-sponsored bills.[10] As shown in Figure 5.1, about 75 to 80 percent of

---

[10] The term *reported bills* is a slightly inaccurate description of our set of bills. The variable in the *Congressional Bills Project* data that indicates whether a bill was reported from committee codes bills that were discharged from committee by unanimous consent as having been reported from committee; as in the *Congressional Bills Project* data, bills discharged from committee are included in our analysis as bills that were reported from committee (hence our use of phrases such as "bills that got out of committee"). For the

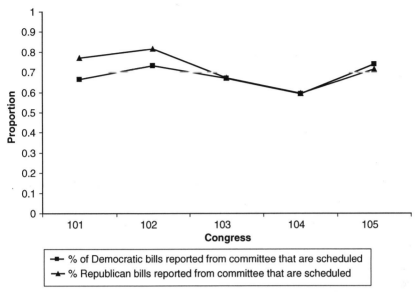

FIGURE 5.2. Share of Bills Scheduled by Party, 101st through 105th Congresses.

reported bills in each of these Congresses were majority-sponsored, with a sharp partisan change when Republicans became the majority party.[11]

Of these reported bills, roughly two-thirds (67.2 percent) are scheduled across our time series.[12] We can take a first, crude look at whether Hypothesis 5.1 holds by looking at the proportion of each party's reported bills that are scheduled in each Congress and looking for a switching pattern similar to that in Figure 5.1. The data shown in Figure 5.2 reveal no such pattern; rather, the proportion of each party's committee-reported bills that are scheduled is roughly the same for the minority party as for the majority party, with striking consistency across the period. In fact, a

sake of parsimony, in the remainder of the chapter we use the term *reported* to refer to all bills that got out of committee.

[11] There is a similar but less pronounced pattern in the proportion of bills introduced by the majority party in each of these Congresses. The majority proportion is .630, .623, .645, .598, .598 in the 101st through 105th Congresses, respectively. The number of seats held by the majority is 55, 56, 57, 52, 55, respectively.

[12] For individual Congresses, the proportion scheduled is .685 (101st), .747 (102nd), .669 (103rd), .51 (104th), and .714 (105th).

slightly larger share of minority-sponsored bills is scheduled in three of the five Congresses.

Of course, this figure does not control for many other factors. We address this by using probit (with robust standard errors) to estimate the following:

$$Scheduled_{it} = \alpha + \beta_1 Democrat_i + \beta_2 Majority_{it}$$
$$+ \beta_3 Democrat_i * Majority_{it} + \beta_4 MajoritySize_t$$
$$+ \beta_5 Majority_{it} * MajoritySize_t + \beta_6 Noncentrist1_{it}$$
$$+ \beta_7 Noncentrist2_{it} + \beta_8 CommMember_{it} + \beta_9 Cosponsors_i$$
$$+ \beta_{10} MultipleReferral_i + \beta_{11} YearsServed_{it} + \beta_{12} CommChair_{it}$$
$$+ \beta_{13} CommRank_{it} + \beta_{14} Leader_{it} + \varepsilon.$$

The key variables are *Scheduled*, a dummy variable coded 1 if bill *I* in Congress *t* was scheduled; *Democrat*, a dummy variable coded 1 if the bill's sponsor is a Democrat; *Majority*, a dummy variable coded 1 if the sponsor's party is the majority party in Congress *t*; and *Democrat * Majority*, an interaction term. Hypothesis 5.1 predicts that the coefficient for *Majority* (which captures the change in probability that a Republican-sponsored bill will be scheduled as Republicans go from minority to majority status) will be positive, as will the sum of the coefficients for *Majority* and *Democrat * Majority* (which captures the change in probability that a Democrat-sponsored bill will be scheduled as Democrats go from minority to majority status). Hypothesis 5.1$_{Null}$ predicts that they will not statistically differ from zero.

Other variables are control variables. They are *MajoritySize*, the number of seats held by the majority party in Congress *t*; *Majority*$_{it}$ * *MajoritySize*, an interaction; *Noncentrist1*, the absolute value of the bill sponsor's first-dimension DW-Nominate score, included as a rough measure of how ideologically extreme the sponsor is; *Noncentrist2*, an analogous second-dimension Nominate score; *CommMember*, a dummy coded 1 if the sponsor was a member of a committee to which the bill was referred; *Cosponsors*, the number of cosponsors of the bill; *MultipleReferral*, a dummy coded 1 if the bill was referred to more than one committee; *YearsServed*, the number of years served in the Senate by the bill's sponsor; *CommChair*, a dummy coded 1 if the sponsor was the chair of a committee in Congress *t*; *CommRank*, a dummy coded 1 if the sponsor was the ranking member of a committee in

TABLE 5.1. *Effect of Majority Status on the Probability of a Bill Being Scheduled, 101st through 105th Congresses*

Variable	Coefficient	Standard Error	*p* Value
Democrat	−0.1497	0.1898	.430
Majority (H 5.1: positive)	−1.276	3.530	.718
*Democrat * Majority*	0.0492	0.2140	.818
MajoritySize	0.0607	0.0565	.283
*Majority * MajoritySize*	0.0180	0.0636	.777
Noncentrist1	−0.4903	0.2238	.028
Noncentrist2	−0.1975	0.1167	.091
CommMember	−0.0144	0.0744	.846
Cosponsors	−0.0006	0.0023	.775
MultipleReferral	−0.2405	0.1508	.111
YearsServed	0.0018	0.0086	.830
CommChair	0.0706	0.0897	.431
CommRank	−0.1909	0.1535	.214
Leader	−0.0971	0.1498	.517
Constant	−2.307	3.169	.467
*Majority + Democrat * Majority* (H 5.1: positive)	−1.227	3.448	.722

Note: N = 1,902; pseudo-R^2 = .0128; log-likelihood = −1170.5098.

Congress *t*; and *Leader*, a dummy coded 1 if the sponsor was a party leader in Congress *t*.

The results of this probit, shown in Table 5.1, paint a picture similar to that in Figure 5.2. Both the key coefficients (bold in the table) are negative, not statistically different from zero, and do not allow us to reject the null hypothesis. In fact, the model explains little variation in the dependent variable. Only the *Noncentrist* variables are significant at greater than the 90 percent level; both are negative, indicating that, as bills' sponsors are less centrist, bills are less likely to be scheduled.[13]

These results suggest that bills sponsored by members of either party have about the same chance of being scheduled once they have come out of committee. Given that the majority gets far more bills out of committee in the first place, this translates into far more majority- than minority-sponsored bills being scheduled in each Congress, as shown in Figure 5.3. The figure closely mirrors the pattern in Figure 5.1, with roughly

---

[13] We have also run this analysis including dummy variables for committee origin, which does not change the inferences we draw about the hypotheses.

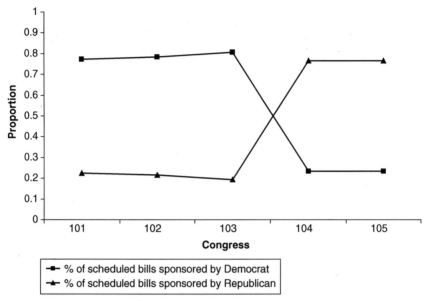

FIGURE 5.3. Share of Scheduled Bills Sponsored by Each Party, 101st through 105th Congresses.

75 to 80 percent of scheduled bills in each Congress being sponsored by a majority party senator, and with Democrats and Republicans seeing a sharp change in fortunes in the 104th Congress.

Do Scheduled Majority Bills Differ from Scheduled Minority Bills?

At this point one caveat is in order: the preceding analysis considers only the probability of bills being scheduled, without considering the content of scheduled bills. It is possible that the preceding results reveal no majority advantage in scheduling bills that come out of committee because of a shortcoming in our research design. Our analysis assumes implicitly that the sample of bills sponsored by members of one party is identical to the sample of bills sponsored by the other, aside from factors for which we have added controls. But it is possible that one factor we have not controlled for, the contentiousness of a bill, differs between the two groups. It may be that the set of scheduled minority bills is composed predominantly of uncontroversial and easy-to-schedule bills but that the set of scheduled majority bills includes a larger share of controversial and harder-to-schedule bills. In other words, the majority may have an

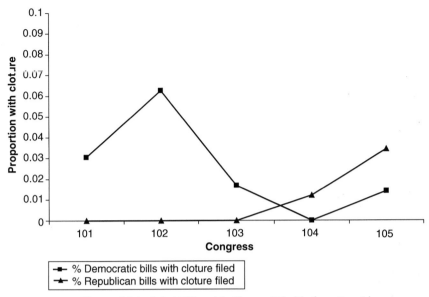

FIGURE 5.4. Share of Scheduled Bills with Cloture Filed before Consideration.

advantage that is not captured by the probability of a bill being scheduled but that does show up in the nature of scheduled bills. In this section we explore this possibility.

We do not have a reliable means of measuring how contentious each scheduled bill is and thus cannot analyze each party's level of success in scheduling such bills. We can, however, look at a few different indicators that provide circumstantial evidence that scheduled majority bills are more contentious than scheduled minority bills. First, for the set of scheduled bills, we compare the percentage of each party's bills for which cloture was filed prior to the bill being scheduled. We assume that if cloture is filed early, it indicates that the bill is at least somewhat controversial. For most scheduled bills from either party, cloture is not filed before scheduling. Within the subset of bills for which cloture is filed, however, we see a familiar pattern (shown in Figure 5.4): each party has a higher proportion of bills subject to cloture when it is the majority than when it is the minority. In fact, there is only one minority-sponsored bill (in the 105th Congress) on which cloture is filed.

Another way of roughly gauging bills' contentiousness is by looking at the set of each party's scheduled bills that go on to pass the chamber and comparing the proportion for each party that passes on voice

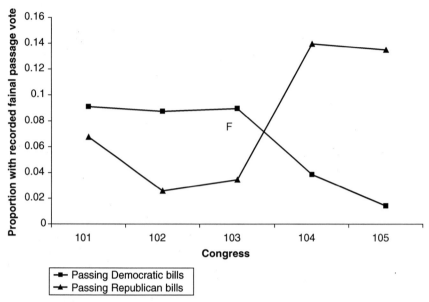

FIGURE 5.5. Share of Each Party's Passing Bills with Recorded Vote on Final Passage.

versus recorded votes.[14] A downside of this approach is that it does not account for the possibility that the bills being voted on were amended between being scheduled and the votes on final passage, in which case the contents of the bill being voted on at final passage may be quite different from the contents of the bill that was introduced and may not reflect the original sponsor's intent. However, as long as such cases do not introduce a bias that is systematically related to bill sponsors' partisan affiliation, it is not problematic. Figure 5.5 shows this proportion for each party, and we see a similar pattern, with a low proportion of minority bills and a higher proportion of majority bills, getting recorded votes in each Congress.

Our final approach gets around the potential problem of bias introduced via the amendment process by focusing on the subset of bills that passed the Senate without amendment. For such bills, we can draw a confident inference from individuals' votes on final passage about the nature

[14] We are assuming here that uncontentious bills are likely to pass on voice votes and that contentious bills are more likely to pass on recorded votes, so a higher proportion of bills with recorded votes indicates more contentious bills being scheduled.

of the bill that was scheduled, since the bill is identical at each stage. A downside of this approach is that relatively few bills fall into this category, and inferences drawn from this sample may not be representative of the larger set of bills in which we are interested.

If it is the case that scheduled minority-sponsored bills are uncontentious, scheduled majority-sponsored bills are sometimes contentious, and contentious bills are less likely to roll members of the bill sponsor's party than to roll a member of the other party (where a roll is defined as a senator voting against a bill that passes), we can draw the following hypotheses about patterns that we should see on final passage votes:

Hypothesis 5.2. For majority-sponsored bills, minority senators are more likely than majority senators to be rolled, ceteris paribus.

Hypothesis 5.3. For minority-sponsored bills, there is no difference between majority and minority senators' probability of being rolled, ceteris paribus.

Hypothesis 5.4. For majority senators, the probability of being rolled is no greater on minority-sponsored bills than on majority-sponsored bills, ceteris paribus.

Hypothesis 5.5. For minority senators, the probability of being rolled is greater on majority-sponsored bills than on minority-sponsored bills, ceteris paribus.

The basic logic here is that uncontentious bills shouldn't roll anyone at a high rate. That is, these bills should pass, but almost no one will vote against them. Thus, if minority party senators are getting only uncontentious bills out of committee, Hypotheses 5.3 and 5.4 follow: bills that pass with nearly universal support should produce low roll rates for members of both parties. On the other hand, if some (or many) of the majority-sponsored bills making it out of committee are contentious, but not in a way that will go against the wishes of a large portion of the majority caucus, then Hypotheses 5.2 and 5.5 should follow. That is, these bills should sometimes pass, against the nay votes of many minority senators (thus rolling them), but with little opposition by majority senators.

For each of the 1,379 S. bills that passed the Senate in our time series (drawn from the *Congressional Bills Project* data), we have coded whether the bill passed with or without amendment. Of the 530 that passed without amendment, only 10 were subject to recorded votes on final passage.[15] Using a dataset with an observation for each senator on each of these votes, we test the hypotheses with the following probit:

$$Roll_{ijt} = \alpha + \beta_1 MajoritySenator_{it} + \beta_2 MajoritySponsor_j$$
$$+ \beta_3 MajoritySenator * Sponsor_{ijt} + \beta_4 Distance_{it} + \varepsilon_{ijt}$$

$Roll_{ijt}$ is a dummy variable coded 1 if senator i was rolled on vote j in Congress t; $MajoritySenator_{it}$ is a dummy variable coded 1 if senator i is a member of the majority party in Congress t; $MajoritySponsor_j$ is a dummy variable coded 1 if the bill being voted on in vote j was sponsored by a member of the majority party; $MajoritySenator * Sponsor_{ijt}$ is an interaction of the previous two variables; and $Distance_{it}$ is the absolute value of senator i's first-dimension DW-Nominate score in Congress t, included as a rough measure of the senator's ideological extremity.

We estimate the model using robust standard errors. The hypotheses predict the following about these variables' coefficients:

Hypothesis 5.2. *MajoritySenator$_{it}$ + MajoritySenator * Sponsor$_{ijt}$ will be negative.*

Hypothesis 5.3. *MajoritySenator$_{it}$ will not differ from zero.*

Hypothesis 5.4. *MajoritySponsor$_j$ + MajoritySenator * Sponsor$_{ijt}$ will not be positive.*

Hypothesis 5.5. *MajoritySponsor$_j$ will be positive.*

Table 5.2a shows the results of this probit, which are consistent with the predictions of all four hypotheses. Table 5.2b shows these results as estimated probabilities of a senator being rolled on final passage of an unamended bill. The leftmost data column shows that, for majority-sponsored bills, majority senators have a low probability of being rolled (.03), and minority senators are significantly more likely to be rolled (.33). In contrast, for minority-sponsored bills, neither majority nor minority senators are likely to be rolled (the rightmost column shows the estimated probabilities, .03 and .01, respectively), though the difference is marginally significant. For majority senators, the probability of being rolled is low and does not differ significantly whether the bill sponsor is a majority or minority member (.03 in each case). For minority senators, however, the probability of being rolled is low for bills sponsored by

[15] By contrast, of 848 bills that passed with amendment(s), 114 were subject to a recorded vote on final passage.

TABLE 5.2a. *Estimated Effect of Majority and Minority Bill Sponsorship on Majority and Minority Senators' Probability of a Senator Being Rolled on Final Passage of an Unamended Bill, 101st through 105th Congresses*

Variable	Coefficient	Standard Error	p Value
MajoritySenator (H 5.3: zero)	0.6599	0.4127	.110
MajoritySponsor (H 5.5: positive)	2.0973	0.3818	.001
*MajoritySenator * Sponsor*	−2.1313	0.4477	.001
Distance	1.320	0.4175	.002
Constant	−2.9855	0.4672	.001
MajoritySenator + *MajoritySenator * Sponsor* (H 5.2: negative)	−1.4714	0.1522	.001
MajoritySponsor + *MajoritySenator * Sponsor* (H 5.1: less than or equal to zero)	−0.0339	0.2097	.872

Note: N = 1,005; pseudo-R^2 = .2778; log-likelihood = −256.68667.

TABLE 5.2b. *Estimated Probability of a Senator Being Rolled on Final Passage of an Unamended Bill, by Senator Party and Bill Sponsor Party, 101st through 105th Congresses*

		Bill Sponsor	
		Majority	Minority
Senator	Majority	.0314 (.0171–.0524)	.0338 (.0146–.0655)
	Minority	.3392 (.2840–.3978)	.0092 (.0006–.0338)

Note: Cells contain estimated probability of amendment being adopted; 95% confidence intervals shown in parentheses, estimated via CLARIFY (Toms, Wittenberg, and King 2001) with *AbsDW1* set at its mean value. CLARIFY software and documentation are available on Gary King's webpage at http://gking.harvard.edu/.

minority members (.01) but is sharply and significantly higher (.33) for bills sponsored by majority members.

As noted, these results are based on a small, nonrandom sample of bills; inferences drawn from them may or may not apply to scheduling decisions more generally. But the results are consistent with our conjecture that scheduled majority bills are more contentious than scheduled minority bills – which is in turn consistent with the majority having a scheduling advantage over the minority.

Summary

Is the majority better than the minority at getting bills that have come out of committee onto the floor? In this chapter, we have used a wide variety of data and approached the question from a number of angles to argue that there are good reasons to believe that the majority does have a floor scheduling advantage. While a large part of the majority advantage stems from control of committee decision making, our analysis reveals evidence of other subtle but important advantages that occur at the scheduling stage. Thus, the consideration cost advantage from the committee stage is clearly maintained and, to some extent enhanced, at the scheduling stage.

The first part of our empirical analysis shows that, for the set of bills that have gotten beyond the committee stage, majority-sponsored bills are no more or less likely than minority-sponsored bills to be scheduled; this seems to indicate that there is not a majority advantage at the scheduling stage. However, the majority's control of committees means that the set of bills getting beyond the committee stage in the first place heavily favors the majority, and this bias carries over into the set of bills that is scheduled.

We also examine the content of scheduled bills and find circumstantial but consistent evidence across a variety of indicators that scheduled majority bills are more often contentious than are scheduled minority bills. This leads us to amend our initial finding that there is no majority advantage at the scheduling stage; the majority seems to be better than the minority at scheduling its bills when they are controversial.

We neither suggest nor believe that the majority is able to unilaterally dictate what reaches the floor; rather, we agree with the conventional view that scheduling decisions result from bargaining between and within parties. Unlike the authors of much of the literature, however, we believe the majority has advantages that allow it to bargain more effectively than the minority; and, critically, this bargaining advantage translates into lower consideration costs.

6

The Effects of Filibusters

It sometimes seems that Senate observers perceive all (threats of) filibusters as similar to those of Huey Long, Strom Thurmond, Alfonse D'Amato, and Jimmy Stewart – that is, as insurmountable obstacles to the majority party agenda. Even from more moderate perspectives, scholars often characterize the chamber's legislative process as requiring 60 votes to pass any significant legislation, which is portrayed as a serious obstacle for the majority party that typically forces it either to give up on a proposal or to water it down so seriously that the resultant legislation does not clearly constitute majority party success.[1]

We rethink this characterization. We agree that the filibuster presents the kind of obstacle just described under some circumstances; indeed, it is perhaps the most significant and consistent component of the majority party's consideration costs. We argue, however, that the filibuster does not present this kind of insurmountable obstacle under other circumstances. In many cases, the majority party is able to pay the consideration costs associated with breaking through or sidestepping a filibuster. We believe, moreover, that Senate literature focuses disproportionately on cases of the first type, creating a bias toward overestimating the extent to which filibusters undermine the majority party.

In the remainder of the chapter, we make our case by first analyzing the logic of potential filibuster fights, then presenting cloture and scheduling data consistent with our argument.

---

[1] For example, both Sinclair (2002) and Rohde and Shepsle (2007) use "60-vote Senate" in their titles; others, such as Krehbiel (1998) and Chiou and Rothenberg 2003, build the 60-vote threshold into formal models.

The Logic of Potential Filibuster Fights

The Partisan Distribution of Filibusters

In our costly-consideration terms, filibusters, whether actual or expected, create one part of the costs a proposal's proponents must bear to get the proposal to final consideration. This is the case regardless of whether the proponent is the majority party, another coalition, or an individual senator, raising the question of why people see the filibuster as being, first and foremost, a tool used against the majority party by opponents of the majority's efforts.

We suspect the answer begins with the more general distribution of consideration costs created by Senate rules and procedures. If the majority leadership wants to block something, filibustering is last on a long list of potential blocking strategies. The majority can use procedural powers held by majority senators at the committee and scheduling stages, as well as floor procedures such as points of order, tabling motions, and filling the amendment tree, to block proposals. Given that filibustering often requires significant sacrifices by the filibusterer and that these other dilatory strategies are less burdensome, it makes sense that the majority generally prefers blocking via methods other than the filibuster.

Senators outside the majority leadership can also try to use some of these other methods (such as tabling motions and points of order). But using them successfully requires gaining the votes of at least a majority of the chamber. Majority leaders have a procedural coalition standing by that meets this threshold if it is unified, but a minority leaders' coalition does not meet this threshold, even if unified.

Of course, neither party's leaders can assume levels of procedural unity as high as is often the case in other legislatures, including the House or Representatives. There are clear examples of low procedural unity thwarting majority leaders' efforts. But comparatively low procedural unity and anecdotal evidence of majority losses do not imply that procedural failure is the norm for majority leaders. What really counts is how often they get enough votes to accomplish their procedural objectives, not how often party members defect. Even when enough majority senators defect that the remaining majority senators no longer constitute a majority, the leadership can sometimes pick up sufficient votes from the minority party (whose members are also less than perfectly unified in many cases). Unless we assume the majority finds it harder than the minority to hold together its procedural coalition, we should expect to see the majority win more procedural battles. In the next two chapters, we present evidence supporting this expectation.

This has two implications. First, since the majority prefers nonfilibuster blocking strategies, and these strategies are more difficult for others to use, the filibuster is often the most viable tactic for blocking majority proposals. Thus, we *should* see more filibusters directed against the majority than against the minority. Second, and more important for our purposes, the majority leaders' advantage in using procedural blocking tools means such tools will be used to raise consideration costs for opposition proposals more often than for majority proposals. In other words, such tools impose higher consideration costs on others than on the majority party.

Effects of Filibusters on Majority Proposals

This leaves unanswered the big question: when opponents filibuster a majority proposal, what are the consequences? We argue that, in many instances, majority leaders have substantial resources for paying the costs of overcoming a filibuster. Their influence over committee and scheduling decisions allows them to raise or lower consideration costs of other senators' proposals, which creates sticks and carrots they can offer in exchange for support on a cloture vote. Similarly, their influence over committee assignments, staff, and other resources can raise or lower consideration costs. And leaders' influence over substantial amounts of campaign support creates another set of incentives that can be used to gain votes on cloture motions (Groseclose and Snyder 1996; Lee 2000).

We are at pains to clarify, however, that we do not claim that the majority party is willing or even able to bear the costs of overcoming a filibuster. There are many examples in which the majority clearly does not bear these costs and fails to achieve its goals. Rather, our aim is to reinforce two points: first, the costs of overcoming a filibuster are lower for the majority than for the minority, and second, such costs are not always prohibitive for the majority.

A Typology of Potential Filibuster Fights

In this section, we present a typology of possible outcomes that can result from instances in which the majority party wants to push a proposal that the minority party opposes. We group these outcomes into four categories representing scenarios that range from worst- to best-case outcomes for the majority party.

In any such case, majority and opposition leaders need to answer three questions. First, if the majority tries to push its proposal forward, will it be filibustered? Second, how many votes would majority leaders need to pick up to invoke cloture? And third, what sacrifices would leaders have to make to get the needed number of votes? From the answers to these questions, leaders can calculate the expected consideration costs the majority needs to pay to overcome a filibuster or the possibility of a filibuster.

Observers often treat the Senate's hold system as a dilatory mechanism. As Evans and Lipinski (2005) point out, however, it also serves as an information-gathering mechanism for majority leaders that reduces the cost of answering the first question by inducing opponents to reveal their intent to filibuster. In addition, the parties' whip organizations facilitate the gathering of such information. The whip organizations also serve as networks for efficiently transmitting information that helps leaders answer the second and third questions (Bradbury, Davidson, and Evans 2008). Our typology depends on the answers to these questions, which allow leaders to estimate the likelihood of an opponents' filibuster if the majority pushes a bill, the consideration costs the majority would have to pay to overcome a filibuster, and whether the majority would find it worthwhile to pay these costs.

In cases falling into the first of our four categories, the majority leader estimates that pushing the proposal in question would trigger a filibuster and that the costs of overcoming the filibuster are greater than the benefits of passing the bill. Thus, the majority leader does not push the bill in the first place.[2] Such cases feature prominently in Senate literature, which often emphasizes the effectiveness of filibuster threats. Instances in this category obviously constitute losses for the majority party and wins for the minority, and these losses should clearly be attributed to the power opponents gain from the ability to filibuster. Observers may or may not attribute the outcome to the filibuster, though, since such cases do not entail an actual filibuster, let alone a filibuster fight.[3]

In the second category, unlike the first, the majority decides to push its proposal and triggers a filibuster fight. But as in the first category, opponents win the fight and the filibuster thwarts the bill. This scenario should

---

[2] Note that this does not imply that majority leaders are *unable* to bear the costs of cloture. They might be unable – or they might be able but calculate that the payoff would be insufficient to offset the costs.

[3] Thus, even bills that die in committee might sometimes do so because of anticipation of an eventual, effective filibuster against the bill.

not occur if everyone has perfect information, since fighting the filibuster is itself costly to the majority. Still, there is ample room for uncertainty, miscalculation, and risk acceptance to lead the majority into such losing battles. In contrast to those in the first category, cases in this category produce observable filibuster fights.

The third category comprises instances in which the majority pushes a proposal, triggers a filibuster fight, and ultimately wins the fight. Like the previous cases, such instances entail an incorrect estimation of the parameters of the fight, but in this case it is the minority that miscalculates and enters into a fight that it loses. Like the preceding type of fight, this kind produces an observable struggle. In contrast to both of the first two types of fights, however, the third type results in a majority win.

Finally, there are cases in which the majority pushes its proposal, and opponents do not resist because it is clear that the majority can and will overcome the filibuster. Like the first category, this produces no visible fight but nonetheless represents a majority triumph over the filibuster.

Others note the problems of identifying filibusters, since differentiating filibusters from lengthy but nondilatory debate is sometimes difficult (Beth and Bach 2003; Binder and Smith 1997). One effect of the first and last categories not producing visible filibuster fights is to compound the difficulty of identifying instances in which a filibuster or a possible filibuster shapes the outcome of a legislative struggle. Our take is that the literature focuses heavily on the second category, somewhat less on the first and third categories, and hardly at all on the fourth category. For instance, examples of the majority not pursuing a goal due to fear of a filibuster are common, but examples of the minority not filibustering due to fear of losing the filibuster fight are rare.

In fact, we do not know the distribution of cases across the categories. We often observe instances of the second and third categories but have little information about the frequency of cases in the first or fourth categories. Put another way, filibusters often succeed or fail in ways that are underappreciated in Senate literature, making it difficult to estimate their overall effect on Senate legislation. It is apparent, however, that each scenario occurs sometimes. In the following sections we sketch examples of each category, fleshing out some details about how each type of conflict can unfold.

Category 1: The Taxpayer Relief Act of 1998

The Taxpayer Relief Act of 1998 (H.R. 4579), a tax cut proposal favored by the Republican majority, provides an example of the first type of situation (i.e., one in which the majority party does not pursue its policy because it believes it would lose the ensuing filibuster fight).[4]

In early September 1998, in the looming shadow of the Clinton impeachment, House speaker Newt Gingrich and Senate majority leader Trent Lott agreed to push for passage of a tax cut package before the November elections. Republicans expected to reap electoral benefits from the tax cuts and hoped that electoral pressure stemming from voters' fondness for tax cuts would garner enough Democratic support to overcome a filibuster (Republicans held 55 Senate seats). Clinton and congressional Democratic leaders, however, opposed the measure (Hosansky 1998a,b).

House Ways and Means Committee chair Bill Archer introduced the bill on September 16 and the House passed the bill on September 26, with Republicans voting in favor by a 210–11 margin, and Democrats voting against 183–19.

The bill was placed on the Senate calendar three days later. By that point, however, Republican hopes for the bill had dimmed. Democrats framed the issue largely as a matter of protecting the Social Security trust fund – another electorally popular position – and remained broadly united in their opposition (Hosansky 1998b).

Ultimately, the proposal attracted the support of few, if any, Democratic senators. Moreover, even some members of Lott's own caucus were, at best, lukewarm in their support for the measure. By the time the bill reached the Senate, it was unclear whether the measure could even garner the simple majority needed for passage; Lott's whip count on a cloture vote showed fewer than the 51 yes votes needed for passage. Some Republicans objected on budget-balancing grounds; others objected because they wanted to see a bigger tax cut. Moreover, it was unclear whether any Democrats would support the measure (Hager 1998; Hosansky 1998b). Whether Lott could have rounded up a majority in favor of passage is uncertain, but he clearly could not get the 60 votes needed to get the bill to a final passage vote.[5] In the end, Lott never attempted to bring the bill to the floor and it died on the calendar.

Category 2: Repeal of the Estate Tax

The fight for repeal of the estate tax during the 109th Congress (2005–2006) provides a vivid example of the majority party fighting hard for 60 votes in order to pass a bill yet failing to achieve its goal.

---

[4] We thank Larry Evans for suggesting this example to us and for sharing the whip count information discussed here.

[5] In this case, Republicans needed 60 votes not only for cloture, but also to waive the Budget Act.

The Republican majority held 55 seats. Permanent repeal of the estate tax was a "central element of President Bush's economic agenda" (Rosenbaum 2005) and "a cherished goal of many conservatives" (Stolberg et al. 2005). In April 2005, the House – for the fourth straight year – passed a bill (H.R. 8) to repeal the tax (Rosenbaum 2005).

The bill then sat on the Senate calendar with little action until July, at which point Senate majority leader Bill Frist hoped to enact the bill before the August recess (Stolberg et al. 2005). After initially planning a July vote on scheduling the measure, however, Frist decided to wait until after the break (Schatz 2005).

Congress's return from the recess, however, coincided with Hurricane Katrina. Frist planned a cloture vote, but in the midst of the political turmoil created by Katrina and sharply rising gas prices, he quickly back-tracked. On September 7, he again put on hold his plans to pursue the bill (Murray and Babington 2005; Weisman 2005).

The bill then sat on the calendar until the following summer. In early June 2006, Frist made a motion to proceed. It was not clear that he could gain 60 votes in support (Andrews 2006a), though pro-repeal activist groups simultaneously made concerted efforts to pressure centrist Democrats and Republicans to support the bill (Murray and Babington 2006). Frist got a vote on June 8 but garnered only 57 votes for cloture.

At that point, Republicans effectively gave up on passage of a complete, permanent repeal and instead debated whether to pursue a compromise that would reduce, but not eliminate, the estate tax. Frist reversed his previous course and indicated he was willing to pursue such a compromise (Andrews 2006b).

For more than a year, Republican senator Jon Kyl had worked to forge a compromise that centrist Democrats would support (Rosenbaum 2005; Schatz 2005). Following the rejection of outright repeal of the tax, Kyl and other Republicans pursued a compromise with greater urgency (Van Dongen and Retter 2006), arriving quickly at a deal that passed the House (as H.R. 2638) on June 22. In addition to compromising on the estate tax, the bill featured a sweetener granting tax breaks to lumber companies, in the hope of gaining support from Democratic senators Maria Cantwell of Washington and Mark Pryor of Arkansas (Van Dongen 2006a).

Passing the compromise, however, presented Frist with a tricky balancing act. Republican officials and activists had been divided all along between those willing to compromise and those unwilling to accept anything less than full, permanent repeal of the tax (Andrews 2006a,b; Stolberg et al. 2005). Even once full repeal was clearly dead, it was unclear whether conservative Republicans would back a compromise measure in sufficient numbers to enact a bill.

Frist put off action indefinitely while trying to round up votes (Van Dongen 2006b); Republican leaders soon agreed to include additional sweeteners, which the House passed on June 29 as H.R. 5970. This bill packaged the estate tax reduction with a minimum wage increase, which was a prominent Democratic goal.[6] And in addition to the lumber tax breaks, it included a mine cleanup program aimed at gaining the support of West Virginia Democrats Robert Byrd and Jay Rockefeller (it worked with Byrd but not with Rockefeller), rural development bonds aimed at Mark Pryor, and tax deductions aimed at Democrat Daniel Akaka of Hawaii. In the end, however, the Senate refused to invoke cloture, on a 56–42 vote, on August 3 (Nather and Van Dongen 2006a,b).[7] That vote effectively ended the fight over the estate tax. Frist did not pursue the issue again before retiring from the Senate at the end of the 109th Congress.

Category 3: The Motor Voter Fight

The National Voter Registration Act (NVRA) of 1993 was a contentious piece of legislation from the outset. Initially proposed in 1991 as S. 250, the bill sought to mandate that states offer voter registration at their respective offices handling vehicle registration and driver licensing. Debate over the bill, which took place during the Democrat-controlled 102nd and 103rd Congresses, was quite partisan. On the surface, Republicans objected that the passage of the law would make it easier to commit voter fraud, while Democrats argued that making registration simpler and more accessible could increase turnout and be a boon to the democratic process (Krauss 1992). These positions, however, were little more than public cover for the true political character of the disagreement. The real fight was over the electoral implications of expanding registration: both parties believed that making registration easier would lead to higher Democratic registration and turnout.

The Republican attack focused on three main objections to the bill, contending that it would make it easier to commit voter fraud, be a costly burden on states, and offer unnecessary expansion of voter registration

---

[6] The bill also included unrelated tax cut extensions that both Republicans and Democrats supported.

[7] Frist voted against cloture for procedural reasons, and Democrat Max Baucus of Montana, who had supported full repeal by voting for the June cloture motion, missed the vote due to a family tragedy (Nather and Van Dongen 2006a). So, in effect, Byrd's was the only vote gained by all the compromises and sweeteners.

efforts. On the last point, Republicans relied on the assumption that low voter turnout was a sign of a generally content electorate and was not due to difficulty of registration. Senator Mitch McConnell of Kentucky, who led the Republican effort against the bill, vocalized this philosophy by referring to the bill as "a solution in search of a problem" (Krauss 1992).

In the first round of fighting over the bill, in the 102nd Congress, Republicans submitted amendments addressing these concerns. Among those submitted were amendments to establish voter fraud as a federal crime with a mandatory minimum penalty and a program that would allow states to be federally compensated for the costs of implementing the act. One amendment, proposed by Senator John McCain of Arizona, would have barred individuals from being registered by an agency from which that individual received aid; this would have effectively barred welfare and unemployment offices from offering registration. All these amendments were tabled. The bill was not passed easily; it took a total of three cloture votes to bring about a vote on the bill. The final passage vote in the Senate was 61–38, with just one Democrat voting against the bill and five Republicans voting in favor.[8]

The legislation was given another chance in the 103rd Congress (proposed as H.R. 2 in the House and S. 460 in the Senate) after the election of Democratic president Bill Clinton. Under Clinton, Republican opposition to the bill was stronger due to the lack of a veto safety net. Senate Republicans, led by Senator Mitch McConnell and minority leader Bob Dole, mounted a determined stalling campaign. The filibuster of the Senate version of the bill (S. 460) began on March 5. Dole and McConnell gathered enough votes to prevent the bill from receiving cloture and being brought to the floor for initial debate; the vote failed 52–36, with only one Republican voting for cloture and 12 senators not voting. After four days of lobbying and negotiating, however, Democrats finally won over enough Republicans to muster the 60 votes needed to bring the bill to the floor. On March 9 the Democrats invoked cloture on a 62–38 vote, with the help of five Republicans.

Though Democrats had succeeded in bringing the bill to the floor, the fight was not over. Over the next two weeks, Republican opposition organized further stalls in Senate action. During these two weeks, negotiations took place in the Senate and through White House phone lines. The result of this bargaining was a package of amendments proposed by Senator Ford on March 16. The package included concessions to make

---

[8] The House passed the bill, but Congress did not override President Bush's veto.

the bill more palatable to the GOP, including, most notably, striking the automatic registration of welfare recipients, who were seen as likely Democratic voters; in the revised form of the bill, this was made optional, to be decided at the state level. In addition, a concession was made to a proposal from Senator McCain allowing for registration to occur in military recruitment offices, serving a more conservative demographic (Wines 1993a). Finally, language was added to the bill to ensure that those voters being registered would not be pressured into registering for any particular party. These concessions were sufficiently satisfactory to sway five Republicans to join the 57 Democrats in calling for cloture once again. On May 17 Congress sorted through and tabled amendments to the bill until it reached the bill's scheduled cloture vote at 2 P.M., when the Senate voted 62–38 to send the bill to conference.

In conference committee, the bill was altered so that registration would be offered in both welfare offices and military recruitment offices, though it would not be the type of automatic enrollment originally proposed (Wines 1993b). The Senate approved the final version of the bill with a margin of 62–36, the partisan nature of the bill underlined by the fact that all 36 nays came from Republicans. The NVRA was signed into law on May 20, 1993.

The NVRA illustrates the nature of the bargaining over cloture in the Senate. The final effect of this bargaining process was a bill that retained most of the Democrats' plans, with minimal concessions made to win over the small number of votes to effectively cloture debate on the bill.[9] It was *not* a bipartisan bill in that it did not represent the interests of the parties equally. Rather, as Senate majority leader George Mitchell put it, "The important point is that we [Democrats] passed a bill to expand the right to vote. This legislation is not perfect, but we accomplished most of our objectives."[10] The concessions made, which bought the necessary votes for cloture, represent incremental moves to moderate the initial, majority-proposed bill, not changes that represented equal satisfaction for both parties.

Category 4: The Central American Free Trade Agreement
Soon after his election to a second term, President George W. Bush began pushing Republican trade policies through the 109th Congress. The

---

[9] The literature on vetoes (e.g., Cameron 2000; Kiewiet and McCubbins 1988) employs a similar logic in describing the bargaining process between Congress and the president.

[10] Associated Press, Eugene Register-Guard, "Senate Approves Motor Voter Bill," March 18, 1993.

Central America Free Trade Act (CAFTA) spread free trade to the countries of Costa Rica, El Salvador, Guatemala, Honduras, and Nicaragua, and added a separate agreement for the Dominican Republic. This bill intended to add to the area covered by the North America Free Trade Act (NAFTA), which included the United States, Canada, and Mexico.

Even though many Democrats and some Republicans did not believe NAFTA lived up to what was intended, President Bush made agreements with the countries involved and presented the agreements to be adopted by Congress. While the power to make trade agreements was delegated to Congress in the Constitution, presidents have been allowed to make agreements and have them put through Congress as bills that may not be amended (CQ Weekly 2006). CAFTA became a partisan issue, as evidenced by the statements of two House members: Republican Bill Thomas and Democrat Sherrod Brown both agreed that the bill was more about politics than actual trade policy. But Thomas blamed the Democrats for making the bill "a major political vote," while Brown referred to the Republicans' efforts as "an exercise in strong-arm tactics" (Norton 2005). In the House, minority leader Nancy Pelosi fought hard against the bill, even to the point of suggesting that an "ethics inquiry might result from deals offered by Republicans to round up votes" (Norton 2005).

Early on, in the Senate Finance Committee, the bill lacked enough support to reach the floor. Several members of the committee were worried about the effect of sugar imports, which would hurt their constituencies. To secure some support, Rob Portman, U.S. trade representative, and Mike Johanns, secretary of agriculture, promised to keep sugar imports and other deals permitted under CAFTA out of U.S. markets for two years as protected under a farm bill (CQ Weekly 1993). While a majority of committee members did not support CAFTA, they allowed it to pass to the Senate floor (CQ Weekly 1993).

The bill reached the floor on a 61–34 vote on a motion to proceed (CQ Weekly 1993). This vote is interesting in that it raises some questions about potential opposition to the bill. Roll call votes on a motion to proceed are relatively rare, especially in the absence of a preceding (successful) vote for cloture. Typically, if there is no attempt to filibuster, the motion to proceed is voted on by unanimous consent. A roll call vote on the motion to proceed implies that there was enough opposition to force a roll call vote. Given the vote tally, however, it may have been a test for the opposition, which indicated that the majority leadership did have enough votes to overcome a potential filibuster. After debate, the bill passed the Senate 54–45. At the same time, H.R. 3045, the House companion bill, passed in that chamber 217–215 (Norton 2005). The Senate then voted again on this House version of the bill, by a similar margin of 55–45.[11]

CAFTA faced intense opposition from many Democrats who would have liked to block the bill. Yet opponents did not attempt a filibuster. In part, at least, this is because they simply did not have the votes to block, a fact that shows up in the motion-to-proceed vote tally. It is important that the bill itself, on final passage, fell 5 votes short of the 60 that would have been needed for cloture. But the 61 votes it got on the motion to proceed suggest that, on a procedural motion, the majority Republicans could have found the support they needed to get final consideration of the bill. One might argue that Democrats did not step in to block final consideration of the bill because they felt that Republicans from protectionist states would be forced to support the party, and thus suffer some electoral distress. Certainly, this is part of the story. However, had they had the votes, it seems likely that Democrats would have preferred to kill the legislation and deny the Bush administration a win. Because they did not, they instead almost unanimously opposed the bill on final passage, forcing Republicans to hold ranks and setting themselves up to avoid any blame the might have followed from the passage of CAFTA.

Cloture Motions and Scheduling

Another indication that the majority often overcomes the possibility of a filibuster can be found in patterns of cloture and scheduling. In the next chapter, we study bill-scheduling patterns in detail for the 101st through 105th Congresses. In collecting data for that chapter, we coded which bills – from the set of all Senate bills that were either reported from committee or never referred to committee – ultimately reached the Senate floor. For each bill we also coded whether a cloture motion was filed before the bill was scheduled.[12]

If we take the filing of a cloture motion as an indication that it was plausible there would be a filibuster fight on a bill, these data enable us to examine how often such potential fights are followed by a bill being scheduled and how often they lead to a bill not being scheduled. In the cases of 41 bills, cloture was filed prior to any floor action. Of these, 34

---

[11] "H.R. 3045 Dominican Republic–Central America–United States Free Trade Agreement Implementation Act (Engrossed as Agreed to or Passed by House)," 2006, http://thomas.loc.gov/.

[12] We have not coded whether cloture motions were filed after each bill reached the floor.

eventually reached the floor. We can break the results down further by looking at what came of the cloture motion. On 15 bills there was no actual cloture vote (at least not before the bill reached the floor); of these, 14 reached the floor. On 19 bills there was a successful cloture vote; all 19 bills reached the floor. On 6 bills there was an unsuccessful cloture vote; none of these bills reached the floor. And, finally, on 1 bill there were both successful and unsuccessful cloture votes; the bill reached the floor.

The first point we want to make here is that, consistent with our categorization, there are instances in which there is uncertainty about whether a cloture fight will occur. The second point is that, in many such situations, we observe neither a filibuster nor a cloture vote, and the bill is scheduled. Finally, in 20 of the 26 cases in which there were cloture votes, the bill in question reached the floor.

Summary

The conventional view portrays the filibuster as the great equalizer of the Senate; individuals and minority coalitions are able to block extreme legislation, preventing majority party bias in policy outcomes. We argue for a more nuanced view of filibustering that includes two key points. First, the majority party leadership is better equipped to pay the costs of overcoming a filibuster than any other individual or coalition in the chamber. In this sense, the filibuster represents yet another instance where majority party consideration costs are lower than their opponents'. And, second, the majority party sometimes overcomes filibusters, even when the opposition is highly organized, partisan, and motivated.

We also offer a typology of potential filibuster fight cases, some of which are often ignored or overlooked in the literature. Our examples illustrate how each type sometimes plays out and support our contention that majority party agenda-setting efforts are not necessarily doomed by the filibuster.

7

The Disposition of Majority and Minority Amendments

The two preceding chapters show a majority party advantage in getting its bills through committee and onto the floor, consistent with our claim that the majority faces lower consideration costs. Of course, this advantage might mean little if, as is commonly suggested, floor amendments serve as powerful weapons that majority party opponents can use to gut majority proposals and to bring majority-opposed policies directly to the floor – thereby undermining majority party agenda-setting efforts. In this chapter and the two that follow, we argue that the amendment process constitutes a far more limited weapon than is often believed to be the case. We highlight the difference between offering an amendment and having the chamber cast an up-or-down vote on the adoption of an amendment, emphasizing that, although it is easy to offer an amendment, it is much more difficult to get an adoption vote on an amendment – especially if the majority party strongly opposes the proposal. Our findings in these chapters indicate that the amendment process is a less potent weapon than is sometimes supposed for exactly this reason: once offered, minority floor amendments still face substantial consideration costs. This allows the majority party to retain substantial influence over the chamber's agenda.

In this chapter, we use an original dataset with an observation for each amendment offered in the 101st through 106th Congresses (1989–2000) to examine the disposition of amendments – that is, what happens to amendments after their sponsors offer them on the floor.

In our first cut at this question, we study the probability of adoption for majority- and minority-sponsored amendments and find that, for both Democrats and Republicans, party members' amendments are less likely to be adopted when the party is in the minority than when it is in the majority. We then take a more fine grained look at the data, looking not just at adoption, but also at what happens to amendments that are offered but not adopted. We find that each party's amendments are more likely to be killed by procedural means (before coming to a straight up-or-down floor vote on adoption) when the party is in the minority than when it is in the majority; stated differently, minority amendments face higher consideration costs than majority amendments.

This chapter also fills a significant empirical gap in the literature on Senate procedure. Despite broad agreement that floor amendment fights are crucial to Senate decision making, previous work brings surprisingly few data to bear on this topic. As far as we are aware, ours is the most comprehensive empirical study to date of the introduction and disposition of amendments.[1]

Amendments and Agenda Setting

As noted, our take on the conventional view of the Senate is that there is relatively broad agreement that the majority party has an advantage at the committee stage but that whatever remains of this agenda-setting advantage among the set of bills that reach the floor is subject to attack via amendment.[2] Since, in the absence of a unanimous consent agreement to the contrary, there are rarely restrictions on either the ability of any senator to offer an amendment or the content of amendments, the majority's opponents can circumvent majority attempts to block proposals; moreover, amendments can be used to water down the majority's bills or to add elements that the majority finds objectionable (Oppenheimer and Hetherington 2008; Sinclair 2005, 2007; Wawro and Schickler 2006).

---

[1] The most extensive quantitative study of amendments is Smith's (1989) study of floor activity. Using data from a number of congresses roughly equal to the number we use (but from an earlier time frame), Smith examines a variety of amendment-related data, such as restrictions imposed by unanimous consent agreements, tabling of amendments, and the distribution of amendments across committees. In terms of amendment disposition, he examines adoption of the amendments. Our analysis of amendment disposition goes into greater detail by examining the probability of adoption while simultaneously examining the probabilities of an amendment being disposed of in another manner before adoption. We also use multivariate analysis to estimate the effects of partisanship on type of disposition.

[2] Sinclair (1989: 85), e.g., points out that "[minority] Republicans' greater frequency of amendment sponsorship from the 86th through the 96th Congresses and the [minority] Democrats' greater rate in the 97th through 99th is in part due to dissatisfaction with bills written by committees controlled by the opposition party."

This line of thinking places the amendment process at the heart of the matter of majority agenda influence in the Senate. But there is substantial reason to believe that it overstates amendments' effectiveness as antimajority weapons.

First, it at least mildly overstates the ease of offering amendments. Under some circumstances, such as following cloture or during consideration of a budget resolution, there are some restrictions on the content of amendments. Also, unanimous consent agreements often *do* restrict amendments. Smith (1989: 128) observed that "[unanimous consent agreements] are far less effective than [House] special rules in reducing the volume of amending activity"; but "less effective" does not imply that they are completely ineffective. To whatever extent the argument we made about unanimous consent agreements in Chapter 5 holds true – that is, that the majority leader gains a first-proposer advantage in negotiations over them – majority opponents' ability to offer amendments will decline at least marginally. Finally, the Senate's amendment trees create a finite number of opportunities for offering amendments during consideration of a bill. The majority leader sometimes uses the right of first recognition to "fill the tree" – that is, to monopolize amendment-offering opportunities and thereby prevent other senators from offering an amendment during consideration of the given bill (Campbell 2004). Majority leaders used this strategy sparingly until recent Congresses, but its use has increased sharply since 2005 (the 109th Congress) (Beth et al. 2009; King, Orlando, and Rohde 2010; Oleszek 2011).

For example, in 2007 majority leader Harry Reid "filled the tree" on the continuing appropriations bill for that year (H.J. Res. 20) with five amendments (CQ Weekly 2007). The first would have added a single line to the bill: "The division ... shall take effect 2 days after date of enactment." The second simply changed that to one day. The third, fourth, and fifth amendments all made motions to recommit the bill but specified different effective dates three, four, and five days after enactment, respectively. In other words, none of the amendments were real amendments; they were simply components of a strategy to fend off other unwanted amendments, raising consideration costs for majority party opponents.

Setting aside that concern, however, and assuming that a majority opponent can offer a proposal via amendment, there is a more significant oversight in the conventional thinking: it rests on the implicit assumption that, if a senator proposes an amendment, the chamber will vote on whether to adopt it, creating an opportunity to undermine majority agenda-setting efforts. But this assumption often does not hold; the Senate kills many floor amendments via procedural decisions without ever voting on whether to adopt the measure.[3] A great many proposed amendments never reach the point of an adoption vote.

An Illustration: Amendments to the Education Tax Credits Bill

The case with which we began the book, the Education Savings Act, illustrates some of the ways in which the majority can combat unwanted amendments. As noted in the opening paragraphs of the book, Republicans struggled to bring the bill to the floor and eventually agreed to a unanimous consent agreement allowing Democrats to propose several amendments (and also allowing Republican amendments).

When the Senate worked on the bill, Democrats offered 10 first-degree amendments. Of these, three were tabled (i.e., killed), with no more than 14 percent of Democrats supporting the tabling motion and at least 92 percent of Republicans supporting it in any of the three cases. Another amendment was ruled out of order when the Senate voted not to waive the Budget Act point of order for the amendment, with 93 percent of Democrats voting to waive and 92 percent of Republicans voting not to waive. The Senate held adoption votes on the remaining six amendments. At least 97 percent of Democrats supported adoption in all six cases. In three of the cases, however, fewer than 8 percent of Republicans supported adoption and the amendment was rejected. As for the other three cases, the Senate adopted two by voice vote and adopted the third with 54 percent of Republicans voting in favor. In short, the Senate voted on only six of 10 Democratic amendments – with the other four blocked by procedure – and did not adopt a single Democratic amendment opposed by more than half the Republicans.

On the other hand, Republicans offered eight first-degree amendments.[4] Of these, the Senate adopted seven – four on voice votes, one on a unanimous bipartisan roll call, and three despite the objections of at least two-thirds of Democrats. In the remaining case, 82 percent of Republicans voted for adoption, but only 2 percent of Democrats voted in favor, and

---

[3] The array of procedural decisions that kill amendments is vast (see Appendix B). In the next chapter we examine the two most common procedures: tabling motions and point-of-order votes.

[4] This number excludes the committee substitute offered by Roth when the bill first reached the floor. In addition, two of the eight were offered initially as second-degree amendments but were later considered first-degree amendments by unanimous consent.

the Senate rejected the amendment. In short, the Senate voted on all eight Republican amendments – with none blocked by procedure – and adopted three of the four amendments opposed by more than half the Democrats.

Hypotheses

It is not entirely clear what the conventional viewpoint predicts about the expected levels of success of majority or minority party amendments. Some elements of the literature might lead us to expect that the minority will outperform the majority in the amendment process; since the set of bills that reach the floor is biased toward the majority party's preferences, this thinking goes, amendments that move policy closer to the center are more likely to succeed than amendments that do not.

Though we think this is a fair characterization of some parts of the literature, others seem to suggest that the likelihood of adoption for minority amendments need only be similar to the likelihood of adoption for majority party amendments in order to seriously undermine the majority's agenda-setting efforts. This view implies more modest expectations about minority success.

Regardless of which characterization one finds more appropriate, however, it is hard to read the literature as predicting that majority amendments will fare better than minority amendments on the floor. Yet our argument that the majority enjoys various amendment-killing procedural advantages makes exactly such a prediction. We therefore test the following hypotheses:

> **Hypothesis 7.1.** The probability of an amendment being adopted is higher for an amendment sponsored by a majority party senator than for an amendment sponsored by a minority party senator, ceteris paribus.
>
> **Hypothesis 7.2.** The probability of an amendment being killed by a procedural tactic is higher for an amendment sponsored by a minority party senator than for an amendment sponsored by a majority party senator, ceteris paribus.

We note two points about these hypotheses. First, the null hypothesis for each – that majority amendments are no more likely to be adopted and minority amendments are no more likely to be killed by procedures – is the prediction of the conventional view, however one construes it. By setting up our research design in this way, we create a tough standard for rejection of the conventional wisdom and place the burden of proof squarely on our predictions, since a finding of no advantage for the majority party will be taken as support for the conventional wisdom.

Second, Hypothesis 7.2 in particular represents a crucial point of divergence between our thinking and conventional thinking. In our view, the majority's ability to kill amendments via procedures is a fundamentally significant component of majority agenda influence. The conventional view, however, emphasizes the wide distribution of procedural power across all individual senators, with little suggestion of a majority advantage in the use of such procedural power.

Amendment Data, 101st through 106th Congresses

We test these hypotheses using a dataset with an observation for each of the 22,972 Senate amendments submitted from the 101st through 106th Congresses; we collected these data from Congress's Web site, Thomas.[5] In the remainder of this section we describe our data in more detail.

The observation for each amendment includes the amendment sponsor's name, party, and first-dimension DW-Nominate score; the number of the underlying measure that the amendment proposes to alter; the number of amendment cosponsors; and the last action taken by the Senate on the amendment. For the 2,239 amendments on which the last action entailed a recorded vote, we also have party and chamber yes/no vote totals for that vote.[6]

A key variable in this dataset is the last action taken on the amendment. There is great variation not only in the actions taken, but also in the way Thomas reports a given action; we have thus done a substantial amount of data cleaning and recoding to produce a usable "last-action" variable. We discuss this in more detail in Appendix B; here, we focus on the categorical variable, *Disposition*, that we produced to encapsulate this last-action data.

[5] We collected the data from Thomas's "Search Bill Summary & Status for the [XXX] Congress" pages (http://thomas.loc.gov/bss/XXXsearch.html), where XXX is the Congress number. The "Senate Amendments" link at the bottom of this page leads to a list of all Senate amendments submitted in that Congress, along with data about each. Our research assistant, Feilong Chen, wrote a program to collect these data and produce from them a text file for each Congress included. This is the basis of our dataset.

[6] We thank Keith Poole and Howard Rosenthal for sharing their DW-Nominate and roll call vote data, available at voteview.com.

For *Disposition*, we grouped all last actions listed on Thomas into seven categories, then coded the last action for each amendment as falling into one of these categories. The categories are as follows:

"Modified," indicating the Senate modified the amendment (usually by unanimous consent) after having previously adopted it;

"Adopted," indicating the Senate adopted the amendment by voice or recorded vote;

"Rejected," indicating the Senate rejected the amendment by voice or recorded vote;

"Killed by Procedure," indicating the Senate's final action on the amendment was a procedural decision (and the amendment was not adopted);

"Considered," indicating the Senate's last action was consideration of the amendment;

"Submitted/Withdrawn," indicating the amendment either was submitted but never brought up on the floor or was withdrawn;

"Indeterminate," indicating it is unclear how to classify the final action.[7]

Frequencies for each of these categories, as well as a first take on the question of whether majority and minority amendments face different fates in the Senate, are shown in Table 7.1a. First, 50.9 percent of the 22,972 amendments were submitted by majority senators, while 49.1 percent were submitted by minority senators. Also, nearly half (48.2 percent) were never called up on the floor. Adoption was the last action for 42.1 percent (another 0.2 percent were amended after adoption); far fewer fell into each of the Rejected (2.6 percent), Killed by Procedure (6.3 percent), Considered (0.5 percent), and Indeterminate (0.001 percent) categories.

For the purpose of studying how disposition varies by sponsor party, it seems best to omit amendments in the Submitted/Withdrawn and Indeterminate categories, since in the former case it is not clear that they should be treated as serious proposals, and in the latter case it is not clear what can be gleaned from the observations. A note on the amendment submission process may clarify this decision. In order for an amendment to be "offered" – verbally put forth on the floor during work on a bill – it must first be put in writing. Accordingly, senators often "submit" amendments in writing to be printed in the *Congressional Record* a day or more before

---

[7] For the 22 "Indeterminate" observations in our dataset, we code *Disposition* as missing data.

TABLE 7.1a. *Disposition of Amendments by Party of Sponsor, 101st through 106th Congresses*

Disposition	Minority Sponsor	Majority Sponsor	Total
Modified	26	29	55
	(0.2)	(0.2)	(0.2)
Adopted	3,952	5,719	9,671
	(35.1)	(48.9)	(42.1)
Rejected	387	201	588
	(3.4)	(1.7)	(2.6)
Killed by Procedure	956	496	1,452
	(8.5)	(4.2)	(6.3)
Considered	29	76	105
	(0.3)	(0.6)	(0.5)
Submitted/withdrawn	5,909	5,170	11,079
	(52.4)	(44.2)	(48.2)
Indeterminate	9	13	22
	(0.08)	(0.1)	(0.001)
Total	11,268	11,704	22,972

Note: Column percentages shown in parentheses.

they plan to offer the amendment on the floor. At that point, the amendment receives a sequential number and is permanently recorded as having been submitted, even if it is later withdrawn or simply never offered on the floor. Amendments in the dataset categorized as submitted or withdrawn were never actually offered on the floor. We thus emphasize that, as both a theoretical point and a data consideration, submitting a Senate amendment is not the same thing as offering a Senate amendment.[8]

In Table 7.1b we recalculate the percentage of each party's amendments in each category as a percentage of all amendments, excluding Submitted/Withdrawn and Indeterminate amendments. Tabulated in this manner, the data show that majority senators offered 54.9 percent of the amendments, while minority senators offered 45.1 percent.

The data in Table 7.1b are consistent with our prediction that majority party senators do better at passing amendments, and are inconsistent with the null prediction that minority party amendments do no worse than majority party amendments. A larger proportion of majority amendments are adopted than minority amendments (87.7 percent to

[8] This discussion of submission procedure is based on Palmer and Bach (2003: 3). For excellent discussions of the Senate amendment process, see Oleszek (2001b) and Palmer and Bach (2003).

TABLE 7.1b. *Disposition of Amendments Called Up on Floor, by Party of Sponsor*

Disposition	Minority Sponsor	Majority Sponsor	Total
Modified	26	29	55
	(0.5)	(0.4)	(0.5)
Adopted	3,952	5,719	9,671
	(73.9)	(87.7)	(81.5)
Rejected	387	201	588
	(7.2)	(3.1)	(5.0)
Killed by Procedure	956	496	1,452
	(17.9)	(7.6)	(12.2)
Considered	29	76	105
	(0.5)	(1.2)	(0.9)
Total	5,350	6,521	11,871

Note: Column percentages shown in parentheses.

73.9 percent), a smaller proportion of majority amendments are rejected (3.1 percent to 7.2 percent), and a smaller proportion of majority amendments are killed by procedural means (7.6 percent to 17.9 percent).

Amendment Sponsorship and Adoption

To test Hypothesis 7.1, we again use the "switching replications" research design of previous chapters, treating senators of each party as a group and estimating how the adoption of group members' amendments changes when the party is and is not the majority party.[9] Using probit, we estimate the following:

$$Adopt_{it} = \alpha + \beta_1 DemSponsor_i + \beta_2 Majority_i$$
$$+ \beta_3 DemSponsor_i * Majority_i + \beta_4 MajoritySize_t$$
$$+ \beta_5 DW\text{-}Nom_i + \beta_6 Consponsors_i + \varepsilon_{it}$$

The dependent variable, $Adopt_{it}$, is a dummy variable coded 1 if amendment i from Congress t was adopted, and 0 otherwise.[10] The three key variables for testing Hypothesis 7.1 are $DemSponsor_i$, a dummy

[9] Democrats were the majority in the first three Congresses in our sample (101st through 103st); Republicans were the majority in the latter three Congresses (104th through 106th).

[10] For this analysis, we collapse the Adopted and Modified categories into a single category and exclude amendments from the Submitted/Withdrawn and Indeterminate categories.

variable coded 1 if amendment i's sponsor is a Democrat, and 0 otherwise; $Majority_i$, a dummy variable coded 1 if the sponsor is a member of the majority party; and $DemSponsor_i * Majority_i$, the interaction of these two dummy variables.

The coefficient for $Majority_i$ captures the change in the probability of adoption for Republican-sponsored amendments as Republicans go from minority to majority status. Hypothesis 7.1 predicts that this coefficient will be positive; that is, Republicans' becoming the minority will not make Republican amendments more likely to be adopted. The other key test of Hypothesis 7.1 stems from the sum of the coefficients for $Majority_i$ and $DemSponsor_i * Majority_i$. The hypothesis predicts that this sum, which captures the change in the probability of adoption for Democrat-sponsored amendments as Democrats go from minority to majority status, will be positive.

Control variables included in the model are as follows:

$MajoritySize_t$, the number of seats held by the Senate majority in Congress t;

$DW\text{-}Nom_i$, the first-dimension DW-Nominate score of amendment i's sponsor;[11]

$Consponsors_i$, the number of cosponsors for amendment i.

Table 7.2a shows the probit results. Consistent with Hypothesis 7.1 – and contrary to the null hypothesis – the coefficient for $Majority_i$ is positive and significant, indicating that Republican-sponsored amendments are more likely to be adopted when Republicans are the majority party than when they are the minority party. Similarly, the sum of the coefficients for $Majority_i$ and $DemSponsor_i * Majority_i$ is positive and significant, indicating that Democrat-sponsored amendments are more likely to be adopted when the Democrats are the majority than when they are the minority. This allows us to reject the null hypothesis that majority amendments are no more likely than minority amendments to be adopted.

Table 7.2b shows the substantive meaning of these results. Each cell gives the estimated probability that a bill will be adopted, by party and majority status.[12] Again, for each party we see the probability of adoption

---

[11] Seven observations for which this variable is missing data drop out of our analysis. These are observations for amendments introduced by Daniel Akaka in the 101st Congress; Akaka replaced Spark Matsunaga late in the 101st Congress and does not receive a DW-Nominate score for that Congress.

[12] We estimated probabilities and confidence intervals with CLARIFY (King, Tomz, and Wittenberg 2000; Tomz, Wittenberg, and King 2001).

TABLE 7.2a. *Effect of Majority Status on Probability of Amendment Being Adopted for All Amendments Called Up on Floor, 101st through 106th Congresses*

Variable	Coefficient	Standard Error	p Value
DemSponsor	−0.301	0.065	.001
Majority (H 7.1: positive)	0.541	0.028	.001
*DemSponsor * Majority*	0.041	0.037	.263
MajoritySize	0.046	0.011	.001
DW-Nominate	−0.322	0.077	.001
Cosponsors	−0.026	0.003	.001
Constant	−1.672	0.617	.007
Majority$_i$ + *DemSponsor * Majority* (H 7.1: positive)	0.582	0.046	.001

Note: N = 11,869; pseudo-R^2 = .0451; log-likelihood = −5354.7597.

TABLE 7.2b. *Probability of Amendment Being Adopted, by Party and Majority Status*

Sponsor Is:	Sponsor's Party Is:	
	Majority	Minority
Republican	.907	.783
	(0.007)	(0.012)
Democrat	.856	.684
	(0.010)	(0.015)

Note: Cells contain estimated probability of amendment being adopted. Standard errors shown in parentheses, estimated via CLARIFY (with other variables set at means).

increase when the party is the majority party (for Republicans, the increase is from .783 to .907; for Democrats, it is from .684 to .856).

The foregoing analysis could, however, provide a biased picture of amendment activity. Given that many amendments are uncontroversial, excite little interest or opposition, and are adopted by voice votes, it may overstate the likelihood of amendment adoption for senators of one or both parties. We therefore repeat the analysis using only the subset of amendments that received recorded votes on the last action taken, which we see as a reasonable, albeit crude, filter for choosing more controversial amendments. Table 7.3a shows the results of the probit when repeated on this restricted sample; they yield the same conclusions as before regarding Hypothesis 7.1. Table 7.3b shows that, in this sample, the probability of adoption is lower across the board. The most striking difference from the

TABLE 7.3a. *Effect of Majority Status on Probability of Amendment Being Adopted for "Controversial" Amendments Only, 101st through 106th Congresses*

Variable	Coefficient	Standard Error	p Value
DemSponsor	−0.374	0.135	.006
Majority (H 7.1: positive)	0.796	0.058	.001
*DemSponsor * Majority*	−0.049	0.082	.546
MajoritySize	0.016	0.023	.504
DW-Nom	−0.088	0.151	.560
Cosponsors	0.051	0.006	.001
Constant	−1.572	1.258	.211
*Majority + DemSponsor * Majority* (H 7.1: positive)	0.747	0.103	.001

Note: N = 2,235; pseudo-R^2 = .1099; Log-likelihood = −1286.7261.

TABLE 7.3b. *Probability of Amendment Being Adopted, by Party and Majority Status*

Sponsor Is:	Sponsor's Party Is:	
	Majority	Minority
Republican	.601	.296
	(0.034)	(0.029)
Democrat	.434	.181
	(0.035)	(0.024)

Note: Cells contain estimated probability of amendment being adopted. Standard errors shown in parentheses, estimated via CLARIFY with other variables set at means.

unrestricted analysis is a larger increase in the probability for each party as it goes from minority to majority status. For Republicans, the increase is from .296 to .601; for Democrats, it is from .181 to .434.[13]

A More Nuanced Look at Amendment Disposition

In this section, we test Hypothesis 7.2 and in the process take a more nuanced look at what happens to amendments. We do so using a method

---

[13] Our dataset contains both first- and second-degree amendments. In order to account for the possibility that this introduces a bias into our sample, we have rerun each of the foregoing analyses with second-degree amendments excluded (this reduced N to 10,391 and 1,707, respectively). In each analysis, this made little difference in the results and did not affect any of our inferences regarding the hypotheses.

that is the same as the prior analysis, with the exceptions that we substitute the categorical variable *Disposition* for *Adoption* as the dependent variable, and we use ordered rather than regular probit.[14] In other words, we estimate the following:

$$Disposition_{it} = \alpha + \beta_1 DemSponsor_i + \beta_2 Majority_i$$
$$+ \beta_3 DemSponsor_i * Majority_i + \beta_4 MajoritySize_t$$
$$+ \beta_5 DW\text{-}Nom_i + \beta_6 Consponsors_i + \varepsilon_{it}$$

The categories for *Disposition* are "Considered," "Killed by Procedure," "Rejected," and "Adopted."[15] Ordered probit enables us to estimate the probabilities of an amendment falling into each of these categories and to again examine how these probabilities change when a party is in the majority rather than in the minority.

Tables 7.4a and 7.4b show the results. Our main interest here is how the estimated probability of each type of disposition – particularly the probability of being killed by procedure – changes when the sponsor's party goes from minority to majority status. Hypothesis 7.2 predicts positive change; conventional wisdom predicts no change. As before, the results support our prediction (Table 7.4a). For each party, the probability of party members' amendments being killed by procedure drops when it is the majority party; for Republicans, it decreases from .438 to .202; for Democrats, it decreases from .519 to .309 (Table 7.4b).[16] Also,

---

[14] An assumption implied by this methodology is that there is an underlying order to the categories of *Disposition*; that is, "Considered," "Killed by Procedure," "Rejected," and "Adopted" represent an ordered sequence of categories. We believe this is a safe assumption because the categories represent a sequence of events that can occur for an amendment: it must be considered before anything else can happen, it must clear any procedural hurdles before it can come to final vote, it goes no farther than the final vote if it is rejected, and it continues beyond the final vote if it is adopted. See the discussion later in this section for alternative approaches that do not rely on this assumption of ordinality.

[15] We exclude the 55 amendments in the "Modified" category from this analysis. We do so because we think this category does not indicate in any meaningful sense that an amendment went farther through the legislative process than the previous category ("Adopted"), and so it is inappropriate as an additional ordinal category for our dependent variable. In addition, as discussed in Appendix B, lumping these observations into the "Adopted" category could introduce problems for analyses that examine adoption votes, such as the one in this section. In the analysis shown here, we again include only amendments that were subject to recorded votes on final disposition. Dropping this filter and using the entire amendment sample does not affect the inferences we draw regarding the hypotheses and serves mainly to decrease the estimated probability of adoption, all else constant. Similarly, restricting the analysis to first-degree amendments does not affect our inferences.

[16] An interesting aside to these results is that the probability of an amendment making it to an adoption vote and then being rejected does not change significantly for Democrats

TABLE 7.4a. *Effect of Majority Status on Amendment Disposition (Ordered Probit), 101st through 106th Congresses*

Variable	Coefficient	Standard Error	p Value
DemSponsor	−0.201	0.118	.088
Majority (H 7.2: positive)	0.682	0.051	.001
*DemSponsor * Majority*	−0.127	0.071	.072
MajoritySize	0.030	0.020	.129
DW-Nom	0.082	0.130	.527
Cosponsors	0.045	0.005	.001
Cutpoint 1	−1.185	1.082	
Cutpoint 2	1.663	1.073	
Cutpoint 3	2.338	1.073	
*Majority + DemSponsor * Majority* (H 7.2: positive)	0.555	0.088	0.001

Note: N = 2,235; pseudo-R^2=.063; log-likelihood = −2276.1105.

TABLE 7.4b. *Probability of Each Type of Disposition, by Sponsor Party and Status*

Sponsor's Party	Party Status	Disposition			
		Considered	Killed by Procedure	Rejected	Adopted
Republican	Majority	.001 (0.001)	.202 (0.023)	.234 (0.012)	.564 (0.032)
	Minority	.002 (0.001)	.438 (0.029)	.260 (0.001)	.300 (0.027)
Democrat	Majority	.001 (0.001)	.309 (0.027)	.261 (0.010)	.430 (0.030)
	Minority	.003 (0.002)	.519 (0.029)	.245 (0.011)	.233 (0.023)

Note: Cells contain probabilities of amendment disposition falling into each category. Standard errors shown in parentheses, estimated via CLARIFY with other variables set at means.

as before, the probability of adoption is higher for each party when it is in the majority.[17]

when they become the majority party and actually drops a slight but significant amount for Republicans.

[17] To check whether our model violates the parallel regression/proportional odds assumption implied by the use of ordered probit, we estimated the same model using generalized ordered logit, which does not rely on the parallel regression assumption. The results were substantively the same. In addition, a Wald test (in which a significant test statistic would indicate violation of the assumption) did not indicate that the model violates the assumption.

To guard against objections to our assumption that the *Disposition* categories are ordinal, we approached the test using three alternative methods, using the same key independent variables. We summarize the results here. First, we estimated the same model using multinomial logit rather than ordered probit. The predicted probabilities were as hypothesized, though the differences between majority and minority status were significant only for Democrats' amendments; that is, for Republicans' amendments, the estimated differences in the probabilities of an amendment being killed and for an amendment being adopted as the party switched from minority to majority status followed our predicted pattern, but were not significant. Second, we broke the analysis into a probit estimating the probability of an amendment being killed by procedure and a separate probit only on bills that received adoption votes. In this case, all coefficients and significance levels were as predicted. (Notice that, unlike the ordered probit results in Table 7.4, this indicates that even minority amendments that make it to an adoption vote are less likely to be adopted than majority amendments that make it to an adoption vote.) Finally, we ran a Sartori Selection model (Sartori 2003); by using this approach, similar to a Heckman model, we treat the decision whether to kill an amendment procedurally as a selection choice and the decision whether to adopt remaining amendments as an outcome choice. This method also yields results predicted by our hypotheses.

A Closer Look at Amendments That Pass

Notwithstanding the extent to which each party's amendments are more likely to be adopted when the party is the majority party, the estimated probability of minority success in gaining adoption of (controversial) amendments is roughly 20 to 25 percent – leading us to wonder about the nature of these adopted amendments, whether they differ from adopted amendments introduced by majority party members, and, most of all, whether adopted amendments from the minority party tend to generate more or less partisan division than do those from the majority party. Given that we think the majority is good at filtering out amendments it dislikes, we suspect that adopted minority amendments will be less likely than adopted majority amendments to generate controversy. We thus take a brief look at adopted amendments from each party.

Table 7.5 presents three types of data bearing on these questions: the percentage of amendments adopted by recorded vote, which we take as a rough indication of greater partisanship; the percentage of amendments

TABLE 7.5. *Differences Between Adopted Majority and Minority Amendments, 101st through 106th Congresses*

	Majority Amendments	Minority Amendments	All Amendments
Number of adopted amendments	5,719	3,952	9,671
Percent adopted by recorded vote	8.2 (473/5,719)	7.8 (307/3,952)	8.1 (780/9,671)
Number adopted by recorded vote	473	307	780
Percent rolled the majority	5.1 (24/473)	19.9 (61/307)	10.9 (85/780)
Percent rolled the minority	33.8 (160/473)	3.6 (11/307)	21.9 (171/780)

adopted by recorded vote that rolled each party, which we take as a more direct indicator of partisan conflict; and the distribution of adoption votes that passed narrowly. The upper section of the table shows the number of adopted amendments introduced by members of each party and the percentage of those amendments adopted by recorded vote. There appears to be little difference between majority and minority amendments; the Senate adopted 8.2 percent of majority amendments on recorded votes and 7.8 percent of minority amendments on recorded votes.

The second indicator, however, shows a different pattern. The lower part of Table 7.5 shows that, although each party was rarely rolled on amendments offered by its own members (5.1 and 3.6 percent, respectively, for the majority and minority), there was a disparity in the propensity of amendments to roll the other party. About 34 percent of majority amendments rolled the minority, whereas about 20 percent of minority amendments rolled the majority, which is consistent with our other findings indicating a majority advantage (and minority disadvantage) in moving amendments through the floor process.

Finally, we look at the percentage of senators voting yes on the adoption vote for each amendment that was adopted by recorded vote. We surmise that more partisan legislation will generate narrower vote margins, whereas less partisan legislation will generate larger vote margins. Figure 7.1 shows separate histograms indicating the distribution of vote margins on adoption votes for each party's amendments. For each party, the distribution patterns of votes with margins between 60 and 90 percent are broadly similar; also, for each party, around 50 percent of

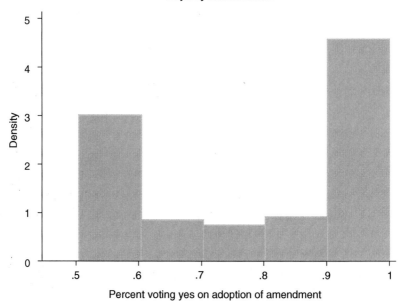

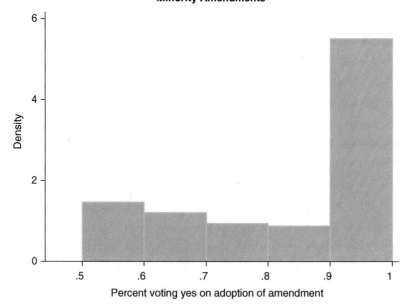

FIGURE 7.1. Histograms of Percentage of Senators Voting Yes on Roll Call Votes on Which Amendments Were Adopted, by (a) Majority Status of Amendment Sponsor and (b) Minority Status of Amendment Sponsor.

amendments are adopted by margins upwards of 90 percent. The striking difference between the two charts is the proportion of votes in the 50 to 60 percent vote margin category; about 30 percent of adopted majority amendments are adopted by margins in this range, whereas only about 15 percent of minority amendments fall into this range.

In sum, the evidence suggests that the minority party does not achieve dramatic policy gains via the 20 to 25 percent of controversial amendments it sponsors that are adopted. Indeed, it appears that, of adopted amendments, far more majority-sponsored than minority-sponsored amendments engender partisan controversy.

Summary

The typical characterization of Senate policy making emphasizes the chamber's open amendment process, which is thought to allow a minority faction to undermine the will of an ill-equipped majority party. This view rests on the implicit assumption that, if an amendment is introduced, it will receive an adoption vote. In other words, it implies that there are low or no consideration costs associated with Senate amendments, for either the majority or its opponents, and thus any majority advantage that existed prior to the floor stage will be negated because of opposition amendments.

Yet many things can prevent an amendment from reaching an adoption vote, and despite the centrality of the conventional assumption, there is little previous quantitative work on the likelihood of an amendment receiving such a vote, let alone on how that likelihood interacts with partisanship. We offer a more comprehensive look at disposition and partisanship and find that there is an important distinction between offering an amendment and getting a preference-based vote on an amendment; that is, there *are* consideration costs associated with Senate amendments.

This distinction highlights the importance of decisions made between these two stages of the process. Using data from recent Congresses, we show that minority-proposed amendments are more likely to be killed by procedural tactics than are majority-proposed amendments and also that minority-proposed amendments are less likely to be adopted by the chamber. These findings suggest that the majority has stronger defenses against minority attacks by amendment than is widely recognized.

8

Killing Amendments with Tabling Motions and Points of Order

> My proposed amendment ought to get 100 votes in the U.S. Senate, but it will not. People will walk up to the door and up to the manager and say, "What is our vote on this?" Well, they will not have to ask, they know what their vote is. They know there has been a motion to table every single amendment. What kind of democracy is that?
>
> Senator Dale Bumpers, *Congressional Record*, February 24, 1995

> Look at what we have been doing this morning. What a joke. We had a vote on a noncontroversial committee amendment saying that a specified amount of money may be used for environment or agriculture in Nicaragua. I think it was a unanimous vote. Then we had a vote on whether or not to sustain the ruling of the Chair. I realize that this body just systemically disregards the ruling of the Chair. If we want to, we go to the substance and do not pay any attention to whether it is germane or not.
>
> Senator Trent Lott, *Congressional Record*, April 27, 1990

These quotes underscore two procedures used frequently to kill amendments on the floor: tabling motions and points of order. Bumpers, a Democrat, made his statement during the early days of the 104th Congress, as the Senate worked on one of the major components of the new Republican majority's Contract with America, a balanced-budget proposal. A long series of Democratic amendments to the measure triggered a long series of successful motions to table (kill) Democratic amendments.[1] Lott's statement suggests that the Senate decides points

---

[1] Technically, Bumpers offered a motion to recommit the balanced-budget measure with instructions, which is functionally similar to an amendment. The Senate tabled his recommital motion a few days later, as he predicted, with all Republicans voting to table and most Democrats voting against tabling.

of order against amendments; that is, it determines whether a proposed amendment runs afoul of chamber rules and procedures, in which case it is disallowed – in a partisan fashion.

In this chapter, we examine more closely how the Senate uses these procedures to kill amendments. We begin by considering generally why procedural motions are more effective amendment-killing instruments than up-or-down votes; then using data from the 101st through 106th Congresses, we find that the Senate is more likely to kill minority-sponsored amendments than to kill majority-sponsored amendments when it votes on tabling motions and points of order.[2] In our model's terms, the findings reinforce our point from the preceding chapter: that majority consideration costs are smaller than minority consideration costs, even at the amendment stage – in other words, amendments face hazards once they reach the floor, and the hazards are greater for minority amendments.

The Appeal of Procedural Motions

Mr. President, the Helms amendment, which apparently will be tabled, is pretty much in a fix that a rustler would get into if he was hung and thereafter given a fair trial.

Senator Jesse Helms, *Congressional Record*, October 5, 1989

One reason the Senate's open amendment process is conventionally seen as a powerful weapon against majority agenda influence is that it creates opportunities for majority opponents to offer amendments that split the majority party and gain support from enough majority senators for the chamber to adopt the amendment. From this point of view, majority senators can be peeled off because they are put in a position in which they are torn between doing what their constituents want and what the party wants, and they sometimes side with their constituents in such cases.

---

[2] We do not examine every type of amendment-killing procedural decision that occurs in our data from the preceding chapter (listed in Appendix B), for several reasons. First, most amendments killed by procedure die by tabling motion or point of order, so we focus on what we see as the two main threats to amendments. Second, some of the procedures do not lead to roll call votes, and we thus cannot analyze them in the same way we analyze tabling motions and points of order. Third, in a small number of cases, we are uncertain of the underlying procedural process and do not want to miscode those cases. Also, we exclude cloture votes on amendments, because no votes do not necessarily kill the amendment and because such votes might be targeted at the underlying measure rather than at the amendment itself.

Procedural decisions to kill amendments often entail a chamber vote on a procedural motion. The result of such votes is usually the same as the result of an up-or-down vote on the adoption of an amendment – the chamber either kills the amendment or accepts it (in practice, Senate rejection of a procedural motion to kill an amendment is usually tantamount to adoption of the amendment) – raising the question, why would procedural votes be any more effective than up-or-down votes in killing amendments?

The answer to this question provided by many House studies also applies to the Senate: it is generally easier for majority leaders to hold together the caucus – or at least to hold together enough of it to win – on procedural votes than on substantive votes. Scholars have long noted that party cohesion is very high on procedural votes in the House and attribute this cohesion to weaker constituent scrutiny on procedural votes than on substantive votes. Members' votes are functions of various factors, prominently including demands from constituents and party leaders; procedural votes and their consequences are often less observable and easier to explain to constituents than are adoption votes; the impact of party demands relative to the impact of constituent demands is thus greater on procedural votes than on adoption votes; so procedural motions are more likely than up-or-down votes to kill amendments that split the party. In other words, procedural votes facilitate cooperation among the majority by reducing the electoral risks faced by caucus members torn between the party and their constituents (Arnold 1990; Jones 1968; Rohde 1991; Van Houweling 2003).

Though less common, similar claims exist regarding the Senate. Oleszek (2004: 236), for example, makes this point regarding procedural votes in general: "If a procedural vote can be arranged to kill or delay a controversial bill, it is likely to win the support of senators who may prefer to duck the substantive issue. Moreover, senators generally support the party leadership on procedural votes. As one senator has pointed out, on a procedural vote, members 'traditionally stick with the leadership.'"

Various scholars describe tabling-motion votes as votes on which many senators feel at least some level of compulsion to side with their party, because a vote on a tabling motion is not as visible to the public and not as easy to interpret as a direct vote on an amendment (Gold 2004; Marshall, Prins, and Rohde 1999; Oleszek 2004; Tiefer 1989; on tabling motions, see also Goodman 2006) – a point emphasized by the following quote: "A motion to table is a procedural motion. It obfuscates the issue, and it makes possible an explanation by a Senator to his constituents ... that his vote was not on the merits of the issue. He can claim that he might have voted this way or might have voted that way, if the Senate had voted up or down on the issue itself. But on a procedural motion, he can state he voted to table the amendment, and he can assign any number of reasons therefore, one of which would be that he did so in order that the Senate would get on with its work or about its business" (Senator Robert Byrd, *Congressional Record*, September 23, 1975; cited in Oleszek 2004: 236).[3]

In addition, ample anecdotal (Bradbury et al. 2008; Davidson 2001; Oleszek 2004; Pearson 2008) and quantitative (King, Orlando, and Rohde 2010) evidence also indicates that senators' procedural votes are more likely than votes on adoption to be influenced by partisan considerations.

Of course, constituents' ability to observe and understand procedural votes is not constant across the spectrum of procedures. For instance, a vote to table an amendment might well be more transparent to constituents than a vote on a motion to table a motion to appeal a decision of the chair (each of which is an example of ways that amendments are sometimes killed). As procedural transparency increases, the relative impact of constituent demands should also increase, making it more likely that some majority senators will not support the party on the procedural vote and less likely that the majority will win.

Clearly, this type of scenario sometimes occurs and minority amendments sometimes succeed in splitting the majority. This seems to us to be a major difference between the House and the Senate: in the Senate, procedural strategies develop in a more ad hoc fashion (as opposed to revolving around the Rules Committee in the House), and the majority party procedural coalition is less reliable.

This, however, does not imply that the majority usually fails on procedural votes. The majority does not necessarily need every caucus member's vote to win; most majorities are large enough to suffer defections and still have a majority. Also, transparency can cut both ways; that is, it can also induce minority senators to vote with the majority. So long as majority senators are no more likely than minority senators to defect

[3] In an interview with the authors (September 6, 2010), Lee Rawls – former chief of staff for Senate majority leader Bill Frist – described a very similar logic behind motions to table: "It's a majority tool. The minority's not tabling anything.... If [the senator has] to go on record about this [he] prefer[s] tabling rather than up or down, because tabling is confusing ... somebody says you voted against, you say I didn't vote against it, that was just the technical tabling motion."

from the party's strategy, the majority's numerical superiority makes it likely the majority will prevail.

Though we do not undertake a systematic analysis here, a brief look at roll call data reveals evidence consistent with claims that senators do not always cast tabling-motion votes strictly on the basis of their policy preferences regarding the amendment in question.[4] We examine all 20 cases from the 101st through 109th Congresses in which a tabling motion failed and was followed by a roll call vote on the amendment in question. For each such vote pair, if tabling-motion votes are nothing more than votes based on policy preferences over the amendment, senators should always vote either against the motion to table and for the amendment, or for the motion to table and against the amendment. In 17 percent (332/1,928) of the cases in which a senator voted on both votes in a pair, the senator did not vote as predicted; that is, the senator either voted for the tabling motion and for the amendment, or voted against both. This seems to indicate unequivocally that tabling-motion and amendment votes are not always based on identical considerations.

To get at whether something like partisan loyalty is a factor, as claimed, we examine the same vote pairs from a different angle. For each pair, we code whether each vote in the pair was a party unity vote (defined as more than 50 percent of one party voting against more than 50 percent of the other party). In 12 of the 20 pairs, both the tabling-motion vote and the amendment vote are party unity votes; in such cases, we cannot distinguish between party- and preference-based voting. In another five pairs, however, the tabling-motion vote is a unity vote but the amendment vote is not, consistent with the claim that senators are at least somewhat more inclined to vote with the party on tabling motions than on amendment votes.

Killing Amendments with Tabling Motions

As we showed in the preceding chapter, the majority party uses a mix of procedural measures to disproportionately block minority amendments;

---

[4] King, Orlando, and Rohde (2010) do conduct a systematic analysis of individual-level vote switching on amendments in cases where there is a roll call on both the motion to table and adoption. Using all such votes from the 95th through 110th Congresses, they show that members are more likely to support the motion to table and then switch and support adoption of the amendment if they are (1) majority party members and (2) ideologically moderate. These results support the main thrust of our argument here, in that they suggest, especially for majority party members, that motions to table are not simply equivalent to votes on adoption.

for instance, the majority leader sometimes fills the amendment tree to prevent unwanted amendments from being offered. This strategy can protect a pending majority party bill from hostile amendments, but it is not a useful strategy if the majority party's goal is to prevent a particular unwanted proposal from *ever* being offered as an amendment. Tabling motions, on the other hand, provide a simple mechanism whereby a simple majority can effectively kill a motion, amendment, or bill.[5] They are nondebatable (and thus not subject to filibuster), are highly privileged, and need only a bare majority for acceptance. This means that what is essentially an up-or-down vote on an amendment can be forced immediately. Without a tabling motion, there is the possibility that debate – and potentially a filibuster – will ensue before the vote on the amendment, thereby imposing opportunity costs on the majority party by consuming scarce floor time.

Tabling-Motion-Vote Hypothesis

This suggests that majority party opponents' attempts to push proposals via the amendment process face a greater likelihood of being tabled than do majority party proposals. If this is the case, then tabling motions constitute another way in which majority party proposals face lower consideration costs than minority party proposals. This leads us to the following:

> Hypothesis 8.1. The Senate is more likely to agree to motions to table minority-sponsored amendments than to agree to motions to table majority-sponsored amendments, ceteris paribus.
> We test it against the following null hypothesis:
> Hypothesis 8.1$_{Null}$. The Senate is no more likely to agree to motions to table minority-sponsored amendments than to agree to motions to table majority-sponsored amendments, ceteris paribus.

Research Design

To test our hypothesis, we use a dataset with an observation for each tabling motion that proposed to table an amendment and that was subject to a recorded vote, from the 101st through 106th Congresses (there are 1,102 tabling motions in the six Congresses we examine). Our

---

[5] Tabling motions are by far the most common type of Senate procedural roll call vote in many Congresses, though there has been a sharp drop in the number of tabling motions in recent years (King, Orlando, and Rohde 2010).

research design is essentially the same as in Chapters 5 (scheduling) and 7 (disposition of amendments). For Democrats and Republicans, we examine how the probability of the Senate agreeing to a motion to table a party member's amendment differs depending on whether the party is the majority or minority. Using probit with robust standard errors, we estimate the following:

$$Agreed_i = \alpha + \beta_1 DemSponsor_i + \beta_2 MajSponsor_i$$
$$+ \beta_3 DemSponsor_i * MajSponsor_i + \beta_4 MajMotioner_i$$
$$+ \beta_5 ByLeader_i + \beta_6 ByChair_i + \beta_7 ByComm_i$$
$$+ \beta_8 MotionerDistance_i + \beta_9 SponsorDistance_i + \varepsilon_i$$

Our main variables are as follows:

$Agreed_i$ is a dummy variable coded 1 if the Senate agreed to tabling motion i and 0 if the Senate rejected the motion;
$DemSponsor_i$ is a dummy variable coded 1 if the amendment sponsor is a Democrat and 0 if a Republican;
$MajSponsor_i$ is a dummy variable coded 1 if the amendment sponsor is a majority party member and 0 if a minority party member;
$DemSponsor_i * MajSponsor_i$ is the interaction of the two prior variables.

The coefficient for $MajSponsor_i$ captures how the probability of the Senate agreeing to a motion to table a Republican-sponsored amendment changes as Republicans go from minority to majority status. Our hypothesis predicts that this coefficient will be negative; that is, becoming the majority will decrease the probability of the Senate agreeing to motions to table Republican amendments. Similarly, the sum of the coefficients for $MajSponsor_i$ and $DemSponsor_i * MajSponsor_i$ captures how the probability of the Senate agreeing to a motion to table a Democrat-sponsored amendment changes as Democrats go from minority to majority status. Our hypothesis predicts that this sum will also be negative.

We also include the following control variables:

$MajMotioner_i$ is a dummy variable coded 1 if the tabling motion was made by a majority party member and 0 if by a minority party member;
$ByLeader_i$ is a dummy variable coded 1 if the tabling motion was made by the leader or whip of either party and 0 otherwise;

ByChair$_i$ is a dummy variable coded 1 if the tabling motion was made by the chair of the committee that reported the underlying bill and 0 otherwise;[6]

ByComm$_i$ is a dummy variable coded 1 if the tabling motion was made by a member of the committee that reported the underlying bill and 0 otherwise;

MotionerDistance$_i$ is the absolute value of the difference between the motioner's ideal point and the chamber median's ideal point on the first dimension of DW-Nominate (Poole and Rosenthal 1997);

SponsorDistance$_i$ is the absolute value of the difference between the amendment sponsor's ideal point and the chamber median's ideal point on the first dimension of DW-Nominate.

We include the majority motioner, leader, chair, and committee member variables to control for possible effects of motioner characteristics on the probability of the Senate agreeing to a tabling motion. We include the distance variables as crude controls for the effects of members' ideology on the probability that their motions to table or amendments are accepted or rejected. Nonpartisan theories suggest that, as table motioners are more ideologically distant from the floor median, the Senate will be less likely to agree to their tabling motions. Such theories also suggest that, as amendment sponsors are more distant from the floor median, the Senate will be more likely to table their amendments.[7]

Results

Table 8.1a shows the results of our probit.[8] As predicted, the coefficient for *MajSponsor* is negative and significant, indicating that the Senate is less likely to agree to a motion to table a Republican amendment when the Republicans are the majority party than when they are the minority party, all else constant. Also as predicted, the sum of the coefficients for *MajSponsor$_i$* and *DemSponsor$_i$* * *MajSponsor$_i$* is negative and significant,

---

[6] For bills referred to more than one committee, we code *ByChair* and *ByComm* 1 if the motioner was the chair or a member (respectively) of any of the committees.

[7] These distance-related conjectures hinge on the assumption that table motioners and amendment sponsors offer tabling motions and amendments, respectively, that reflect their sincere preferences. In other words, as motioners are more extreme, they are more likely to want to kill a bill that the median does not want to kill; and as sponsors are more extreme, they are more likely to propose amendments that the median wants to kill.

[8] Observations for some tabling motions drop out of the analysis because they are motions to table committee amendments, in which case our sponsor variables are missing data.

TABLE 8.1a. *Effect of Amendment Sponsor's Majority Status on Probability of Senate Agreeing to Motion to Table the Amendment, 101st through 106th Congresses*

Variable	Coefficient	Standard Error	p Value
DemSponsor	0.254	0.142	.074
MajSponsor (H 8.1: negative)	−0.416	0.151	.006
DemSponsor * MajSponsor	−0.054	0.212	.798
MajMotioner	0.347	0.151	.022
ByLeader	0.329	0.200	.099
ByChair	0.254	0.129	.049
ByComm	0.047	0.121	.696
MotionerDistance	−0.692	0.335	.039
SponsorDistance	0.367	0.254	.149
Constant	0.494	0.254	.052
MajSponsor + DemSponsor * MajSponsor (H 8.1: negative)	−0.470	0.167	.005

Note: N = 936; pseudo-R^2 = .087; log-likelihood = −426.0400.

TABLE 8.1b. *Probability of a Motion to Table an Amendment Being Agreed to, by Party and Majority Status of Amendment Sponsor*

Amendment Sponsor Is:	Amendment Sponsor's Party Is:	
	Majority	Minority
Republican	.695 (0.041)	.880 (0.020)
Democrat	.762 (0.037)	.880 (0.020)

Note: Cells contain estimated probability of amendment being adopted. Standard errors shown in parentheses, estimated via CLARIFY with other variables set at means.

indicating that the likelihood is also lower for Democrats when they are the majority than when they are the minority.

Table 8.1b shows the substantive meaning of these coefficients. For Republican-sponsored amendments, the probability of the Senate agreeing to a tabling motion is .88 when Republicans are the minority party, but only .695 percent when they are the majority party. For Democrats, the probability changes from .88 percent to .765.

The coefficients for *MajMotioner, ByLeader,* and *ByChair* are all positive and at least marginally significant, suggesting that the Senate is more
likely to agree to tabling motions from majority party senators, party
leaders, and chairs of relevant committees. The coefficient for *ByComm,*
however, is not significant.

Also, the negative and significant coefficient for *MotionerDistance*
indicates that the Senate is less likely to agree to tabling motions made
by more ideologically extreme senators. And the positive but marginally significant coefficient for *SponsorDistance* weakly suggests that the
Senate is more likely to table amendments sponsored by more ideologically extreme senators.

These probit coefficients are useful for testing our hypothesis but less
useful for conveying the extent to which motions to table advantage or
disadvantage members of each party. Of the 1,080 motions for which we
have sponsor party data, 68.2 percent (737) propose to kill a minority-
sponsored amendment. The Senate agreed to 86.3 percent (636/737) of
these motions. On the other hand, of the 343 motions to table majority-
sponsored amendments, the Senate agreed to only 69.1 percent (237).
In short, across our sample, the Senate tabled more than two and a half
times as many minority amendments as majority amendments.[9] Our
results support our hypothesis and indicate that tabling motions pose a
larger obstacle for minority party amendments than for majority party
amendments.

Killing Amendments with Points of Order

When an amendment is pending, an opponent of the amendment can
make a point of order that the amendment violates either the Constitution,
a provision of statutory law (usually the Budget Act), or some aspect
of Senate rules or precedents, such as the germaneness requirement for
amendments to general appropriations bills. If the chamber sustains the
point of order, the amendment dies.

The Senate's decision whether to sustain or reject the point of order can
occur in a variety of ways.[10] Once a senator makes the point of order, the
chair (in consultation with the parliamentarian) can either rule directly

---

[9] See Den Hartog and Monroe (2008b) for a more detailed analysis of relationships
between motioner and sponsor characteristics.
[10] Except as noted, the basis for our discussion of procedure in this section is Frumin and
Riddick (1992).

on the question of order (i.e., sustain or reject it) or put the question to the chamber without first ruling on it.[11] If the chair rules directly and there is no appeal, then the amendment either is allowed (i.e., the chair rejects the point of order) or is ruled out of order and dies (i.e., the chair sustains the point of order).

If the chair puts the question to the chamber without ruling directly, then the chamber, subject to debate, settles the question of order by voting on it. A yes vote sustains the point of order, thus killing the amendment, while a no vote allows the amendment to stand. By rule, the chair submits certain matters, such as questions of germaneness or constitutionality, directly to the floor without first ruling on them – though the chair sometimes rules on such matters directly (Gold 2008: 10).

If a senator appeals the chair's ruling, the chamber votes on whether to sustain or overturn *the chair's ruling*, subject to debate. This gives rise to four possible scenarios: if the chair sustains the point of order and the chamber sustains the ruling, then the amendment is rejected; if the chair rejects the point of order and the chamber sustains the ruling, then the amendment is allowed; if the chair sustains the point of order but the chamber overturns the ruling, then the amendment is allowed; and if the chair rejects the point of order but the chamber overturns the ruling, then the amendment is rejected.

In addition, when the Senate considers budget-related bills that are governed by the Budget Act, an amendment's sponsor can move to waive certain points of order that the act applies to such legislation and amendments offered to such legislation. Motions to waive must be made before the chair or chamber acts on a point of order and are often made preemptively without a point of order having been raised (Gold 2008: 10). The chamber then votes on the motion to waive, which is a de facto vote on the point of order itself. In practice, if the chamber rejects the motion to waive, then the amendment falls, but if the chamber approves the motion to waive, then the point of order fails.[12]

---

[11] If the chair rules directly, there is no intervening debate on the matter, unless the chair solicits debate. If the chair submits the question to the chamber, the matter is debatable. For further discussion of chairs' decisions, see Bach (1989, 1991), Den Hartog and Monroe (2009), Evans (1999), Gold (2008), Heitshusen (2006), Madonna (2009), Preston (2005), Schneider (2005), and Smith (2007).

[12] The Budget Act requires 60 votes in the affirmative to waive some points of order (most notoriously, those stemming from "the Byrd rule"). This supermajority waiver requirement seemingly imposes costs on amendments from senators of either party – though, as we argued before, we believe it is generally more difficult for the minority to bear these costs than for the majority party to do so. For more on the points of order created by the Budget Act, see Saturno (2008).

Finally, Senate practice allows motions to table points of order that the chair submits to the chamber for a decision, to table appeals of chairs' rulings, and to table motions to waive points of order. In each case, the tabling motion cuts off debate and the chamber decides the matter by majority vote, with the votes again comprising de facto votes on the point of order. If the Senate tables a point of order submitted by the chair to the chamber, the point of order falls and the amendment is allowed; but if the Senate does not table the point of order, then the amendment falls. An affirmative vote on a motion to table an appeal of a chair's ruling means the chair's ruling (i.e., finding the amendment either in order or not) stands, while a negative vote on such a motion reverses the chair's decision. When the chamber votes on whether to table a motion to waive a point of order, a yes vote kills the amendment, while failure to table the motion to waive has the effect of rejecting the point of order.

Point-of-Order-Vote Hypothesis
As with motions to table amendments, we think the majority is also likely to use point-of-order votes (by which we mean any of the literal or de facto votes just discussed) to kill amendments in part because such votes are not transparent to the public. We thus test the following hypothesis:

> Hypothesis 8.2. When the Senate votes to decide a point of order, it is more likely to decide the question in a manner that kills the amendment if the amendment is minority-sponsored than if the amendment is majority-sponsored, ceteris paribus.
> Hypothesis 8.2$_{Null}$. When the Senate votes to decide a point of order, it is no more likely to decide the question in a manner that kills the amendment if the amendment is minority-sponsored than if the amendment is majority-sponsored, ceteris paribus.

Research Design
With the exception of the dependent variable, we test this hypothesis using the same research design we used to test our tabling-motion hypothesis. In this case, we use a dataset with an observation for each recorded point-of-order vote that could kill an amendment by sustaining a point of order against it, from the 101st through 106th Congresses (there are 257 votes in our sample). We examine, for Democrats and Republicans, how the probability of the Senate agreeing to a procedural vote that kills a party member's amendment differs depending on whether the amendment

sponsor is a member of the majority or minority party. Using probit with robust standard errors, we estimate the following:

$$Killed_i = \alpha + \beta_1 DemSponsor_i + \beta_2 MajSponsor_i$$
$$+ \beta_3 DemSponsor_i * MajSponsor_i + \beta_4 MajMotioner_i$$
$$+ \beta_5 ByLeader_i + \beta_6 ByChair_i + \beta_7 ByComm_i$$
$$+ \beta_8 MotionerDistance_i + \beta_9 SponsorDistance_i + \varepsilon_i$$

Killed_i is a dummy variable coded 1 if the Senate killed the amendment by voting to sustain the point of order and 0 if the Senate voted so as to reject the point of order.[13]

The coefficient for *MajSponsor_i* captures how the probability of the Senate voting to kill a Republican-sponsored amendment changes as Republicans go from minority to majority status. Our hypothesis predicts that this coefficient will be negative; that is, becoming the majority will decrease the probability. Similarly, the sum of the coefficients for *MajSponsor_i* and *DemSponsor_i * MajSponsor_i* captures how the probability of the Senate voting to kill a Democrat-sponsored amendment changes as Democrats go from minority to majority status. Our hypothesis predicts that this sum will also be negative.

Results

Table 8.2a shows the results of our probit.[14] As predicted, the coefficient for *MajSponsor* is negative and significant, indicating that the Senate is less likely to decide a point-of-order vote so as to kill a Republican amendment when the Republicans are the majority party than when they are the minority party, all else constant.[15] Also as predicted, the sum of the coefficients for *MajSponsor_i* and *DemSponsor_i * MajSponsor_i* is negative

---

[13] More specifically, *Killed* is coded 1 if (1) the chair submitted the question to the chamber and the chamber sustained the point of order, (2) the chair sustained the point of order and was sustained on appeal, (3) the chair rejected the point of order but was overturned on appeal, (4) the Senate votes not to waive points of order against an amendment, (5) the Senate rejects a motion to table a point of order submitted to the chamber, (6) the Senate votes to table an appeal of a chair's ruling that sustained a point of order, (7) the Senate votes not to table an appeal of a chair's ruling that rejected a point of order, or (8) the Senate tables a motion to waive points of order against an amendment.

[14] As before, some observations drop out of the analysis because they involve committee amendments, in which case our sponsor variables are missing data.

[15] The *p* value for the coefficient is .069 for a two-tailed test, but .0345 for the more appropriate one-tailed test.

TABLE 8.2a. *Effect of Amendment Sponsor's Majority Status on Probability of Senate Killing Amendment with a Point-of-Order Vote, 101st through 106th Congresses*

Variable	Coefficient	Standard Error	p Value
DemSponsor	0.420	0.477	.378
MajSponsor (H 8.2: negative)	−0.969	0.533	.069
DemSponsor * MajSponsor	−0.513	0.589	.384
MajMotioner	−0.035	0.505	.945
ByLeader	0.089	0.480	.852
ByChair	0.982	0.508	.053
ByComm	0.496	0.339	.144
MotionerDistance	0.820	0.917	.371
SponsorDistance	−0.360	0.880	.683
Constant	1.224	0.954	.200
MajSponsor + DemSponsor * MajSponsor (H 8.2: negative)	−1.482	0.632	.019

Note: N = 212; pseudo-R^2 = .2355; log-likelihood = −50.6438.

TABLE 8.2b. *Probability of a Point-of-Order Vote Killing an Amendment, by Party and Majority Status of Amendment Sponsor*

Amendment Sponsor Is:	Amendment Sponsor's Party Is:	
	Majority	Minority
Republican	.838 (0.083)	.969 (0.027)
Democrat	.818 (0.088)	.986 (0.017)

Note: Cells contain estimated probability of amendment being adopted. Standard errors shown in parentheses, estimated via CLARIFY with other variables set at means.

and significant, indicating that the likelihood is also lower for Democrats when they are the majority than when they are the minority.

Table 8.2b shows the substantive meaning of these coefficients. For Republican-sponsored amendments, the probability of the Senate voting to kill the amendment is .969 percent when Republicans are the minority party, but only .838 when they are the majority party. For Democrats, the probability changes from .986 percent to .818.

As with tabling motions, the probit coefficients are useful for testing our hypothesis but less useful for conveying the extent to which point-of-order votes advantage or disadvantage members of each party. Of the 252 votes for which we have sponsor party data, 64.3 percent (162) propose killing a minority-sponsored amendment; in 96.3 percent (156) of these cases, the Senate killed the amendment. In contrast, of the 90 motions to kill majority-sponsored amendments, the Senate killed the amendment in 82.2 percent (74) of the cases. In short, across our sample, Senate point-of-order votes killed more than twice as many minority amendments as majority amendments.

Of the remaining variables in the probit, only the coefficient for *ByChair* is close to significant (and positive), indicating that the Senate is more likely to kill an amendment when the motion that triggers the vote comes from the chair of the committee that reported the underlying bill than when it does not, all else constant. This makes sense given that the committee chair often serves as floor manager for the majority party. In fact, in our sample, a remarkable 87 of 88 votes on motions made by the committee chair were decided in a way that killed the amendment. Also, 9 of 10 votes on motions by a majority party leader killed the amendment, and 23 of 26 motions made by majority members of the committee other than the chair resulted in the amendment falling. On the minority party side, 20 of 23 motions made by the ranking member on the committee led to the amendment's death, 5 of 6 motions by minority party leaders led to amendments being killed, and 10 of 11 motions by minority party committee members other than the ranking member ended in the amendment's demise. In sum, 122 motions by majority leaders or majority members of the reporting committee led to an amendment being voted down, whereas only 39 motions by minority leaders or minority members of the reporting committee led to an amendment being voted down.

Summary

Our results support our hypotheses and indicate that tabling motions and points of order pose larger obstacles for minority party amendments than for majority party amendments. Like the rest of Part II, this illustrates that, at yet another step in the Senate's legislative process, majority consideration costs are smaller than minority consideration costs. Moreover, this illustrates two ways in which offering an amendment is not necessarily tantamount to having the Senate consider the amendment based on policy preferences. The majority also has at its disposal other means of fighting opponents' amendments, such as filling the amendment tree to preclude the offering of unwanted amendments at certain times. And even if an unwanted amendment survives these obstacles, "fighting fire with fire" – that is, offering second-degree amendments designed to counter unwanted amendments – remains an option (Campbell 2004; Weingast 1992). In short, notwithstanding the ease with which amendments can be offered, majority party opponents often face uphill battles in their attempts to use floor amendments to push proposals toward final consideration.

In the big picture, this is even more significant than it might at first appear. The majority is able to get many of its proposals through the committee and scheduling stages in the form of bills; hence, floor amendments are not necessarily the party's primary vehicle for its proposals. For the minority party, however, getting controversial bills beyond committee and scheduling is a tall order, so amendments are a primary vehicle for its proposals; but our results indicate that even the floor amendment route presents difficulties for many minority proposals.

9

The Effects of Amendments

According to the conventional view, the ability of strategic minority party members (or maverick majority party members) to offer amendments that move policy away from the majority position – or, worse yet from a majority point of view, amendments that introduce a majority-splitting policy dimension – has the potential to undermine the majority's ability to manage the Senate agenda. Indeed, long before partisan agenda setting entered the lexicon of congressional scholarship, scholars noted that the Senate's open amendment process is a significant causal component of Senate outcomes. Yet to date, no systematic empirical study has directly examined the effects of amendment outcomes on bills that the Senate passes.

In the preceding two chapters, we showed evidence of the majority leadership's ability to dispose of many unwanted amendments by procedural means. Killing many amendments, however, does not necessarily imply that the majority successfully kills all the amendments it needs to in order to produce legislative outcomes it desires. Thus, a critical and unanswered question remains: to what extent do amendments undermine majority party agenda-setting efforts?

To answer this question, we examine the effects of adopting amendments opposed by a Senate party (i.e., party rolls on amendments) on the probability of that party being rolled on a subsequent final passage vote on the underlying measure. If majority party leaders are effective at suppressing or partly suppressing unwanted amendments, then we would expect being rolled on an amendment to have a weaker effect on the probability of being rolled on final passage for the majority party than for the minority party.[1]

---

[1] Note that a party can be rolled on an amendment but not rolled on final passage. We illustrate this point in the next section.

Using data from the 101st through 109th Congresses, we find that the majority party is less likely than the minority party to be rolled on final passage votes, even when rolled on one or more amendments prior to final passage. For the minority party, being rolled on amendments is associated with a much greater increase in the probability of a final passage roll than is the case for the majority party. This result strongly suggests that the majority party wields some level of negative agenda influence – meaning, in this context, some ability to block unwanted amendments – that is underappreciated in the literature.

In the next section, we consider the relationship between amendments and bill outcomes. We use spatial illustrations to demonstrate different versions of the threats posed to majority agenda influence by both germane and nongermane amendments. Next, we present hypotheses regarding unwanted amendments, patterns of rolls on final passage, and majority status, followed by a section with details of our research design and another with empirical results.

How Amendments Affect Outcomes

Figures 9.1a–9.1c illustrate this challenge spatially; each panel in the figure represents a different situation in which the open amendment process threatens the majority party.[2] We begin with the potential threat presented by germane amendments. Figure 9.1a represents a simple version of the basic problem for the majority party. The figure shows a one-dimensional policy space, inhabited by a leftward minority median, a leftward status quo, a floor median, and a rightward majority party median.[3] Here, we imagine that the majority median proposes a bill at her ideal point, which, given the choice, the floor median would prefer to the status quo.[4] If this were the pairing on final passage, the bill would be adopted, representing a major policy gain for the majority median. Consider, however, the germane amendment proposal shown in the figure at the floor median's ideal point. Were a minority party member, or even

---

[2] The spatial examples that follow constitute our attempt to interpret and formalize arguments that are common but not formalized in much of the Senate literature. We acknowledge that these characterizations are not attributable to any specific author(s) but believe they effectively capture the spirit and many of the specific claims of the conventional view.

[3] Our discussion rests on standard assumptions of symmetric, single-peaked preferences.

[4] Note that the mechanics of this example are consistent across a whole class of scenarios in which status quos are on the minority side of the floor median and initial bill proposals are on the majority side of the floor median. Thus, the intuition is much more broadly applicable than this one specific arrangement.

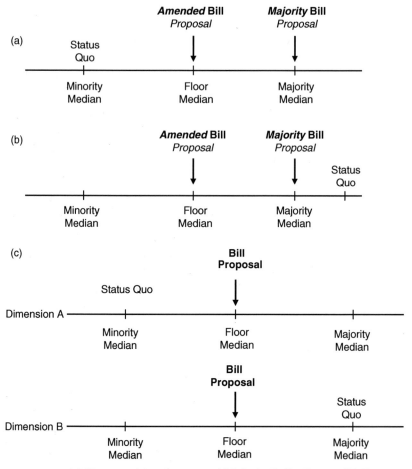

FIGURE 9.1. (a) Germane Amendments and Majority Policy Losses, (b) Germane Amendments and Majority Rolls, and (c) Nongermane Amendments and Majority Rolls.

a rogue majority party member, to offer this amendment, it would defeat the majority proposal, would be unbeatable by other amendments, and would be adopted on final passage. And while this still represents a net gain for the majority median (as she prefers the amended proposal to the status quo), we can see that it is a relative loss compared with the initial majority proposal.[5] The minority median, on the other hand, suffers an

---

[5] In this and the following examples, we use the terms "net" and "absolute" policy gains and losses to refer to differences in utility for a given actor – usually the majority or minority party median – derived from the bill adopted on final passage as compared with the status

absolute policy loss with either proposal but a relative policy gain when the germane amendment defeats the majority's initial proposal.

Figure 9.1b shows a more difficult version of the majority's germane amendment problem. The scenario is identical to that presented in Figure 9.1a, except that now the status quo sits just to the right of the majority median.[6] While the majority is safe if it can secure the proposal on this dimension at its median ideal point, it quickly gets into trouble if the proposal is amended to the far left.[7] If, as the figure shows, the germane amendment proposes moving the bill to the floor median's ideal point, not only is it a relative policy loss compared with the proposal at the majority median, but the bill will pass, rolling the majority and representing an absolute policy loss on that dimension. In other words, the majority would have been better off had the bill never come up in the first place. Meanwhile, for the minority median, the amendment represents a relative policy gain (as compared with the initial majority median proposal), and the final bill at the floor median represents an absolute policy gain on that dimension.

Figure 9.1c presents the case of nongermane amendments. Here, rather than thinking in terms of a single-dimensional policy space, imagine that you are looking at two separate single-dimensional policy spaces (dimensions A and B). For simplicity, we assume that ideal points are similarly situated across dimensions and that the bill proposal on each dimension is at the floor median's ideal point. The scenario plays out as follows. The majority party proposes a bill (or consents to a proposal) at the floor median's ideal point *on policy dimension A*. Some senator takes advantage of the absence of a germaneness rule in the Senate and offers an amendment in the form of a substitute. In so doing, he moves to replace the entire text of the initial bill with the text of a bill addressing the status quo *on dimension B* and proposing to move policy to the floor median's ideal point *on that dimension*. Since the floor median is slightly closer to the minority median (and thus to the dimension A status quo) than to the majority median (and thus to the dimension B status quo), she – and

---

quo. We use the terms "relative" policy gains and losses to describe differences in utility derived from the bill as adopted on final passage as compared with the initial bill proposal.

[6] As in the former example, the mechanics of this example are consistent across a whole class of scenarios. In this case, the example represents situations in which status quos are to the extreme side of the majority median but in which the majority median is still closer to the status quo than the floor median. Once the status quo moves to the right of the point at which the majority median would be indifferent between the floor median and the status quo, the intuition is closer to that represented in Figure 9.1a.

[7] Technically, it still sees policy gains up to the point where the proposal is to the left of the majority median's indifference point between the bill and the status quo.

everyone to her left – derives greater policy gain by agreeing to the substitute and bringing policy on dimension B to her ideal point.

Given these calculations, consider the relative and absolute policy gains and losses for the minority and majority party medians on final passage.[8] Had the substitute amendment been warded off, the status quo on dimension A would have been changed when the bill proposal at the floor median's ideal point was adopted on final passage, and the majority median would have seen an absolute policy gain the size of the distance between the minority median's ideal point and the floor median's ideal point. Instead, with the nongermane substitute passing, the majority median and most of her fellow party members would be rolled on final passage, leaving her with an absolute policy loss the size of the distance between her ideal point and that of the floor median and a relative policy loss (as compared with the scenario in which the substitute is warded off) the size of the distance between her ideal point and that of the minority median. The picture for the minority median is essentially the mirror image. Whereas he would have suffered policy losses (both absolute and relative) had the substitute been warded off, the move to switch to a bill on dimension B allowed him to avoid a final passage roll and realize a significant policy gain.

Before we move on to consider hypotheses, a short aside may be useful. We have not considered the filibuster (or, more precisely, filibuster pivots) in the foregoing examples. Certainly, this would complicate the examples some. But the same basic logic holds either way, and we could construct examples that include filibuster pivots but produce the same intuition. We omit filibusters in order to focus on amendments simply and directly and because we have already addressed them at length in Chapter 6.

Hypotheses

Notice that across the cases in which an amendment passes over the objections of the majority party, some scenarios are worse than others for the majority. Namely, the class of scenarios represented by the example given in Figure 9.1a – in which an amendment represents a relative policy loss, but the final bill still yields an absolute policy gain for the majority – is less problematic for the majority. Indeed, most or all of the majority party members would still have voted for the bill on final passage in Figure 9.1a, whereas most of the minority party members would have voted no and been rolled.

---

[8] Again, the logic and insights of this example apply to a whole class of similar scenarios.

Figures 9.1b and 9.1c, however, are much more troubling for notions of majority party agenda influence. In these scenarios, the majority party suffers both relative and absolute policy losses. In each case, the majority median, along with a large majority of her fellow partisans, was rolled on final passage. The minority party, on the other hand, reaps great policy benefits in both cases as a result of the amendments, turning a final passage roll into an overwhelming final passage success in the example from Figure 9.1c. If the majority consistently suffered the passage of amendments that created absolute policy losses, leading to rolls on final passage, it would be hard to make the case for a majority party bias in the Senate agenda. Nonetheless, there is no reason to believe that the minority party is any less vulnerable to unwanted amendments when conditions support an amendment that would roll the minority party. Hence, in the absence of agenda influence – assuming a uniform distribution of status quos across dimensions and assuming both parties' medians are equidistant from the floor median – parties should be equally likely to suffer rolls on amendments and on final passage votes. This characterization of the conventional wisdom leads us to the following:

Hypothesis 9.1. The majority and minority parties are equally likely to be rolled on a final passage vote, ceteris paribus.
Hypothesis 9.2. Being rolled on an amendment makes both the minority party and the majority party more likely to be rolled on a final passage vote, ceteris paribus.
Hypothesis 9.3. Being rolled on an amendment vote has the same effect on the probability of a final passage roll for the majority party as it does for the minority party, ceteris paribus.

If, in contrast, the majority party is better at killing unwanted amendments than is the minority party – and if the majority is generally better than the minority at influencing the chamber agenda – then we should not expect equal probabilities of amendment and final passage rolls between the two parties. In that case, the majority should be rolled less often than the minority on final passage votes, all else constant, including when the party is rolled on an amendment prior to final passage. Claims of majority agenda-influencing advantages (made by us and by others) therefore lead us to expect to reject these hypotheses.[9]

[9] These hypotheses are similar to those tested by Campbell, Cox, and McCubbins (2002) and Gailmard and Jenkins (2007), though neither group controls for amendment rolls when testing them. The alternative to Hypothesis 9.2 follows from the claim that the Senate majority party enjoys significant advantages in blocking unwanted floor proposals.

Research Design, Data, and Measures

We test these hypotheses using Senate roll call and legislative history data for the 101st through 109th Congresses.[10] The unit of analysis is a party-bill; that is, there is an observation for each party on each bill included in our dataset. The set of bills is 531 bills, joint resolutions, and budget resolutions that received recorded final passage votes in the Senate during our time period.[11]

To test our hypotheses, we employ a two-by-two factorial design (Trochim and Donnelly 2007) in which the factors are majority status and whether or not the party was rolled on an amendment vote before the final passage vote on the measure. This is a strong design that emulates a multigroup experiment and allows us to assess the effects of a treatment (amendment rolls) on two groups with theoretically important differences (majority/minority status). Because majority status changes from one group to the other during our time series, we also take advantage of the "switching replications" (Trochim and Donnelly 2007) nature of our design to assess within-group variation across changing conditions (i.e., for each party, we see how the effect of amendment rolls varies across majority and minority status).

More specifically, we use probit with robust standard errors to estimate the following:

$$Roll_{ik} = \alpha + \beta_1 Majority_{ik} + \beta_2 AmendmentRoll_{ik}$$
$$+ \beta_3 MajAmendmentRoll_{ik} + \beta_4 MajoritySize_k + \varepsilon_{ik}$$

[10] The dataset was assembled by combining the information provided in the roll call tables in the "Legislation and Records" portion of www.senate.gov with roll call vote information provided by Keith Poole at voteview.com.

[11] We conduct our analysis on measures that received recorded final passage votes in part because those are measures for which we can observe our dependent variable unequivocally (i.e., a party being rolled on final passage of a measure). We considered broadening our set of observations by treating the passage of a measure by voice vote as evidence that a party did not oppose the measure and thus was not rolled. In the end, however, we decided against doing so, partly to avoid the possibility of reading too much into voice votes and partly to concentrate on what we think are the most relevant bills theoretically. Including bills that passed the chamber by voice vote would mean including a large number of noncontroversial bills in our analysis. By instead conducting the analysis on more controversial legislation, we focus on instances in which the minority has the greatest incentive to try to use the amendment process to undermine majority party efforts. Put differently, we focus on instances that are most likely to bear out the conventional wisdom predictions that we test. We also considered broadening our set of measures to those that received a floor vote of any type or to those reported from committee but decided against these options for similar reasons. To avoid possible confounding effects of changes made in conference, we do not include measures that received a recorded vote on a conference report but did not receive a recorded vote when initially passed by the Senate.

$Roll_{ik}$ is a dummy variable coded 1 if party i was rolled on the final passage vote on measure k; $Majority_{ik}$ is a dummy variable coded 1 if party i is the majority party at the time measure k was considered;[12] $AmendmentRoll_{ik}$ is a dummy variable coded 1 if party i was rolled on an amendment vote on measure k before the final passage vote;[13] $MajAmendmentRoll_{ik}$ is an interaction of $Majority_{ik}$ and $AmendmentRoll_{ik}$; and $MajoritySize_k$ is a control variable that is the number of seats held by the majority party at the time measure k was considered.

Translated into expectations about the coefficients in our model, Hypothesis 9.1 predicts a coefficient not significantly different from zero for *Majority*; Hypothesis 9.2 predicts a positive coefficient for the sum of *AmendmentRoll* and *MajAmendmentRoll* (i.e., the difference between the majority's probability of a final passage roll if rolled on an amendment and the party's probability of a final passage roll if not rolled on an amendment) and for *AmendmentRoll* (which captures the difference between the minority's probability of a final passage roll if rolled on an amendment and the party's probability of a final passage roll if not rolled on an amendment); and Hypothesis 9.3 predicts a coefficient not significantly different from zero for the sum of *Majority* and *MajAmendmentRoll* (i.e., the difference between the majority's probability of a final passage roll if rolled on an amendment and the minority party's probability of a final passage roll if rolled on an amendment).

Results

Table 9.1 summarizes the incidence of amendment rolls and final passage rolls for both the majority and minority parties. Before turning to the probit results, we note three aspects of the data. First, by far the most

---

[12] Because of the midsession change in majority resulting from Jim Jeffords's switch, the 107th Congress presents complications in the coding of this variable. We have dealt with this by excluding measures that were introduced before the change in majority but received final passage votes after the change. In practice, this resulted in the exclusion of only a handful of measures. For remaining measures from the 107th Congress, the majority variable is coded 1 for Republican observations on measures that got final passage votes prior to the switch and is coded 1 for Democratic observations on measures that were introduced after the switch.

[13] Our definition of amendment rolls is broader than the standard definition of rolls. In addition to coding this variable 1 if an amendment was adopted despite the nay votes of a majority of party i, we have also coded this variable 1 if a majority of party i voted unsuccessfully to table an amendment and the amendment was subsequently adopted on a voice vote. We have run our analysis using both the simpler and the more involved definitions, and it makes a trivial difference in our results.

TABLE 9.1. *Incidence in the Senate of Party Amendment Rolls and Final Passage Rolls, by Majority Status, 101st through 109th Congresses*

Majority Party		On Final Passage, Party Is:	
		Rolled	Not Rolled
On Amendment,	Rolled	2	74
Party Is:	Not Rolled	4	451

Minority Party		On Final Passage, Party Is:	
		Rolled	Not Rolled
On Amendment,	Rolled	21	61
Party Is:	Not Rolled	68	381

Note: Each cell contains the number of bills on which the given combination of amendment and final passage rolls or non-rolls occurred for each party.

common outcome, for each party, is that the party is not rolled either on an amendment or on final passage. Second, the majority party is rolled on final passage only 6 times, whereas the minority party is rolled on final passage 89 times. Third, although the number of amendment rolls is similar for the majority and minority parties (76 and 82, respectively), the number of amendment rolls that lead to final passage rolls is much smaller for the majority party than for the minority party (2 and 21, respectively).[14]

The results of our probit are shown in Table 9.2a and cast serious doubt on the conventional wisdom hypotheses presented earlier. The coefficient for *Majority* is negative and significant (the coefficient is −1.3461, the standard error is 0.1964 and the p value is .000), clearly rejecting the Hypothesis 9.1 prediction that majority status is unrelated to probability of being rolled on final passage. Rather, the majority party is less likely to be rolled on final passage than the minority party, all else equal.

The coefficient for the sum of *AmendmentRoll* and *MajAmendmentRoll* is positive but not significant, which is inconsistent with the prediction of Hypothesis 9.2, that both parties should be more likely to be rolled on final passage, given a prior roll on an amendment. Instead, even when

[14] Note that one limitation of our research design is that it does not reflect the successful use of "killer amendments." A killer amendment would lead either to no final passage vote – in which case it would be excluded from our data – or to a failing final passage vote. Of the 531 bills in our sample, three failed on final passage; the majority had been rolled on a preceding amendment vote in one of these three cases.

TABLE 9.2a. *Effects of Majority Status and Amendment Rolls on Probability of a Final Passage Roll in the Senate, 101st through 109th Congresses*

Independent Variable	Coefficient	Standard Error	p Value
Majority (H 9.1: zero)	−1.3461	0.1964	.000
AmendmentRoll (H 9.2: positive)	0.3730	0.1662	.025
MajAmendmentRoll	0.0674	0.3875	.862
MajoritySize	0.0105	0.0297	.723
Constant	−1.6003	1.6147	.322
AmendmentRoll + *MajAmendmentRoll* (H 9.2: positive)	0.4404	0.3510	.210
Majority + MajAmendmentRoll (H 9.3: zero)	−1.2787	0.3356	.000

Note: N = 1,062; pseudo-R^2 = .1571; log-likelihood = −269.6745.

TABLE 9.2b. *Probability of Being Rolled on Final Passage, by Majority Status and Amendment Roll*

	Majority Party	Minority Party
Not Rolled on amendment	.0097 (0.0031–0.0216)	.1522 (0.1183–0.1889)
Rolled on amendment	.0327 (0.0059–0.0898)	.2588 (0.1708–0.3536)

Note: Top number in each cell is the estimated probability of a final passage roll; numbers in parentheses are 95% confidence intervals for the probabilities, estimated using CLARIFY (King, Tomz, and Wittenberg 2000; Tomz, Wittenberg, and King 2001). *MajoritySize* is held constant at its mean.

rolled on an amendment vote, the majority party is not significantly more likely to be rolled on final passage. Thus, on basis of this result, it appears that the majority party is effective in blocking the most troublesome types of amendments, those that lead to absolute policy losses and final passage rolls.

This is not the case, however, for the minority party. We find the coefficient for *AmendmentRoll* positive and significant, indicating that, unlike the majority party, the minority party is more likely to be rolled on final passage if rolled on an amendment. Thus, despite the supposed protections offered by filibusters and open amendments, the minority struggles to protect itself against final passage policy losses.

Finally, Hypothesis 9.3 is rejected by the coefficient for the sum of *Majority* and *MajAmendmentRoll*, which is negative and significant, demonstrating that being rolled on an amendment has a larger (positive) effect on the minority party's probability of being rolled on final passage than on the majority party's probability of being rolled on final passage.[15] Here, critically, we see that the types of amendments that roll the minority and majority parties, respectively, are systematically different in terms of the policy losses that they produce. That is, the minority is significantly more likely than the majority to suffer amendments that generate absolute policy losses on final passage. If the majority party has no special influence over the Senate agenda, this should not be the case.

Table 9.2b shows the substantive implications of the probit results. Using CLARIFY, we have estimated probabilities of a final passage roll, and 95 percent confidence intervals for these probabilities, as a function of majority status and being rolled (or not) on an amendment. The numbers are striking: if the majority party is not rolled on an amendment, its probability of a final passage roll is .0097; and even if it is rolled on an amendment, the number rises only to .0327. So while amendment rolls do triple the majority roll rate, it goes from an almost nonexistent 0.97 percent to a still tiny 3.3 percent. For the minority party, by contrast, the probability if it is not rolled on an amendment is .1522; if it is rolled on an amendment, the probability rises to .2588. Thus, the minority roll rate on final passage increases by nearly five times as much as the majority roll rate – to more than 25 percent – following an amendment roll for each.

Summary

Contrary to the predictions of the conventional wisdom, our findings support claims that the majority party is better than the minority party at blocking amendments that it opposes – an indicator that the minority pays higher consideration costs than the majority. On final passage, the majority party is rolled less often than the minority, even when it has been rolled on an amendment. Indeed, we find that the majority is no more likely to be rolled on final passage when it is rolled on an amendment

---

[15] We have estimated alternative specifications of our model in which we use a count variable, rather than a dummy variable, for amendment rolls. The results are similar across specifications.

vote than when it is not, suggesting that it is especially apt at blocking the most troubling sorts of amendments. Taken together, these results undermine the idea that the Senate's egalitarian and open amendment process prevents the majority party from engaging in systematic agenda manipulation. Instead, they paint a picture of the majority party using a procedural advantage to bias Senate outcomes in its favor.

In a sense our data provide an upper limit on how much damage the majority suffers via amendment rolls. It demonstrates that hostile amendments rarely lead to the passage of a bill that is so far from the majority members' preferences that the majority is rolled on final passage. But our data do not allow us to rule out the possibility that hostile amendments lead to the passage of bills that are watered down from the majority's point of view or bills that include one or more new dimensions that the majority would prefer were not included.

Conclusion to Part II

Part II includes a great deal of data analysis. At this point we pause to summarize our results and link them to the larger picture. We reiterate the following:

- At each stage except scheduling, a majority-sponsored proposal that has reached that stage is disproportionately likely to move forward in the process.
- The results are meant to establish the majority party's systematic advantage. The party does not need to win at every stage on every bill to have an overall advantage in moving bills to final passage; it needs only to have an advantage at some point that is not undone at a later stage.
- The results are not meant to be taken as independent tests of party effects.
- We are not trying to show that all majority party procedural wins occur due to leaders' efforts to discipline party members.

Summary of Results

In Chapter 4, we argued that the majority party leverages its control of committee chairmanships and committee appointments as a means of paying lower consideration costs in getting its preferred bills reported to the floor; the powers of the chair, with the support of a cohesive majority, reduce the barriers to majority party proposals in committee. This contention found empirical support: majority party bills are reported from committee at higher rates, even accounting for the fact that majority party members introduce more bills.

In Chapter 5, we argued (and demonstrated empirically) that this committee advantage is inherited at the scheduling stage and that the majority party's consideration cost advantage persists by virtue of the majority leader's special floor powers. His or her right of first recognition along with some degree of majority party cohesion on key procedural votes (such as motions to proceed) yield a bargaining advantage over the floor schedule such that majority party proposals have fewer barriers to gaining a final up-or-down vote in the chamber; in other words, the majority leader's bargaining advantage over scheduling reduces majority party consideration costs.

Recall, however, that we do not claim that the majority party faces no consideration costs; rather, we claim that the minority costs are higher. This point is made clearly in Chapter 6's discussion of the filibuster. There are many instances in which the majority party faces consideration costs that are too high for it to bear. Some of those cases result in well-publicized instances of the minority party "thwarting the will of the majority" and creating "legislative gridlock." Yet there are also many instances, often downplayed or overlooked in the literature, where the majority party overcomes a filibuster (or threat thereof) and gets final consideration of a contentious proposal. In much rarer cases, majority party opponents sometimes achieve the same result. In terms of consideration costs, this goes right to the heart of our assumption: all actors pay consideration costs, but the majority party's are systematically lower.

Chapters 7, 8, and 9 demonstrate a consideration cost asymmetry at the floor stage, where amendments are often said to undo the majority party's agenda-setting advantage. Taken together, these three chapters make a compelling case that, contrary to the conventional view, the majority party is much better than its opponents at dispensing with unwanted floor amendments, especially through the use of procedural tactics – such as motions to table and points of order – that allow for higher majority party voting cohesion with lower electoral risk for pivotal moderate members. Notably, the results show that majority-sponsored amendments are less likely to be killed by procedure (Chapter 7), especially when that procedure is a point of order or motion to table (Chapter 8); and even when the majority party is rolled on a floor amendment, it is no more likely to be rolled on the final bill, where the same is not true for the minority party (Chapter 9).

In terms of consideration costs, these results represent strong support for our key assumption. Minority efforts to push proposals through the amendment process face higher hurdles than majority proposals. Also, the majority party is better situated than the minority to sidestep attempts to derail a bill by adding toxic amendments.

Alternative Explanations

A reader could miss the larger implications of Part II by dismissing the results one by one on the grounds that a plausible alternative explanation exists for each finding. In other words, it may be tempting to ask, for any particular result, if there is a partyless explanation that predicts the results that we have presented as evidence of a majority party advantage. We do not wish to discourage this exercise in healthy skepticism. However, we think it essential to remind the reader that while any *one* result might be alternatively (and parsimoniously) explained by an ad hoc partyless theory, no single coherent partyless theory (that we can think of) can explain *all* – or even many – of the results together.

To illustrate this point, let us briefly try to sketch the beginnings of a partyless theory that would predict multiple results from different chapters in Part II.[16] To begin, we might assume a simple median voter model (at both the committee and floor stages), where the median both selects which status quos to address and is able to pull those policies from both directions toward her ideal point. However, assuming she has no preference for moving policy in one direction or another, this model alone is insufficient to explain any of the results favoring the majority party in the previous six chapters. To begin alternatively explaining some of those results, the most obvious (and, in our experience, commonly offered) additional assumptions address either the distribution of status quos or some bias in where proposals come from.

Consider the result from Chapter 4, that majority-sponsored bills are more likely to be reported from committee *and* that this pattern holds even across a change in majority party control. Perhaps the simplest way to explain this without party influence would be to assume that there are more status quos on the minority party side of the floor median. If this

---

[16] It is not clear what alternative model is most charitable to partyless arguments, in part because amendments and procedural votes typically are not explicit parts of such models. Applying Occam's razor, we keep our characterization of alternative explanations as simple as possible. For more on the difficulty of modeling alternative explanations and more detailed efforts to do so, see Koger and Fowler (2006).

were the case, and if we also assume that (1) senators' bills address status quos on the opposite side of the floor median and (2) they always propose bills as close to their preferred ideal point as possible, such that the proposal is still closer to the floor median than the status quo, then we would expect more majority-sponsored bills to be reported. That is, if the chamber median uses some random function to select which status quos to address and chooses from a status quo distribution that is skewed toward the minority party, then majority party bills addressing minority-side status quos have a higher probability of being selected and reported, simply by virtue of the fact that more of the status quos targeted by their bills are likely to come up. Note, however, that our alternative explanation must also account for the fact that the pattern changes direction after the 1994 election. This could be achieved with an additional assumption: with that election, the Senate median moved to the right, leaving a "stack" of policies at the old median's ideal point, now on the minority party side of the median and thus creating a skewed distribution.

But can this alternative model, as constituted so far, explain other results? Skipping forward to Chapter 7, it is hard to see how the median voter model plus a skewed status quo distribution would predict our findings regarding the disposition of amendments. If an amendment is offered, it implies that a proposal to change the status quo has already been made, so at minimum we need additional assumptions about amendment proposals. And if we are to explain this result *as well as* the committee result from Chapter 4, we should begin where we left off.

Accordingly, assume that bills coming out of committee are disproportionately majority party proposals and that this bias persists in the distribution of bills that are scheduled (as we show in Chapter 5). Next, assume that the same basic decision rule that drives the placement of bill proposals also drives amendment proposals: amendment proposers will (1) address bill proposals on the opposite side of the floor median and (2) propose an amendment that moves policy as close to their ideal point as the floor median will allow.[17] Under these assumptions, we should expect to see floor amendment proposals disproportionately attempting to move policy back toward the minority party, since its targeted bills are more likely to make it to the floor.[18] However, in Chapter 7, the opposite result holds. So what additional assumption can we make to explain this?

[17] Note that we could just as easily assume that all proposals are made at the floor median's ideal point and get the same basic result.

[18] For simplicity, we assume here that amendments are on the same dimension as the initial policy. We could just as easily make our point by bringing in other dimensions, though the specific construction of the example would be somewhat different.

One option would be to assume that, disproportionately, successful amendments are sponsored by Senators close to the chamber median, who are more likely to be members of the majority party (also by assumption). That is, even though there are more bills on the majority party side, it could be majority party members on both sides of the floor median that offer most of the chamber amendments (an assumption that embodies the thrust of the median voter model). This would explain higher success rates for majority-sponsored amendments, though it does not necessarily explain minority party amendments being more likely to be killed by procedure. Here again, we would need more assumptions.

To continue on would belabor a point that, by now, must be quite clear: any partyless theory that could explain all of our results would be very complex (and most likely implausible). Certainly, the set of assumptions just described are not the only options for constructing an alternative explanation for our results. They are, however, a good faith effort to construct a simply, partyless alternative, and they are not far from the "models" offered as critiques of our results when we presented early drafts of the chapters in Part II. Moreover, the example just constructed covers only a small fraction of our results; to cover the procedural results of Chapters 7 and 8 and the relationship of amendments and final passage votes in Chapter 9, all under a *unified set of assumptions*, would require considerably more effort and would be extremely unwieldy. Thus, inasmuch as our example here has overlooked a simpler alternative to explain the results in two of our chapters, it has surely understated the complexity and implausibility of what would be required to predict all of our results.

PART III

TESTING THE COSTLY-CONSIDERATION THEORY

10

Testing Our Model

The evidence and anecdotes in the previous chapters have, we think, established the plausibility of our model's key assumption – that the majority party pays lower consideration costs than the minority party (and other rogue senators) in trying to advance its agenda items – and grounded our theory in the procedure and agenda-setting stages of the Senate. They do not, however, test the model's predictive power. In this chapter, we turn to that task.

We focus on our model's predictions about the effects of changes in party control and changes in majority consideration costs on the direction of policy movement and the size of winning coalitions. In the first empirical section, we test our model's predictions against predictions from models that take no account of parties. We focus on the aggregate (i.e., Congress-level) direction of policy movement on final passage votes over a time series spanning 1949–2008, finding support for the prediction that Senate decisions predominantly move policy toward the majority party's side of the political spectrum.

In the second empirical section, we test predictions made by our model that are not made by other party models. We use vote-level data to examine variation in the direction of policy movement and coalition sizes on final passage, across sets of bills that have different majority consideration costs.[1] We find that policy is more likely to move toward the majority party and coalition sizes are smaller on votes involving lower majority

---

[1] Jenkins and Gailmard (2008b), Krehbiel (1998), Madonna (2008), and Wawro and Schickler (2004, 2006) also use coalition size to test theories of Senate decision making.

consideration costs than on votes involving higher majority consideration costs, as predicted by our model.

In the next two sections, we revisit our model and derive hypotheses about the consequences of changes in party control for aggregate policy movement. We also derive hypotheses about aggregate policy movement from two "non-party" models, the median voter theorem and the pivot model. We test these theories with the postwar time series in the section after that. In the fifth section, we derive from our model comparative statics predictions about the effects of changes in majority party consideration costs, which we test in the following section. We end with brief discussions of our results' implications for theories of Congress and of their broader potential significance.

Model Summary

To begin, recall the basic setup of the model. The key players – the majority proposer, M, the floor median, F, and the minority proposer, Mi – have ideal points along a single-dimensional issue space. Each maximizes his or her utility by minimizing the distance between his or her ideal point and policy on a given dimension, minus any cost paid to have a proposal considered. These costs effectively create "no-offer zones" for both M and Mi, so that policy dimensions with status quos in these regions will not merit a proposal from a given actor, because even if they could make utility gains by moving policy closer to their ideal points, the utility losses from consideration costs would negate and surpass these gains.

Though both M and Mi pay costs (c and k, respectively), by assumption, M pays a smaller consideration cost. We also assume that M has the option to make the first proposal, and Mi can then choose to make a counterproposal (or not), before F chooses the closest option of the status quo and any proposals that have been made. These two conditions – the smaller consideration cost and the first move – generate a policy bias for M.

Figure 10.1 summarizes some of the model's implications assuming a Democratic (leftward) majority party. Specifically, note the direction of policy movement for each bracketed region of status quos. First, consider Regions 1 and 4, which expand outward from the left and right edges of the minority no-offer zone (NO_L and NO_R). Given the symmetry of the space, we expect an equal number of status quos to be moved from these regions, thus an equal number of policies moving left and right (note, though, that the distance of policy movement is lopsided, a result we revisit in a later section).

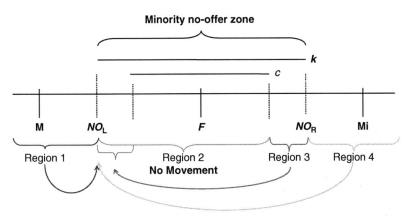

FIGURE 10.1. Summary of Outcomes Assuming a Democratic Majority.

Next consider Region 2. Here, no policy movement occurs at all. For the part of the region covered by both c and k, it is not worthwhile for either actor to pay the costs of having any proposal considered. For the part of this region on the left that is not covered by c, M cannot make a proposal that makes him better off policy-wise that F will prefer to the status quo. Thus, no proposal is made, because it is too costly for Mi.

Region 3, which is the comparable region on the right side of the space, does see policies moved, all to the left. Mi is unable to protect these status quos because she pays larger consideration costs, and thus M can move them to the left side of the space. Region 3 thus represents an asymmetry in the disposition of status quos. In other words, it is an area on the right (minority) side of the spectrum from which status quos will be taken and moved to the left (majority) side; and it is not mirrored by an area of status quos that will be taken from the left side and moved to the right.

Direction-of-Policy-Movement Hypotheses

Assuming a uniform distribution of status quos across all regions, this asymmetry implies that more status quos will move toward the left side of the spectrum than toward the right.[2] Of course, our model assumes a leftward majority merely for convenience. We could just as easily reverse M and *Mi*, and (holding c and k constant) the resulting predictions about

---

[2] We maintain this assumption of uniform status quo distribution throughout the chapter. However, we discuss the implications of relaxing this assumption, with respect to changes in c and k, later in the chapter.

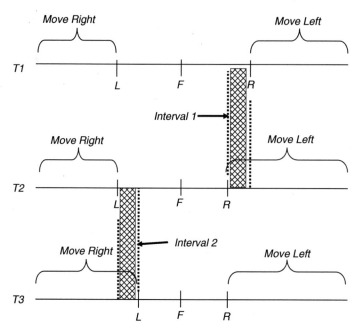

FIGURE 10.2. How Changes in the Pivot Model's Gridlock Interval Affect the Direction of Policy Movement.

which status quos would be moved, and where to, would exactly mirror those shown in Figure 10.1.

This leads to our first two hypotheses:

Hypothesis 10.1. When Democrats become the majority party, the proportion of leftward policy movements should increase, ceteris paribus.

Hypothesis 10.2. When Republicans become the majority party, the proportion of leftward policy movements should decrease, ceteris paribus.

We contrast these hypotheses with alternative explanations. First, and most notably, the pivot model (Krehbiel 1998) yields a very different prediction about the proportion of bills moving left, which is based on the relative area covered by the "gridlock zone" to the right and left sides of the floor median (F). The logic of the prediction is represented in Figure 10.2, which shows the single-dimensional policy space at three consecutive points in time ($T1$, $T2$, and $T3$), at which status quos are assumed to be uniformly distributed. By assumption F falls within the gridlock zone, which is the area between the left pivot (L) and right pivot (R). In the figure, from T_1 to T_2, the only change is that R moves inward toward F, which uncovers a previously blocked set of status quos (Interval 1). By assumption of the pivot model, all of these status quos should now move left, as they are to the right of the floor median. Thus, no new rightward-moving status quos have been uncovered, while some new leftward status quos have been uncovered, implying that this change will lead to an increase in the proportion of policies moving left.

Conversely, the only change from T_2 to T_3 is that L moves inward, uncovering a new set of status quos (Interval 2) on the left side of F, which will move right. Thus, this change should lead to a decrease in the proportion of policies moving left. Critically, however, we must consider the hypothetical in which both L and R move at the same time. If, for example, we skipped straight from T_1 to T_3 (and assuming Intervals 1 and 2 have an equal number of status quos contained within), then we would have an increase in the number of policies moving left and right. But we would have no expected change in the proportion of moves left, because the new leftward moves are canceled out proportionally by the new rightward moves. From this basic observation, we get the following hypothesis:

> **Hypothesis 10.3 (Pivot).** As the area in the gridlock interval on the right side of the floor median increases relative to the area in the gridlock interval on the left side of the floor median, the proportion of leftward policy movements will increase, ceteris paribus.

The second alternative explanation follows from the median voter model (Black 1958; Downs 1957). Represented in Figure 10.3, the setup here is similar to that in Figure 10.2, except that the floor median, F, is the central actor in determining the direction of policy movement. In short, all policy moves toward the floor median's ideal point, without interference from the pivotal actors from Figure 10.2. So as F moves right, as is the case between T_1 and T_2, status quos in Interval 1 that were previously to the right of F, and thus primed to be moved left, are now to F's left and thus primed to be moved right. Thus, this change causes both an increase in the number of policies moving right and a decrease in the number of policies moving left, resulting in a drop in the proportion of policies moving to the left. The reverse happens moving from T_2 to T_3, where F moves back to the left, leaving a block of status quos (Interval 2) that would have moved right at T_2 but will now move left at T_3. The result is an increase in the proportion of policies moving left.

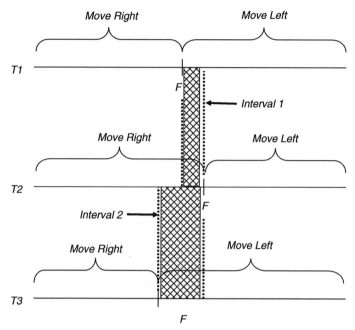

FIGURE 10.3. How Changes in the Floor Median Affect the Direction of Policy Movement.

From this basic logic, we derive the following:

Hypothesis 10.4 (Median Voter). As the floor median moves right, the proportion of leftward policy movements will decrease, ceteris paribus.

Testing Competing Models

Research Design

To test our model's predictions about direction of policy movement against predictions of non-party models, we use a longitudinal analysis of policy movement as a function of variables emphasized by models' predictions. More precisely, using ordinary least squares (OLS) on a post–World War II time series with an observation for each Congress, we estimate the following:

$$ChangePercentLeft_t = \alpha + \beta_1 NewDemMajority_t + \beta_2 NewRepMajority_t$$
$$+ \beta_3 ChangeFloorMedian_t + \beta_4 ChangeNetRightCovered_t$$
$$+ \beta_7 ChangeDemClotureVotesNeeded_t$$
$$+ \beta_6 LaggedChangePercentLeft_t + \varepsilon_t$$

Our dependent variable, *ChangePercentLeft*, is the change in the proportion of final passage votes moving policy in a liberal direction from Congress $t-1$ to Congress t.[3] To generate this variable, for each Congress we first identify votes moving policy to the left and votes moving policy to the right, using Poole and Rosenthal's (1997) DW-Nominate roll call vote data file.[4] We calculate the proportion moving left as the number of left-moving votes divided by the total number of leftward and rightward moves. We then take the difference between the proportions in Congress t and Congress $t-1$ (hence, an increase in the proportion from one Congress to the next takes a positive value).

The key variables for testing our model's predictions are *NewDemMajority* and *NewRepMajority*. Each is a dummy variable that indicates whether there was a new Democratic or Republican Senate majority in Congress t. These variables capture changes in majority status, as well as which party became the majority, in Congress t. The omitted category – that is, the condition captured when both dummies take the value zero – is that there was no change in majority status in Congress t. The coefficient for *NewDemMajority* should be positive – that is, we should see an increase in the proportion of bills moving left – and the coefficient for *NewRepMajority* should be negative, indicating a decrease in the proportion moving left.

The key variables for testing non-party models' predictions are *ChangeFloorMedian* and *ChangeNetRightCovered*, which measure change in the floor median's ideal point and change in the amount of leftward and rightward space between the pivots, respectively. We define *ChangeFloorMedian* as the difference between the Senate median first-dimension DW-Nominate score in Congress t and the median in Congress $t-1$. Since for Nominate scores rightward moves are scaled as positive, a positive value of this variable for a given Congress indicates that the floor median is farther right than was the floor median in the prior Congress. Since median voter models imply that policy will move with the median,

---

[3] We include final passage votes on House and Senate bills and joint resolutions. We exclude votes on simple and concurrent resolutions, as well as conference reports.

[4] We use the data available at the "Roll Call Estimates 1st to 110th Senates (Stata 8 File, 49,079 lines)" link at http://pooleandrosenthal.com/default.htm. We thank Keith Poole and Howard Rosenthal for sharing their data. For our analysis, votes moving policy in a leftward or rightward direction are defined as those votes that scale as moving policy left or right on the first dimension of Nominate. More specifically, the "spread1" variable contained in the roll call data has a direction attached to it; a negative value indicates that the bill moved right, and a positive value indicates that the bill moved left. Votes that do not scale on the first dimension are excluded from our analysis.

they predict that this variable will be negatively related to changes in the proportion of bills moving left.

The other non-party variable, *ChangeNetRightCovered*, is the sum of the rightward movement of the left pivot from Congress $t - 1$ to Congress t and the rightward movement of the right pivot from Congress $t - 1$ to Congress t.[5] In other words, for each Congress we identify the amount of rightward space that has become "covered" by the right pivot and add this to the amount of leftward space that has become uncovered by the left pivot. Each space represents status quos that the pivot model predicts will be associated with a lower proportion of leftward moves, so the model predicts that increases in this variable will be negatively related to changes in the proportion of bills moving policy left.

We include two additional variables as control variables. The first, *ChangeDemClotureVotesNeeded*, is the change in the number of votes Senate Democrats would have to gain to reach the cloture threshold. For each Congress, we calculate the number of Democratic seats and subtract it from the number of votes needed for cloture.[6] The other control variable is a lag of the dependent variable, *LaggedChangePercent Left*, which we include to account for possible serial correlation.

The time series we use to construct the dataset is the 79th through 110th Congresses (1945–2008). However, because we use change variables, the 79th Congress drops out of our analysis; and because we use the lag of the dependent variable, the 80th Congress also drops out. In addition, we treat the 107th Congress as two different Congresses (before and after Jeffords's switch). This leaves us with 31 observations. In addition, we estimate the regression using robust standard errors.

Intuitively, this research design has a straightforward quasi-experimental interpretation. For each Congress, we have a "pre-test" observation on the dependent variable from the prior Congress; for each key independent variable (i.e., each treatment) we observe changes, if any, that occurred between the prior Congress and the current Congress; we then observe "post-test" values of the dependent variable.

Results

Table 10.1 shows the results of this regression. The coefficients for the new Democratic and new Republican majority dummy variables are

---

[5] We again use first-dimension DW-Nominate scores. In identifying pivots, we use only Senate Nominate scores.

[6] In coding the number of Democratic seats for each Congress, we have made several judgment calls about how to code independents (such as Wayne Morse) and how to code midsession changes in Senate membership. Details are available upon request.

TABLE 10.1. *Effects of Changes in Majority Party, Floor Median, and Pivots on Change in the Proportion of Final Passage Votes Moving Policy Left, 81st through 110th Congresses*

Variable	Coefficient	Standard Error	*p* Value
NewDemMajority (H 10.1: positive)	0.2865	0.0407	.000
NewRepMajority (H 10.2: negative)	−0.2989	0.0653	.000
ChangeFloorMedian (H 10.4: negative)	−1.099	0.6566	.107
ChangeNetRightCovered (H 10.3: negative)	−0.0340	0.1774	.850
ChangeDemClotureVotesNeeded	−.0090	0.0097	.362
LaggedChangePercentLeft	−0.2859	0.1015	.010
Constant	−0.0035	0.0228	.880

Note: N = 31; R^2 = .8393.

significant in the predicted directions. With a new Democratic majority, the estimated change in the proportion of bills moving left (relative to the change expected with a continuing majority) is a 28.6 percentage point increase. Conversely, with a new Republican majority, the estimated change in the proportion of bills moving left (again relative to the change expected with a continuing majority) is a 29.9 percentage point decrease.

The results for the floor median variable also support the predictions of the floor median model. As the floor median moves to the right, the expected proportion of leftward moves decreases (the coefficient is significant at the 94.65% level with the appropriate one-tailed test). Note that this result is also consistent with our model. That is, in our model, as just presented, holding all else constant, we expect changes in the floor median to have the effect that we find here. However, it is neither a distinguishing nor a central feature of our theory, and so we have not emphasized it as a test of our model.

The coefficient for *ChangeNetRightCovered*, however, is not close to significant, yielding little support for the prediction that changes in the pivots affect changes in the proportion of leftward moves. Similarly, the coefficient for the Democratic-votes-needed-for-cloture control variable is not close to significant. The lagged dependent variable coefficient is negative and significant, indicating that an increase in the proportion of leftward moves from Congress *t* − 2 to Congress *t* − 1 is associated with a decrease in the proportion of leftward moves from Congress *t* − 1 to Congress *t*.

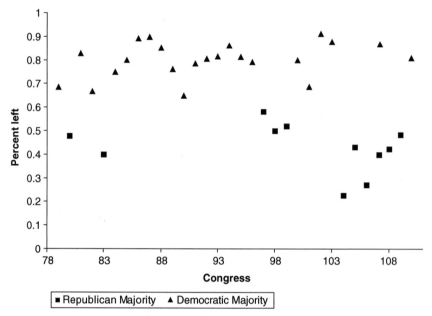

FIGURE 10.4. Percentage of Passing Bills Moving Policy Left, 79th through 110th Congresses (1945–2008).

We wish to make a final point about the data used. For the most part, this book focuses on the past 20 years or so; since this period is often described as one of intensifying partisanship, a potential critique is that our findings might be specific to this period. In other words, the partisan effects that we find throughout the book might be specific to this partisan era and might be absent in other eras. Figure 10.4 shows the percentage of bills moving policy to the left for each Congress from 1945 through 2008, giving us at least a rough picture of how things worked in the Senate before the partisan era. Though there is interesting variation in the data (such as the percentage of bills moving policy in the conservative direction during Republican majorities usually being smaller than the percentage of those moving in the liberal direction during Democrat majorities), one pattern jumps out above all others: the percentage of bills moving left with Democratic majorities *always* exceeds the percentage of those moving left under Republican majorities.

Majority-Consideration-Costs Hypotheses

The hypotheses from our model that we tested against nonpartisan theories in the preceding section are consistent with other partisan theories

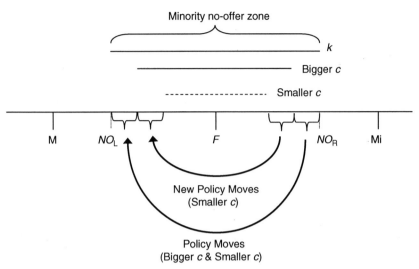

FIGURE 10.5. Effect of a Decrease in the Size of Majority Cost (c).

(Aldrich and Rohde 1998, 2001; Chiou and Rothenberg 2003; Cox and McCubbins 1993, 2005). In this section, to assess our theory against these others, we derive hypotheses from our model that do not follow from other partisan models. These predictions deal with the effects of changes in costs on direction of policy movement and coalition size.

Figure 10.5 represents the basic spatial illustration of our theory (similar to Figure 10.1), with summary outcomes for two different sizes of majority cost, c. In our model, changes in the majority's consideration costs can affect outcomes only of policies with status quos that lie between the floor median, F, and the right edge of the minority no-offer zone, NO_R. Thus, we focus here on that region.

The general result can be stated as follows. All status quos that lie between the right edge of the majority no-offer zone and the right edge of the minority no-offer zone will be moved as far left as F will agree to let them move. However, status quos that fall between F and the right edge of the majority no-offer zone will not move. Thus, as c gets smaller – and as the majority no-offer zone shrinks – a new set of status quos, previously protected, will now move left.[7]

---

[7] For simplicity, we maintain the assumption here that status quos are uniformly distributed across the policy space. However, to understand the implications of relaxing this assumption, the reader need only note that our key comparative static tests focus on status quos in the region between the right edges of the two no-offer zones. In short, whenever a status quo distribution causes this region to be more densely populated with status quos relative to the uniform distribution, the effects of changes in c and k should

This is graphically represented in Figure 10.5, showing the size of the majority no-offer zone under two different sizes of c depicted with the lines labeled "Bigger c" and "Smaller c." Notice that the first hypothesis, regarding the relationship between c and the direction of policy movement, is plain to see from the figure. As the majority no-offer zone shrinks under the "Smaller c," there is a new region of status quos that move left. Thus, we expect the following:

> **Hypothesis 10.5.** As majority consideration costs decrease, policy is more likely to move toward the majority party side of the spectrum, ceteris paribus.[8]

The movement of these previously uncovered status quos also has implications for coalition size. To see this, first note that all of the new policy moves associated with a smaller c should produce minimum winning coalitions, since M will propose bills so far left that F is nearly indifferent. Other policy moves, specifically those associated with status quos that fall outside of the minority no-offer zone both to the left and right, will produce larger than minimum winning coalitions.

Figure 10.6 gives an example of these contrasting policy moves with respect to coalition size. First consider Status Quo 1 (SQ 1). Our model predicts that the majority actor, M, will propose a bill (Bill 1) at the left edge of the minority no-offer zone (NO_L) to address this status quo. The resulting cutpoint (Cutpoint 1) will fall halfway between SQ 1 and Bill 1, which implies that the winning coalition will consist of everyone to the left of the cutpoint, including all members to the left of the floor median and some to the right of the floor median. Thus, this is larger than a minimum winning coalition. The same basic result is true of all policy moves for status quos to the right of NO_R and, by similar logic, to the left of NO_L: they will pass with larger than minimum winning coalitions.

be more pronounced; and the reverse will also be true. With this in mind, consider the effects of changing the status quo distribution in obvious ways. If we move to a normal distribution, assuming this increases the density of status quos in our critical region, then decreasing c will yield an even larger bias in favor of the majority party (for example). On the other hand, a "majority-skewed" distribution, where there are relatively fewer status quos on the minority side of the space, implies that changes in majority consideration costs will have a somewhat smaller effect on the level of majority party policy bias.

[8] Note that this increase in probability is theoretically expected to be focused on the set of bills associated with status quos in a particular interval. However, since we cannot match up bills with status quos, we instead assume that bills are equally likely to fall in this interval, and thus that there should be an increased probability that any given bill will move left.

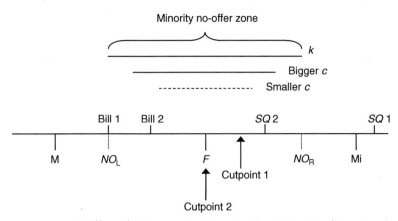

FIGURE 10.6. Effect of a Decrease in Majority Cost (c) on Coalition Size.

Status Quo 2 (SQ 2), on the other hand, falls in the interval of newly uncovered status quos due to the reduction in c. In this case, the majority will propose a bill (Bill 2) as far left as it can and still get the approval of F. Thus, the cutpoint will be just to the right of F, meaning that the bill will pass with the support of F and everyone to her left, a minimum winning coalition. To generalize from this, although every status quo in this newly uncovered region will be moved to a slightly different position to the left of F, they all will move just far enough to produce minimum winning coalitions.

The juxtaposition of these two examples should clarify the grounds for the next hypothesis. As c changes, it does not affect the number of policy moves like those in the first example (associated with SQ 1), which produce larger coalitions. But as c shrinks, the number of policy moves producing minimum winning coalitions should go up. Thus:

Hypothesis 10.6. As majority consideration costs decrease, coalition sizes decrease, ceteris paribus.

A key reason for testing Hypotheses 10.5 and 10.6 is that they do not follow from the cartel or conditional party government (CPG) models. The key independent variables in those models – locations of majority, minority, and floor ideal points in the cartel model; intra-party cohesion and inter-party polarization in the CPG model – are more or less fixed in any given Congress. These models thus are not well equipped to predict variation within a given Congress. In the analysis that follows, we take advantage of variation in consideration costs across different types of bills, within a given Congress, to test our predictions.

Testing the Effects of Changes in Majority Consideration Costs

Research Design

To test our model's predictions about the consequences of changes in majority consideration costs (c in our model), we use both direction of policy movement and coalition size data taken from final passage roll call votes in the Senate, on both House and Senate bills and joint resolutions, as well as budget resolutions, from the 101st through 109th Congresses.

Our analysis rests on the premise that Senate rules and procedures are such that majority consideration costs are lower for budget resolutions and reconciliation bills than they are for other bills (more on this later). We take advantage of this variation by categorizing each vote in our sample as being about passage of a "budget bill" – by which we mean a budget resolution or a reconciliation bill – or of a regular bill.[9] This gives us two sets of bills – those subject to regular consideration and those that get the "treatment" of lower majority consideration costs. We predict that, for budget bills, the probability of policy movement toward the majority will be higher and coalition sizes will be smaller than for regular bills.

To test the direction of movement predictions, we estimate the following model using probit with robust standard errors:

$$MajorityMove_{jt} = \alpha + \beta_1 BudgetBill_{jt} + \beta_2 MajoritySize_t + \beta_3 Congress102_t$$
$$+ \beta_4 Congress103_t + \beta_5 Congress104_t + \beta_6 Congress105_t$$
$$+ \beta_7 Congress106_t + \beta_8 Congress107_t + \beta_9 Congress108_t$$
$$+ \beta_{10} Congress109_t + \varepsilon_{jt}$$

Our dependent variable, *MajorityMove*, is a dummy variable that is coded 1 if a vote moves policy toward the majority (i.e., the vote moves policy left when there is a Democratic majority or right when there is a

---

[9] We exclude appropriations and debt limit bills, as well as continuing resolutions, from our analysis. We do so in part because consideration of them may be affected by budget resolutions and in part because it is plausible that appropriations politics differ markedly from politics of regular bills, so it is unclear what we should expect regarding coalitions on such bills.

Republican majority) and 0 if it moves toward the minority party.[10] Our key independent variable is *BudgetBill*, a dummy variable that is coded 1 for votes on the passage of a budget resolution or a reconciliation bill and 0 for regular bills. Our hypothesis predicts that the coefficient for this variable will be positive, indicating that a vote is more likely to move policy toward the majority for votes on bills subject to lower majority consideration costs.

We also include a control variable for the number of seats held by the majority party in Congress *t*, *MajoritySize*, and a series of fixed-effects dummy variables for each Congress (the 101st Congress is the excluded category).

To test the coalition size prediction, we conduct essentially the same analysis, with the following exceptions: first, the dependent variable, *PercentYes*, is the proportion of senators who voted on vote *j* in Congress *t* who voted for passage; second, we use OLS rather than probit; and third, our hypothesis predicts that the coefficient for the *BudgetBill* variable will be negative, indicating that coalition sizes are smaller for bills subject to lower majority consideration costs.

A key to our research design is the premise that Senate procedures imply lower majority consideration costs for budget resolutions and reconciliation bills than for regular bills. This premise follows from Senate procedures. Since the creation of the contemporary budget process in 1974, unlimited debate – hence, filibustering – is not allowed on budget resolutions or reconciliation bills. Debate is capped at 50 hours for the former and at 20 hours for the latter (Oleszek 2007). Since we see the cost of overcoming a potential filibuster as one of the main components of *c* in our model, budget bills provide a clear case in which we can categorize *c* as being lower than for regular bills.

Results

Table 10.2 shows the direction-of-movement probit results. As predicted, the coefficient for *BudgetBill* is positive and significant in the probit, indicating that the probability of movement toward the majority is greater for budget bills than for regular bills. Substantively, the estimated probability of movement toward the majority is .760 for regular bills (with a

[10] For the regressions in this section, we again use data from Poole and Rosenthal's "Roll Call Estimates 1st to 110th Senates (Stata 8 File, 49,079 lines)" file at http://pooleandrosenthal.com/default.htm. Also as before, we exclude from the direction-of-movement analysis votes that do not scale on the first Nominate dimension.

TABLE 10.2. *Effect of Majority Consideration Cost on Direction of Policy Movement, 101st through 109th Congresses*

Variable	Coefficient	Standard Error	*p* Value
BudgetBill (H 10.5: positive)	1.069	0.4681	.022
MajoritySize	−0.0692	0.1003	.491
Congress102	1.000	0.3885	.010
Congress103	0.7809	0.4332	.071
Congress104	0.7307	0.3311	.027
Congress105	0.5052	0.3704	.173
Congress106	0.5524	0.3653	.130
Congress108	0.1444	0.4418	.744
Congress109	0.5159	0.3485	.139
Constant	3.958	5.400	.464

Note: $N = 258$; pseudo-R^2 = .0630; log-pseudo-likelihood = −129.9851. The dummy variable for the 107th Congress was dropped by Stata due to collinearity.

standard deviation of 0.028), while the probability rises to .947 for budget bills (with a standard deviation of 0.050).[11]

Table 10.3 shows the coalition size OLS results. In this case, the coefficient for *BudgetBill* is negative (−0.213) and significant (the *p* value is .000). This indicates that, consistent with our hypothesis, coalition sizes are smaller for votes on bills that entail lower majority consideration costs than for votes on regular bills.

Discussion

The results of all three regressions in this chapter support our costly-consideration model. Here, we briefly take stock of these results' implications for other models of Senate behavior.

First, in our time-series analysis, our model compares favorably with non-party models such as the median voter and pivot models. Majority status explains a significant amount of variation in the proportion of leftward moves, above and beyond variation explained by movement in the floor median; in addition, we find little indication that movement in the pivots affects the proportion of leftward moves.

The longitudinal analysis does not, however, allow us to differentiate our model from other partisan models such as the cartel (Cox and

---

[11] We simulated standard deviations and estimated probabilities using CLARIFY (King, Tomz, and Wittenberg 2000; Tomz, Wittenberg, and King. 2001), with all variables other than *BudgetBill* set to their means.

TABLE 10.3. *Effect of Majority Consideration Cost on Coalition Size, 101st through 109th Congresses*

Variable	Coefficient	Standard Error	p Value
BudgetBill (H 10.6: negative)	−0.2135	0.0246	.000
MajoritySize	0.0009	0.0106	.934
Congress102	−0.0765	0.0453	.093
Congress103	−0.0807	0.0447	.072
Congress104	−0.0714	0.0341	.037
Congress105	−0.0091	0.0350	.795
Congress106	−0.0129	0.0332	.699
Congress108	−0.0040	0.0478	.934
Congress109	−0.0651	0.0352	.065
Constant	0.8256	0.5707	.149
N	388		
R^2	0.0976		

Note: $N = 388$; $R^2 = .0976$. The dummy variable for the 107th Congress was dropped automatically by Stata.

McCubbins 1993, 2005) or CPG models (Aldrich and Rohde 1998, 2001; Cooper and Brady 1981; Rohde 1991). Indeed, we find it likely that any partisan model would predict the results of our longitudinal analysis. In our second empirical section, examining the effects of changes in majority consideration costs allows us to differentiate our model from cartel and CPG models, whose parameters do not vary across the subsets of bills that we compare. We believe this underscores an important contribution of our model: unlike other partisan models, it explains how we can get majority-favoring outcomes, notwithstanding well-known agenda-setting obstacles presented by Senate procedures. In doing so, it allows us to explain variation in majority success at a more fine grained level than other models.

Our theory overlaps significantly, however, with both the cartel and CPG models. It builds intentionally on foundational ideas, set out in cartel theory, that majority party members band together to form a party organization in order to deal with intra-party collective action problems and that a permanent majority party agenda-setting advantage results from this organization. However, like CPG, ours is a theory of conditional majority party power in the sense that it models agenda influence as a partially qualified function of various factors. Of course, we focus on consideration costs rather than intra- and inter-party preference homogeneity, but we suspect the two are related, at least inasmuch as preference homogeneity most likely affects the consideration costs faced by each party. For example, a more homogeneous minority party seemingly makes it more difficult (i.e., costly) for the majority to overcome a filibuster and have a proposal considered. Similarly, as argued by CPG theory, a more homogeneous majority is likely to delegate more agenda-setting power to party leaders, thereby lowering majority consideration costs and perhaps also raising minority proposal costs. But neither the cartel nor CPG theory was developed in the context of the Senate. We have set out to build on their insights, as well as insights from the substantial nonformal literature on the Senate, to explain legislative behavior in the Senate.

Summary

We have tested the implications of our costly-consideration agenda-setting model and found various types of empirical support for its predictions. In particular, we have found that passing bills are more likely to move policy in the direction of the majority party than in the direction of the minority party; that this is truer when majority consideration costs are lower; and that measures pass with the support of less broad coalitions as these costs decrease.

A related implication of our tests is that the majority party is more successful, on average, on budget resolutions and budget reconciliation bills than on regular legislation. Though we differentiate budget bills from other bills because they provide a clean operationalization of a key parameter in our model, and our purpose here is not to address literature on congressional budgeting and appropriations (Fenno 1966; Kiewiet and McCubbins 1991), our results seem to have significant implications with respect to majority power in the Senate. Specifically, budget resolutions and reconciliation bills are among the most significant measures the Senate handles. They affect appropriations, revenues, and sometimes even authorizations across many government programs, according to Oleszek (2007: 65), who notes, "Given their policy-making significance, [reconciliation] bills, not surprisingly, are shepherded through Congress by party leaders and key committee leaders." Rawls (2009: 53) calls reconciliation "[o]ne of the most powerful offensive weapons" in the majority's arsenal.

An important caveat is that the majority's ability to enact policy via reconciliation might be constrained by the Byrd rule, which prohibits "extraneous" provisions. If the presiding officer sustains a Byrd rule objection, the provision in question is struck from the bill, and it takes

60 votes to reverse the decision – meaning the majority party rarely has enough votes to overturn an objection unilaterally.[12] Some contentious policy areas, however, clearly do not violate the Byrd rule. Reconciliation was used to cut welfare and food stamps in 1981, to change welfare, Medicare, and Medicaid in the 1990s, and to pass tax cuts early in George W. Bush's presidency (Faler 2009). In fact, the procedure came under fire for its blunt partisan usage in the spring of 2010, when Democrats turned to reconciliation to get some essential changes to the health care bill through the Senate, after the House and Senate failed to execute a conference agreement before the Senate Democrats lost their 60th vote in a special election that replaced the late Senator Ted Kennedy.

Put in terms of our theory, the Byrd rule raises the cost of consideration for the majority party on some types of legislation; it does not, however, prohibit the majority from using the budget and reconciliation process as a means of passing highly contentious policy over the objections of potentially all but a bare majority of the Senate's membership. Rawls (2009: 58–59) argues that, even with Byrd rule limitations, reconciliation "allows the majority of the Senate to once a year ... pass far-reaching legislation."

The significance of reconciliation was underscored when it was used to push through health care reform in early 2010. It is clear that Senate majorities sometimes use filibuster-proof budget resolutions and reconciliation bills to push legislative priorities (Hulse 2009; Oleszek 2007).

Certainly, there are limits to what can and cannot be changed through the budget and budget reconciliation process. Presumably, however, the majority generally gains greater power from disproportionate influence over these budgeting measures than it would from disproportionate influence over regular measures. To the extent that this is the case, the majority-thwarting effects of constraints such as the filibuster may be overstated.

---

[12] There are several bases for declaring part of a reconciliation bill extraneous. The most common is that the provision in question does not change either outlays or revenues; others include a provision making "budget changes [that are] merely incidental to non-budgetary components" and a provision falling outside committee jurisdiction (Keith 2008b).

Implications of Costly Consideration

We began with a puzzle in the Senate literature: how do we square findings of party effects (Bargen 2003; Campbell, Cox, and McCubbins 2002; Crespin and Finocchiaro 2008; Den Hartog and Monroe 2008a; Gailmard and Jenkins 2007; Koger 2003; Koger and Fowler 2006) with Senate procedures that seem to preclude party effects? Applications of House-based theories to the Senate (Campbell, Cox, and McCubbins 2002; Chiou and Rothenberg 2003) are supported empirically but are not widely accepted as explanations of Senate behavior (Smith 2007), in large part because they assume, rather than explain, majority agenda-setting power. This assumption flies in the face of decades of literature arguing that individual senators and minority coalitions are powerful agenda-setting actors (Huitt 1961; Lehnen 1967; Matthews 1960; Ripley 1969; Sinclair 1989; Smith 1989).

Our solution to this puzzle centers on the idea that agenda setting is costly – meaning senators must sacrifice scarce resources, such as time, energy, staff, and political chips, to gain final consideration of their proposals. The distinction between getting a proposal to the floor and getting the floor to vote on the proposal is crucial to our take on the Senate – where, unlike the House, much of the significant agenda-setting action happens *after* legislation is initially proposed on the floor. In the absence of an analog to the House Rules Committee, the Senate majority must battle to get its proposals to the floor, to protect them on the floor, and to move them beyond the floor.

However, the minority party must also fight if its proposals are to pass, and it is in a less advantageous position to engage in such fighting. The majority faces lower consideration costs and enjoys first-proposal power, which allows it to bias outcomes in its favor.

A strength of our theory is that it incorporates conventional beliefs about aspects of Senate behavior. Another is that the premises we add to conventional thinking have firm grounding in Senate procedural practice, which we examined in detail in Part II. One of the important lessons we draw about Senate procedure is that, when it comes to pushing its proposals through various stages of the legislative process, the majority is never worse off than its opponents, and is often better off. Taken in isolation from one another, each of our results in Part II paints an incomplete picture of majority power; in aggregate, however, they provide a comprehensive perspective on the majority's advantages throughout the process. Moreover, making sense of the results simultaneously is difficult unless partisan influence is included as an explanatory factor.

Perhaps most important, our theory explains results that were previously puzzling, correctly predicts new empirical patterns, and provides a parsimonious framework for thinking about parties in the Senate. We see it as a useful step forward in a literature that lacks compelling theory, but of course not as the final word on the matter. We hope others will scrutinize, criticize, test, and improve upon our work. In the sections that follow, we discuss possible extensions of our tests and possible applications of our theory in different contexts.

Extensions of Our Tests

A more comparative approach might be used to conduct additional tests of our theory. One general research design that could be used for this purpose is a kind of "history as a laboratory" approach discussed by Brady and McCubbins (2002); that is, for a given legislature, one can compare periods of time before and after changes in consideration costs, effectively treating each change as a treatment being applied to the legislature. Given the many changes over time both in Congress and in other legislatures, that would generate excellent opportunities for operationalizing costs. Indeed, the use of filibusters and the rules governing them in both the House and Senate have changed dramatically over the course of those chambers' histories, along with many other procedures and factors that significantly affect consideration costs. The rich literature on institutional change (Binder 1996, 1997; Dion 1997; Fink and Humes 1996; Schickler 2000; Schickler and Rich 1997) might even be revisited with a costly-consideration framework in mind. One could extend this approach to examine the effect of changing consideration costs across many legislatures.

A more ambitious strategy would be to combine the prior approach with a most-similar-cases design (Lijphart 1971), effectively creating a control group and a treatment group. For instance, one might use two neighboring states with similar legislatures and politics, one of which experiences a change in consideration costs. By comparing behavior before the change with behavior after the change in each state, then comparing the states, one could test predictions about the effect of changing consideration costs.

Other Applications of the Costly-Consideration Theory

We argue that it is preferable to conceptualize agenda setting in terms of costly consideration rather than in terms of absolute veto gates. This approach is flexible enough to be applied to other legislatures and perhaps to some constitutional structures more broadly. Certainly, some legislatures, at some points in their histories, approach the conditions for absolute vetoes by certain actors; but many legislatures do not. An advantage of thinking in terms of consideration costs is that it can accommodate both situations: an absolute veto occurs when one actor pays no consideration costs and other actors' consideration costs are prohibitively large; alternatively, one can imagine a legislature where agenda-setting power is much more uniformly distributed, and thus consideration costs are relatively equal across actors. In short, our theory is applicable to a wide range of legislatures, potentially including the House of Representatives and state legislatures in the United States, as well as other countries' legislatures.

The House of Representatives

A great deal of debate about House agenda setting revolves around Krehbiel's pivot model (1998) and Cox and McCubbins's cartel model (2002, 2005). Like ours, each is a one-dimensional agenda-setting game; unlike ours, each assigns absolute veto power to one or more actors. We think our model offers extra theoretical purchase on the House; from our point of view, the contemporary House is a case of the costly-consideration model in which the majority's consideration costs are low, and the minority's consideration costs high, due to majority party control of the Rules Committee.[1] Our model explains more readily than the pivot

---

[1] Under these conditions, our model is essentially a modified version of the cartel model, in which the chamber considers a bill that reaches the floor under a closed rule rather

model why most policy movement is toward the majority party and also explains more readily than the cartel model why the majority party is occasionally rolled.[2]

In addition, our approach provides a concise framework for thinking about and formally modeling changes over time. For example, Cox and McCubbins (2005) show that majority party negative agenda influence remained "unconditional" – that is, strong – even during the period of "committee dominance" and the Conservative Coalition; what did change, however, was the ability of the Conservative Coalition to block majority leaders' legislative proposals. In our model's terms, minority (including Conservative Coalition) consideration costs remained high across this period, but majority consideration costs increased substantially relative to the periods before and after.

Similarly, the 19th-century "Reed revolution" can be concisely explained in terms of consideration costs. By the late 1880s, explosive growth of the House's workload combined with House procedures in such a way that the floor became chaotic and it was difficult for any party or coalition to bring proposals to a vote. The Rules Committee was able to put bills on the floor; but, once there, they were frequently filibustered via dilatory motions or the disappearing quorum (Alexander 1916; Binder 1997; Dion 1997; Follett 1896; Galloway 1976; McConachie 1974 (1898); Peters 1990; Robinson 1930; Schickler 2001; Strahan 2002). Reed's "revolution" consisted largely of eliminating the disappearing quorum and dilatory motions (Den Hartog 2004); in other words, he sharply reduced consideration costs faced by majority proposals.

U.S. State Legislatures

We can also imagine applications both across and within state legislatures, which are understudied in absolute terms and underutilized as laboratories for testing legislative theories. Broad variation across state legislatures and over time within individual legislative chambers makes them prime candidates for the study of costly consideration.

For instance, Kim (2005) explores cross-sectional variation in procedural arrangements across state legislative chambers with partisan

---

than an open rule. For a theoretical explanation of this modification, see Monroe and Robinson (2008).

[2] Each theory can explain the patterns we mention, but only under certain conditions. The pivot model predicts policy movements being biased toward the majority party if most status quos outside the gridlock interval are on the minority party side of the interval; and Cox and McCubbins (2005) extend the cartel agenda model to incorporate instances in which blocking minority proposals is costly to the majority, which can lead to majority rolls.

deadlocks (i.e., each party holds the same number of seats). In these cases, where parties essentially tie for majority status, the parties often strike power-sharing agreements that create relatively equal consideration costs across parties. One could compare these legislative sessions to the sessions that precede and follow, to study how changes in costs affect outcomes.

Colorado's state House provides another example. In 1988, an externally imposed procedural change mandated that all bills get committee votes and, if reported, be considered by the chamber; effectively, this mandate lowered consideration costs for all bills. Cox, Kousser, and McCubbins (2005) show that, following the change, majority party roll rates increased dramatically.

Costly Consideration in Comparative Perspective

Moving to a comparative institutions perspective, first consider the potential application of a consideration costs framework to presidential systems. In many presidential democracies, such as Brazil, Colombia, and Argentina, the chief executive has some form of legislative agenda power – either through the use of decrees (i.e., the unilateral creation of laws that then require legislative action) or direct proposal power within the legislature (Magar 2001; Shugart and Carey 1992). This means the first proposer can vary across proposals, creating a potential case for applying our model. Also, if decree power is limited – or if the legislature's ability to amend decrees is limited – a costly-consideration approach might be more appropriate than the typical absolute veto and proposal power approach. States in which a president's decree power changes over time are especially fertile ground for our theory. For example, in 1988, constitutional reforms in Brazil altered the president's decree and legislative proposal powers in ways that lowered the cost for the president to get items onto the agenda and that left the president with less than absolute decree power (Amorim Neto, Cox, and McCubbins 2003; Figueiredo and Limongi 2000).

A consideration costs framework yields testable comparative statics both over time and across policies, analogous to those we tested in Chapter 10. As constitutional reforms make it less costly for presidents to get final consideration of legislative proposals or decrees, we should see policy outcomes closer to their preferred positions. Similarly, after reforms, presidents should get more of what they want in policy areas in which they have clearer, less costly paths to final consideration. And if conditions *do* approach absolute vetoes over the agenda, either for a majority coalition in the legislature or for the president, a costly-consideration model still fits. Here, the model simply ascribes a low and constant cost for proposals by either the relevant legislative actor or the president (or both, depending on the specific theoretical setup).

Consideration costs may also have applications to parliamentary settings. In many parliaments – perhaps most quintessentially the British House of Commons – the party in government is viewed as having open access to propose things on the agenda, while the opposition party rarely if ever gains final consideration of its preferred measures. Put in our terms, the party in government pays a very low consideration cost, while the opposition pays a very high cost. Even in these cases, however, there is probably some cost to the party in government, even if only an opportunity cost based on the scarcity of plenary time (i.e., the party simply does not have time to consider everything it would like to).

The consideration costs framework might also be applied to parliamentary settings in which the ruling coalition is a majority coalition of parties. Here, for the majority coalition, there may be highly variable consideration costs across issues and over time, depending on the internal cohesion of parties within the governing coalition. Indeed, depending on the procedures of a particular parliamentary body – such as Israel – it may be useful to consider each party within a ruling coalition as paying a separate consideration cost, which could be a function of size, proximity to the ideological center of the coalition, or both. And in coalition settings, the opposition parties are, we suspect, likely to pay lower consideration costs than their counterparts that face single ruling parties – a proposition that could be tested in future work on a broad, cross-national level using predictions from the model we have laid out here.

Our framework also has potential applications to bicameral settings. Rich and varied literatures focus on how the number of veto gates and control of veto gates affect the functioning of governments (Cox and McCubbins 2000; Linz 1994; Mainwaring and Shugart 1997; Sartori 1994; Shugart and Carey 1992; Stepan and Skach 1994; Tsebelis 1995; Tsebelis and Money 1997). There is a tendency to draw conclusions based on conceptions of veto power as absolute; that is, an actor either has veto power or does not. In many instances, however, an actor's negative agenda power is not absolute. Rather, the actor can make agenda setting by another actor more difficult, and sometimes thereby block another actor's initiative, but cannot with certainty veto such initiatives.

For example, under some circumstances, the British House of Lords and the German Bundesrat can make it more difficult for the government to enact laws but cannot out-and-out veto legislation. By focusing on the ability to impose costs on the agenda-setting powers of others, we offer a more nuanced conception of "quasi-veto" power that might fruitfully be applied in many comparative contexts. That is, we move away from the dichotomous contrast between absolute veto power and absolute lack of veto power, to allow for conditions under which actors have a disproportionate, but not absolute, ability to block legislation from moving forward. By extension, our work also has implications regarding the nature of representation in a given polity. The ability to impose costs on others can grant otherwise powerless legislators some level of influence over policy, implying some level of representation for their constituents that might be either over- or understated by sticking to an all-or-nothing veto concept.

Back to the Big Picture

We began the book with the puzzle presented by conflicting characterizations of the contemporary Senate. The upper chamber is often described as the bottleneck of U.S. lawmaking, where a mix of partisan polarization, individualism, and minority power stifles the majority party's agenda and produces seemingly endless gridlock; but at the same time, Congress has enacted major policy changes. These controversial policies were subject to severe partisan attacks but passed nonetheless. Our consideration costs framework helps us to understand the disconnect in thinking about the Senate.

Our theory reorients our legislative expectations away from conceptions of absolute proposal power, veto power, or agenda control. Perhaps because the majority party in the modern House seems to so routinely get its way, we are conditioned to seeing legislative power as concentrated and unfailing. And as a result, we are quick to mistake the Senate's arena of fierce legislative bargaining and delay as a place of inaction. But if we instead understand agenda power, even in the House, as a matter of scarce resources being dedicated to the pursuit of legislative goals, we improve our ability to explain legislatures that do not fit the all-or-nothing notion of agenda influence. It gives us a better understanding of how and why the extremes of absolute majority party control or legislative gridlock are not the only, or even the most common, stable legislative states.

Certainly, there are times when the consideration costs are beyond the means of the Senate majority party or any other coalition and gridlock ensues, causing widespread frustration with the chamber. But in many other instances, often on important issues, the majority overcomes those costs to enact policies that voters elected them to pursue.

Appendix A

Relaxing the Model's Assumptions

By and large, the implications of the model hold even when we relax the simplifying assumptions. Nonetheless, in this appendix, we consider some small changes in outcomes that follow from relaxing two of our assumptions: that (1) k (and c) $< |M - Mi|$ and (2) M and Mi are equidistant from F.

Expanding k and c

First, as k grows beyond $|M - Mi|$ (i.e., as the minority's consideration cost becomes larger than the distance between the majority and minority ideal points), more status quos to the left of M become part of the minority no-offer zone, meaning that the majority party does not have to "defend" them with preemptive offers that reduce majority utility. Figure A.1 shows an example of this result. Here, k has grown, pushing the edges of the minority no-offer zone well beyond M and Mi. Under our normal assumptions, the status quo in this example – which is to the extreme side of M – would have been moved right by M, leapfrogging his ideal point with a proposal at NO_L (see Figure 3.6a). However, with the expansion of k, the status quo in Figure A.1 will remain unchanged, as Mi can no longer make a proposal that will improve her policy utility enough to offset the consideration cost. Thus, M can simply leave the status quo where it is, avoiding paying a consideration cost himself to keep policy from leaving his side of the space.

If the majority party's costs also grow large – in particular, if $k > c > |M - Mi|$ – several notable things change. First, for some status quos left

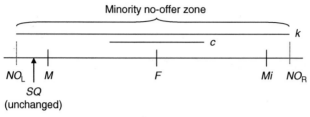

FIGURE A.1. Example of $k > |M - Mi|$.

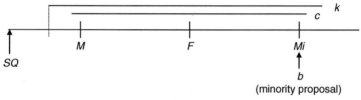

FIGURE A.2. Example of k & $c > |M - Mi|$: Leftward Status Quo.

of M, there are conditions under which no preemptive proposal by M will be worth the cost of its consideration. In such cases, the majority will prefer to let policy move far from its ideal point, perhaps even to Mi, rather than make an offer.

To see this, consider the example laid out in Figure A.2 with a far-left status quo. As before, under our normal assumptions, with both c and k smaller than $|M - Mi|$, this status quo would have seen a preemptive proposal by M, moving to NO_L (again see Figure 3.6a). In the present example, M could make a preemptive proposal at his ideal point, warding off a counterproposal by Mi that would pass. The problem is that this proposal is not enough of an improvement over the alternative policy outcome – letting Mi move policy to her ideal point – to offset the consideration cost c, because as we can see in Figure A.2, c is larger than the distance between M and Mi. So, here, M chooses the best of two bad options and allows policy to move to the other side of the policy space.

Note, however, that this is not true for *all* status quos to the left of M. For example, a status quo that is just slightly to the left of $F - k/2$ will not change, because the distance between the status quo and Mi is still smaller than k. Thus, the policy improvement for Mi is not sufficient to offset the cost of getting a proposal considered, even if that proposal can pass right at Mi. This observation marks a significant shift in the calculation of important intervals in our model, as hinted at by our change in terminology, using $F - k/2$ rather than NO_L. When both c and k grow

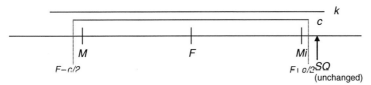

FIGURE A.3. Example of k & $c > |M - Mi|$: Rightward Status Quo.

larger than $|M - Mi|$, the no-offer zones for both actors become more complicated and no longer simply mirror the size of the consideration cost centered on F.

This discrepancy also shows up for status quos on the minority side of the space. For example, Figure A.3 shows a status quo that falls just to the right of $F + c/2$. Under our normal assumptions, the equilibrium outcome would have been a proposal by M, just to the left of $F - c/2$ (see Figure 3.6c). However, in this case, the maximum policy improvement for M – the distance between the status quo and M – is smaller than his consideration cost, c. Thus, even though the status quo does not fall within the F to $F + c/2$ interval, it is still effectively in the majority no-offer zone under these relaxed assumptions.

Working to present exhaustive equilibrium outcomes based on the new no-offer zones under these relaxed assumptions would be laborious and, we think, without significant theoretical advantage. Most of the results, and the basic intuition of the model, remain unchanged.

Allowing Mi to Move
Similarly, we could spend pages exploring variations of the model based on different spacing scenarios of M, F, and Mi. However, we see little substantive, real-world demand for such an exhaustive exercise. But there is one important exception: the movement of Mi. As we have already discussed, in our view, the analog for the minority proposer is best thought of as any opposition actor who might try to assert some agenda influence that competes with the majority party's plans. Thus, it makes sense to consider briefly how the model changes if Mi's ideal point shifts.

Holding all else constant, no matter how far Mi moves outward away from F (i.e., as the minority party becomes more extreme), the outcomes of the model do not change for any status quo. The same is true as Mi begins to move closer to F. However, once Mi moves closer than $F + k/2$ (i.e., crosses the NO_R point in our standard model), the minority no-offer zone begins to *grow*, and the majority policy advantage actually increases.

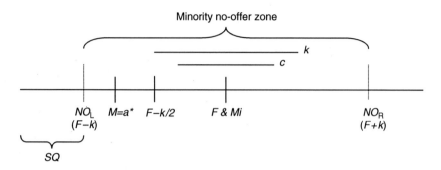

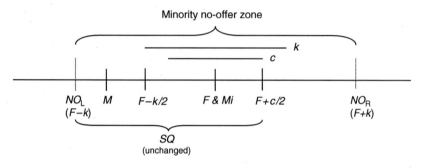

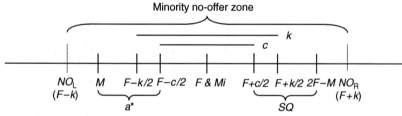

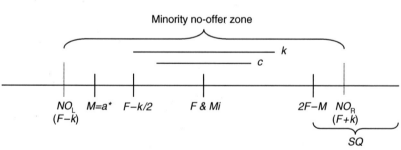

FIGURE A.4. (a) $F = Mi$: $SQ < NO_L$, (b) $F = Mi$: $NO_L < SQ < F + c/2$, (c) $F = Mi$: $F + c/2 < SQ < 2F - M$, and (d) $F = Mi$: $2F - M < SQ < 2F - M$.

To see this at its extreme, consider the scenario presented in panels a through d of Figure A.4, in which F and Mi share an ideal point. (One can think of this as the hypothetical case in which the chamber median is the "minority proposer," though F could in this example be a maverick majority party senator.)[1] The first thing to notice is that the minority no-offer zone has doubled in size, to $2k$ centered on F. This has favorable implications for the majority proposer as compared with our normal assumption that Mi is equidistant from F. For the farthest-left status quos, shown in Figure A.4a, the majority still will make a preemptive proposal. However, notice that in Figure A.4a, this region of status quos begins at $F - k$ as compared with $F - k/2$ in the normal model (cf. Figure 3.6a). Thus, all of the status quos between those two points are now protected, which is preferable for the majority actor. The second difference for these far-left status quos is that M can move them to his ideal point (signified by a^* in Figure A.4a), as opposed to $F - k/2$ in the normal model. Because of the consideration cost, he would still prefer to have some of these status quos remain in place rather than pay the consideration cost to move them to his ideal point, but the option to move them to M at least maximizes his pure policy utility.

Moving right, the next interval of status quos, shown in Figure A.4b, runs from NO_L to $F + c/2$. All of the status quos in this interval remain unchanged. This is the same as in the normal model, in terms of the *labels* that bookend the interval (cf. Figure 3.6b). However, as already noted, here, NO_L has moved left by $k/2$, which creates protection for more majority party favorable status quos.

Next we see in Figure A.4c that some of the status quos in the interval between $F + c/2$ to $2F - M$ yield the same outcomes as the normal model; that is, for all of the status quos between $F + c/2$ and $F + k/2$ the majority proposes a^* that is exactly as far to the left of F as the status quo is to the right of F (cf. Figure 3.6c). M does the same for status quos in the rest of this interval, from $F + k/2$ to $2F - M$, but that is a departure from the normal model. Under our normal assumptions, these status quos can be moved only to the left edge of the minority no-offer zone, which is at $F - k/2$. Thus, if the minority proposer is the floor median, the majority proposer can move policy closer to his ideal point than under our normal assumptions.

The same is true for status quos in our farthest-right interval, running to the right of $2F - M$, as shown in Figure A.4d. Like the second part of

---

[1] This example also relies on the assumption that $k > |F - M|$.

the preceding interval, under our normal assumptions all of these status quos would be moved by majority proposal to $F - k/2$ (i.e., the normal NO_L; cf. Figure 3.6d). However, in the present scenario, the majority actor will instead move these status quos to a^* at his ideal point, thereby maximizing his policy utility in each case.

In sum, if proposal (or counterproposal) power is assumed to fall in the hands of a moderate member of the legislature, it does not undermine the majority advantage revealed in our bargaining model; instead, that advantage is enhanced. This result is a function of the fact that, although moderate legislators may suffer under a majority policy bias, they suffer less than partisans on the other side of the legislative space, and thus have less incentive to bear the costs of pushing legislation to final consideration.

Appendix B

Last Actions and Coding Amendment Disposition

The list in this appendix shows how we have grouped different "last actions" into the categories we use for our *Disposition* variable. Under the header for each category, we list last actions that we have grouped into that category.

Unfortunately, the phrasing used to report this information on Thomas – and hence in our dataset – is not uniform, either across or within Congresses. For example, if the last action is the tabling of the amendment, this action might be described either as "Fell when tabled" or as "Motion to table amendment agreed to in Senate by yea–nay vote." In the following list we have standardized such alternative descriptions of the same action.

In our coding we have made some subjective decisions, which we discuss briefly. First, we have separate Modified and Adopted categories, rather than a single Adopted category, in order to easily distinguish these categories from one another, although we think it probably makes little sense to distinguish them for many purposes. One situation in which distinguishing them might be useful is the study of roll call votes on amendment adoption. Because our data include only the last action on an amendment, and modification comes after adoption, it is possible for amendments in the Modified category that there was a roll call vote on adoption that is not included in our data.

The "Killed by Procedure" label may in some cases be misleading, inasmuch as it is not entirely clear in every such case whether the procedure listed as the last action actually killed the amendment, as opposed to being an action that did not kill it but that turned out to be the last action taken. For most amendments in this category, it is apparent that this concern is not applicable and that the procedure did kill the bill, which is why we have labeled it as we have. In every case, moreover, the category captures the fact that an introduced amendment did not make it to a vote on adoption, which is our primary interest. Nonetheless, the wide variety of procedures that constituted the Senate's final action on an amendment suggests interesting directions for additional research.

We group "Submitted" and "Withdrawn" together because each marks an instance in which the amendment sponsor killed his or her own amendment. In the case of submission, the sponsor essentially reserves the right to call up an amendment but never does so. Indeed, in many cases, submitted amendments state no purpose and appear to be little more than placeholders giving the sponsor the prerogative of introducing an amendment later. It seems most reasonable to us to treat cases in which the sponsor withdrew the amendment after having called it up as being akin to cases in which the amendment was submitted but never called up. There are few withdrawals in our data; overwhelmingly, amendments in our Submitted/Withdrawn category were submitted but never called up for consideration.

Disposition Categories

Amendment Modified after Adoption
- Amendment as previously agreed to, was modified by unanimous consent
- Amendment as previously agreed to, was further modified by unanimous consent

Amendment Adopted
- Agreed to by yea–nay vote
- Senate amendment agreed to

Amendment Rejected
- Fell when rejected
- Senate amendment not agreed to
- Senate rejected the motion to reconsider the vote by which the amendment was rejected

Amendment Killed by Procedure
- The amendment was tabled
- The amendment fell when the committee amendment was tabled

- The motion to reconsider the motion to table the amendment was rejected
- The motion to table the motion to reconsider was agreed to
- The amendment fell when the motion to table the motion to postpone the motion to proceed to the consideration of the conference report was agreed to
- The amendment was referred to a committee
- The amendment fell when the motion to refer was tabled
- The amendment fell when the motion to recommit was agreed to
- The amendment fell when the bill was recommitted
- The amendment fell when the motion to recommit was withdrawn
- The amendment fell when the motion to recommit was tabled
- The amendment fell when the motion to recommit was ruled out of order
- The amendment fell when the motion to commit was withdrawn
- The amendment fell when the motion to commit with instructions was tabled
- The amendment was determined nongermane by yea–nay vote
- The amendment was ruled out of order by the chair
- The amendment fell when the bill was ruled out of order
- The amendment fell when point of order was sustained against the bill
- The amendment was determined out of order by yea–nay vote
- The amendment fell when the point of order was sustained
- The motion to waive the Budget Act with respect to the amendment was rejected
- The point of order that the amendment violates the Constitution was agreed to
- The amendment fell when cloture was invoked
- The amendment fell when cloture was not invoked
- Motion to suspend Rule XXII to permit the consideration of the amendment was not agreed to in Senate
- Second cloture motion on the amendment was not invoked in the Senate

Amendment Considered
- The amendment was proposed on the floor
- The motion to table was rejected in the Senate

Amendment Submitted/Withdrawn
- A Senate amendment was submitted

- The amendment fell when withdrawn
- The proposed amendment by unanimous consent was withdrawn in Senate
- Previous action on the amendment was vitiated by unanimous consent
- Senate vitiated previous adoption by voice vote
- Adoption was vitiated by unanimous consent
- The Senate agreed to a motion to strike the amendment that had been agreed to previously
- All Senate action on the amendment for September 9 was vitiated by unanimous consent
- The amendment fell when its provisions were accepted as a modification of the committee substitute amendment by unanimous consent

Indeterminate Last Action
- The sponsor withdrew appeal regarding the ruling of the chair
- The amendment was determined germane by yea–nay vote
- The amendment is considered an amendment in the first degree
- The amendment was considered a first-degree amendment by unanimous consent
- The committee substitute was modified to incorporate the language of the amendment
- The amendment was incorporated into another amendment by unanimous consent
- The amendment was incorporated into the modification of another amendment
- The amendment was modified by unanimous consent
- Cloture motion on the amendment was rendered moot in Senate
- Division was withdrawn in Senate
- The amendment fell when it was rendered moot
- The amendment fell when another amendment was withdrawn
- A motion to reconsider was made in Senate
- A motion to reconsider the vote by which the amendment was agreed to was entered in Senate
- A motion to strike the language of the amendment was rejected in Senate by yea–nay vote

Works Cited

Adler, E. Scott, and John Wilkerson. 1989–1998. *Congressional Bills Project: 1989–1998*, NSF 00880066 and 00880061. Online at http://www.congressionalbills.org/index.html.

Ainsworth, Scott, and Marcus Flathman. 1995. "Unanimous Consent Agreements as Leadership Tools." *Legislative Studies Quarterly* 20: 177–195.

Alchian, Armen A., and Harold Demsetz. 1972. "Production, Information Costs, and Economic Organization." *American Economic Review* 62(5): 777–795.

Aldrich, John, and David W. Rohde. 1998. "Measuring Conditional Party Government." Paper presented at the annual meeting of the Midwest Political Science Association, Chicago, April 23–25.

2000. "The Republican Revolution and the House Appropriations Committee." *Journal of Politics* 62: 1–33.

2001. "The Logic of Conditional Party Government: Revisiting the Electoral Connection." In Lawrence Dodd and Bruce Oppenheimer, eds., *Congress Reconsidered*, 7th ed. Washington, DC: Congressional Quarterly Press, pp. 269–292.

2005. "Congressional Committees in a Continuing Partisan Era." In Lawrence Dodd and Bruce Oppenheimer, eds., *Congress Reconsidered*, 8th ed. Washington, DC: Congressional Quarterly Press, pp. 249–270.

Alexander, De Alva Stanwood. 1916. *History and Procedure of the House of Representatives*. Boston: Houghton Mifflin.

Ames, Barry. 2001. *The Deadlock of Democracy in Brazil: Interests, Identities, and Institutions in Comparative Politics*. Ann Arbor: University of Michigan Press.

Amorim Neto, Octavio, Gary W. Cox, and Mathew D. McCubbins. 2003. "Agenda Power in Brazil's Câmara dos Deputados, 1989 to 1998." *World Politics* 55: 550–578.

Andrews, Edmund L. 2006a. "Estate Tax Showdown Is Splitting the G.O.P." *New York Times*, June 7.

2006b. "G.O.P. Fails in Attempt to Repeal Estate Tax." *New York Times*, June 9.

Arnold, R. Douglas. 1990. *The Logic of Congressional Action.* New Haven, CT: Yale University Press.

Bach, Stanley. 1989. "Points of Order and Appeals in the Senate." *CRS Report for Congress,* Order Code 89–69 RCO.

     1991. "The Senate's Compliance with Its Legislative Rules: The Appeal of Order." *Congress and the Presidency* 18: 77–92.

Bargen, Andrew. 2003. "Senators, Status Quos, and Agenda Setting: A Spatial Story of Policy Making in the U.S. Senate, 1953–1996." Paper presented at the annual meeting of the American Political Science Association, Philadelphia, August 27–31.

     2004. "Party Power in the U.S. Senate: Shaping the Ideological Content of the Legislative Agenda." Paper presented at the annual meeting of the American Political Science Association, Chicago, September 2–5.

Bawn, Kathy, and Gregory Koger. 2008. "Effort, Intensity, and Position Taking: Reconsidering Obstruction in the Pre-Cloture Senate." *Journal of Theoretical Politics* 20: 67–92.

Beeman, Richard R. 1968. "Unlimited Debate in the Senate: The First Phase." *Political Science Quarterly* 83(3): 419–434.

Bell, Lauren. 2002. "Senatorial Discourtesy: The Senate's Use of Delay to Shape the Federal Judiciary." *Political Research Quarterly* 55: 589–607.

Beth, Richard. 1995. "What We Don't Know about Filibusters." Paper presented at the annual meeting of the Western Political Science Association, Portland, OR, March 20–23.

Beth, Richard S. 2002. "Motions to Proceed to Consider in the Senate: Who Offers Them?" Congressional Research Service Report No. RS21255, Washington, DC.

     2003. "How Unanimous Consent Agreements Regulate Senate Floor Action." Congressional Research Service Report No. RS20594, Washington, DC

Beth, Richard S., and Stanley Bach. 2003. "Filibusters and Cloture in the Senate." Congressional Research Service Report No. RL30360, Washington, DC.

Beth, Richard S., Valerie Heitshusen, Bill Henniff, Jr., and Elizabeth Rybicki. 2009. "Leadership Tools for Managing the U.S. Senate." Paper presented at the annual meeting of the American Political Science Association, Toronto, September 3–6.

Binder, Sarah. 1996. "The Partisan Basis of Procedural Choice: Allocating Parliamentary Rights in the House, 1789–1991." *American Political Science Review* 90: 8–20.

Binder, Sarah A. 1997. *Minority Rights, Majority Rule: Partisanship and the Development of Congress.* New York: Cambridge University Press.

     1999. "The Dynamics of Legislative Gridlock." *American Political Science Review* 93: 519–533.

     2003. *Stalemate: Causes and Consequences of Legislative Gridlock.* Washington, DC: Brookings Institution Press.

     2008. "Taking the Measure of Congress: Response to Chiou and Rothenberg." *Political Analysis* 16: 213–225.

Binder, Sarah A., and Forrest Maltzman. 2002. "Senatorial Delay in Confirming Federal Judges, 1947–1998." *American Journal of Political Science* 46: 190–199.

Binder, Sarah, and Steven S. Smith. 1997. *Politics or Principle: Filibustering in the U.S. Senate*. Washington DC: Brookings Institute Press.

Black, Duncan. 1958. *The Theory of Committee and Elections*. Cambridge: Cambridge University Press.

Bradbury, Erin M., Ryan A. Davidson, and C. Lawrence Evans. 2008. "The Senate Whip System: An Exploration." In Nathan Monroe, Jason Roberts, and David Rohde, eds., *Why Not Parties? Party Effects in the United States Senate*. Chicago: University of Chicago Press, pp. 73–99.

Brady, David W., Richard Brody, and David Epstein. 1989. "Heterogeneous Parties and Political Organization: The US Senate: 1880–1920." *Legislative Studies Quarterly* 14: 205–223.

Brady, David W., and Mathew D. McCubbins. 2002. "Party, Process, and Political Change: New Perspectives on the History of Congress." In David W. Brady and Mathew D. McCubbins, eds., *Party, Process, and Political Change in Congress: New Perspectives on the History of Congress*. Stanford, CA: Stanford University Press, pp. 1–16.

Brady, David W., and Craig Volden. 2006. *Revolving Gridlock: Politics and Policy from Carter to George W. Bush*, 2d ed. Boulder, CO: Westview.

Bullock, Charles E. III, and David W. Brady. 1983. "Party, Constituency, and Roll-Call Voting in the US Senate." *Legislative Studies Quarterly* 8: 29–43.

Burdette, Franklin L. 1940. *Filibustering in the Senate*. Princeton, NJ: Princeton University Press.

Cameron, Charles M. 2000. *Veto Bargaining: Presidents and the Politics of Negative Power*. New York: Cambridge University Press.

Campbell, Andrea C. 2001. "Party Government in the United States Senate." Ph.D. dissertation, University of California, San Diego.

2004. "Fighting Fire with Fire: Strategic Amending in the 105th Senate." Paper presented at the annual meeting of the American Political Science Association, Chicago, April 15–18.

Campbell, Andrea C., Gary W. Cox, and Mathew D. McCubbins. 2002. "Agenda Power in the U.S. Senate, 1877 to 1986." In David Brady and Mathew D. McCubbins, eds., *Party, Process, and Political Change in Congress: New Perspectives on the History of Congress*. Stanford, CA: Stanford University Press, pp. 146–165.

Carr, Thomas P. 2005. "Preparation for Senate Committee Markup." *CRS Report for Congress*, Order Code 95–243 GOV.

Chiou, Fang-Yi, and Lawrence S. Rothenberg. 2003. "When Pivotal Politics Meets Partisan Politics." *American Journal of Political Science* 47: 503–522.

2006. "Preferences, Parties, and Legislative Productivity." *American Politics Research* 34: 705–731.

2008a. "Comparing Legislators and Legislatures: The Dynamics of Legislative Gridlock Reconsidered." *Political Analysis* 16: 197–212.

2008b. "The Search for Comparability: Response to Binder." *Political Analysis* 16: 226–233.

Clausen, Aage R., and Richard B. Cheney. 1970. "A Comparative Analysis of Senate House Voting on Economic and Welfare Policy: 1953–1964." *American Political Science Review* 64: 138–152.

Coase, Ronald H. 1937. "The Nature of the Firm." *Economica*, New Series 4(16): 386–405.

Cooper, Joseph, and David W. Brady. 1981. "Institutional Context and Leadership Style: The House from Cannon to Rayburn." *American Political Science Review* 75: 411–425.

Cox, Gary W., and Mathew D. McCubbins. 1993. *Legislative Leviathan: Party Government in the House.* Berkeley: University of California Press.

    1994. "Bonding, Structure, and the Stability of Political Parties: Party Government in the House." *Legislative Studies Quarterly* 19: 215–231.

    2000. "The Institutional Determinants of Economic Policy Outcomes." In Stephen Haggard and Mathew D. McCubbins, eds., *Presidents, Parliaments, and Policy.* New York: Cambridge University Press, pp. 21–63.

    2002. "Agenda Power in the U.S. House of Representatives." In David Brady and Mathew D. McCubbins, eds., *Party, Process, and Political Change in Congress: New Perspectives on the History of Congress.* Stanford, CA: Stanford University Press, pp. 107–145.

    2005. *Setting the Agenda: Responsible Party Government in the U.S. House of Representatives.* New York: Cambridge University Press.

Cox, Gary W., Thad Kousser, and Mathew D. McCubbins. 2005. "What Polarizes Parties? Preference and Agenda Control in American State Legislatures." Paper presented at the annual meeting of the American Political Science Association, Washington, DC., September 1–4.

CQ Weekly. 2006. "Senate Vote 170: Central America Trade Liberalization." *CQ Weekly* (January 9): 112.

    2007. "Filling the Appropriations Bill's Amendment Tree." *CQ Weekly* (February 12): 488.

Crespin, Michael H., and Charles Finocchiaro. 2008. "Distributive and Partisan Politics in the U.S. Senate: An Exploration of Earmarks, 1996–2005." In Nathan Monroe, Jason Roberts, and David Rohde, eds., *Why Not Parties? Party Effects in the United States Senate* Chicago: University of Chicago Press, pp. 229–252.

Davidson, Roger H. 1985. "Senate Leaders: Janitors for an Untidy Chamber?" In Lawrence C. Dodd and Bruce I. Oppenheimer, eds., *Congress Reconsidered*, 3d ed. Washington, DC: Congressional Quarterly Press, pp. 225–252.

    1989a. "The Senate: If Everyone Leads, Who Follows?" In Lawrence C. Dodd and Bruce I. Oppenheimer, eds., *Congress Reconsidered*, 4th ed. Washington, DC: Congressional Quarterly Press, pp. 275–306.

    2001. "Senate Floor Deliberation: A Preliminary Inquiry." In Nicol C. Rae and Colton C. Campbell, eds., *The Contentious Senate.* Lanham, MD: Rowman & Littlefield, pp. 21–42.

Davidson, Roger H., Walter J. Oleszek, and Frances E. Lee. 2008. *Congress and Its Members*, 11th ed. Washington, DC: Congressional Quarterly Press.

Demsetz, Harold. 1968. "The Cost of Transacting." *Quarterly Journal of Economics* 82: 33–55.

Den Hartog, Christopher F. 2004. "Limited Party Government and the Majority Party Revolution in the Nineteenth-Century House." Ph.D. dissertation, University of California, San Diego.

Den Hartog, Chris, and Nathan W. Monroe. 2008a. "The Value of Majority Status: The Effect of Jeffords's Switch on Asset Prices of Republican and Democratic Firms." *Legislative Studies Quarterly* 33: 63–84.

2008b. "Agenda Influence and Tabling Motions in the U.S. Senate." In Nathan W. Monroe, Jason R. Roberts, and David W. Rohde, eds., *Why Not Parties? Party Effects in the United States Senate.* Chicago: University of Chicago Press, pp. 142–158.

2009. "Partisan Support for Chairs' Rulings in the House and Senate." Paper presented at the Bicameralism Conference, Vanderbilt University, October 23–24.

Dewar, Helen. 2004a. "For Specter, a Showdown over Judiciary Chairmanship; GOP Senator Battles Conservatives Angered by His Comments," *Washington Post,* November 15.

2004b. "Specter Panel Backs Specter; GOP Senators Elicit Pledge Not to Block Antiabortion Judges." *Washington Post,* November 19.

Dion, Douglas. 1997. *Turning the Legislative Thumbscrew: Minority Rights and Procedural Change in Legislative Politics.* Ann Arbor: University of Michigan Press.

Downs, Anthony. 1957. *An Economic Theory of Democracy.* New York: Harper and Row.

Eisele, Albert. 2004. "Turmoil in New Senate," *The Hill,* November 10.

Endersby, James W., and Karen M. McCurdy. 1996. "Committee Assignments in the U.S. Senate." *Legislative Studies Quarterly* 21: 219–233.

Evans, C. Lawrence. 1991. *Leadership in Committee: A Comparative Analysis of Leadership Behavior in the U.S. Senate.* Ann Arbor: University of Michigan Press.

1999. "Legislative Structure: Rules, Precedents, and Jurisdictions." *Legislative Studies Quarterly* 24: 605–624.

2001. "Committees, Leaders, and Message Politics." In Lawrence C. Dodd and Bruce I. Oppenheimer, eds., *Congress Reconsidered,* 6th ed. Washington, DC: Congressional Quarterly Press, pp. 217–244.

Evans, C. Lawrence, and Daniel Lipinski. 2005. "Obstruction and Leadership in the U.S. Senate." In Lawrence C. Dodd and Bruce I. Oppenheimer, eds., *Congress Reconsidered,* 8th ed. Washington, DC: Congressional Quarterly Press, pp. 227–248.

Evans, C. Lawrence, and Walter J. Oleszek. 1997. *Congress under Fire.* Boston: Houghton Mifflin.

2001. "Message Politics and Senate Procedure." In Colton Campbell and Nicol Rae, eds., *The Contentious Senate.* Landham, MD: Rowman and Littlefield.

Faler, Brian. 2009. "Alan Frumin May Rise From Obscurity to Craft Senate Health Bill." Bloomberg.com., August 12.

Fenno, Richard F., Jr. 1966. *The Power of the Purse: Appropriations Politics in Congress.* Boston: Little, Brown.

Figueiredo, Argelina C., and Fernando Limongi. 2000. "Presidential Power, Legislative Organization, and Party Behavior in Brazil." *Comparative Politics* 32: 151–170.

Fink, Evelyn C., and Brian D. Humes. 1996. "Party Conflict and Rules Changes in the United States House of Representatives, 1st–104th Congresses." Revised version of paper presented at the 1996 annual meeting of the American Political Science Association, San Francisco, August 29–September 1.

Follett, Mary Parker. 1896. *The Speaker of the House of Representatives.* New York: Longmans, Green.

Frisch, Scott, and Sean Kelly. 2004. "Democratic Leaders and Democratic Committee Requests and Assignments in the U.S. Senate." Paper presented at the annual meeting of the American Political Science Association, Chicago., September 2–5.

Frumin, Alan S., and Floyd M. Riddick. 1992. *Riddick's Senate Procedure: Precedents and Practices.* U.S. Senate Document 101–28.

Gailmard, Sean, and Jeffrey A. Jenkins. 2007. "Negative Agenda Control in the Senate and House: Fingerprints of Majority Party Power." *Journal of Politics* 69: 689–700.

2008a. "Examining Minority Party Power in the Senate and House." In Nathan Monroe, Jason Roberts, and David Rohde, eds., *Why Not Parties? Party Effects in the United States Senate.* Chicago: University of Chicago Press, pp. 181–197.

2008b . "Coalition Size in the Senate and House of Representatives." Paper presented at the annual meeting of the Midwest Political Science Association, Chicago , April 2–5.

Galloway, George B. 1976. *History of the House of Representatives,* 2d ed. New York: Thomas Y. Crowell.

Gilligan, Thomas W., and Keith Krehbiel. 1990. "Organization of Informative Committees by a Rational Legislature." *American Journal of Political Science* 34: 531–564.

Gold, Martin B. 2004. *Senate Procedure and Practice.* Lanham, MD: Rowman & Littlefield.

2008. *Senate Procedure and Practice,* 2d ed. Lanham, MD: Rowman & Littlefield.

Goodman, Craig. 2006. "Partisan Agenda Control in the United States Senate: The Strategic Use of Motions to Table." Unpublished manuscript, Texas Tech University.

Groseclose, Tim, and James M. Snyder, Jr. 1996. "Buying Supermajorities." *American Political Science Review* 90: 303–315.

Hager, George. 1998. "GOP Tax Cut May Die in Senate; Hill Leaders Say $80 Billion Package Needs a Trim to Survive; Little Optimism for Tax Cut Measure." *Washington Post,* October 1.

Heitshusen, Valerie. 2006. "Points of Order, Rulings, and Appeals in the Senate." *CRS Report for Congress,* Order Code 98–306 GOV.

Hershey, Marjorie R. 2007. *Party Politics in America,* 12th ed. White Plains, NY: Pearson Longman Press.

Hosansky, David. 1997. "Education: Expansion of 'Education IRAs' Approved by Ways and Means." *CQ Weekly Online* (October 11): 2478, http://library.cqpress.com/cqweekly/WR19971011-40SCHOOLTAXoo1 (accessed September 9, 2009).

1998a. "Taxes: GOP Seeks Pre-Election Vote on a Tax Cut Package Despite Long Odds." *CQ Weekly Online* (September 12): 2401, http://library.cqpress.com/cqweekly/WR19980912-36TAXESoo1 (accessed June 17, 2009).

1998b. "Taxes: Tax Bill's Chances Fade as Senate Democrats Savor an Opportunity to Unite." *CQ Weekly Online* (September 26): 2579–2580. http://library.cqpress.com/cqweekly/WR19980926-38TAXES001 (accessed June 17, 2009).

Huitt, Ralph K. 1961. "Democratic Party Leadership in the Senate." *American Political Science Review* 55(2): 333–344.

Hulse, Carl. 2009. "Battle Brewing over Reconciliation, Which Is Anything but That." *New York Times* online ed., March 29.

Jenkins, Jeffrey A., and Timothy Nokken. 2008 . "Partisanship, the Electoral Connection, and Lame-Duke Sessions of Congress, 1877–2006." *Journal of Politics* 70 : 450– 465.

Jones, Charles O. 1968. "Joseph G. Cannon and Howard W. Smith: An Essay on the Limits of Leadership in the House of Representatives." *Journal of Politics* 30: 617–646.

Keith, Robert. 1977. "The Use of Unanimous Consent in the Senate." In U.S. Senate, *Committee and Senate Procedures*, 94th Cong., 2nd Sess. Washington, DC: Government Printing Office.

2008a. "Introduction to the Federal Budget Process." *CRS Report for Congress*, Order Code 98–721 GOV.

2008b. "The Budget Reconciliation Process: The Senate's Byrd Rule." *CRS Report for Congress*, Order Code RL30862.

Kiewiet, D. Roderick, and Mathew D. McCubbins. 1988. " Presidential Influence on Congressional Appropriations Decisions." *American Journal of Political Science* 65: 131–143.

1991. *The Logic of Delegation: Congressional Parties and the Appropriations Process*. Chicago: University of Chicago Press.

Kim, Henry A. 2005. "Partisan Deadlocks and Agenda-Setting in American State Legislatures." Paper presented at the annual meeting of the Midwest Political Science Association, Chicago, April 9–11.

King, Aaron S., Frank J. Orlando, and David W. Rohde. 2010. "Beyond Motions to Table: Exploring the Procedural Toolkit of the Majority Party in the United States Senate." Paper presented at the annual meeting of the Midwest Political Science Association, Chicago, April 22–25.

King, Gary, Michael Tomz, and Jason Wittenberg. 2000. "Making the Most of Statistical Analyses: Improving Interpretation and Presentation." *American Journal of Political Science* 44: 347–361.

Kirchhoff, Sue. 1998. "Education: Senate Agrees on Debate Terms for Savings Accounts Bill." *CQ Weekly Online* (March 28): 824. http://library.cqpress.com/cqweekly/WR19980328–13EDUCATION001 (accessed June 17, 2009).

Kloha, Philip. 2006. "Majority Party Reliability: The Vital Role of Party in the Structure and Composition of Legislative Committees." Ph.D. dissertation, Michigan State University.

Koger, Gregory. 2003. "The Majoritarian Senate: 'Nuclear Options' in Historical Perspective." Paper presented at the annual meeting of the American Political Science Association, Philadelphia, August 27–31.

2004. "Pivots for Sale: Transaction Costs, Endogenous Rules, and Pivotal Politics." Paper presented at the annual meeting of the American Political Science Association, Chicago, September 2.

2006. "Cloture Reform and Party Government in the Senate, 1918 to 1925." *Journal of Politics* 68: 708–719.

2007. "Filibuster Reform in the Senate." In David Brady and Mathew McCubbins, eds., *Process, Party, and Policymaking: Further New Perspectives on the History of Congress.* Stanford, CA: Stanford University Press, pp. 205–225.

2008. "Filibustering and Majority Rule in the Senate: The Contest over Judicial Nominations, 2003–2005." In Nathan Monroe, Jason Roberts, and David Rohde, eds., *Why Not Parties? Party Effects in the United States Senate.* Chicago: University of Chicago Press, pp. 159–177.

2010. *Filibustering: A Political History of Obstruction in the House and Senate.* Chicago: University of Chicago Press.

Koger, Gregory, and James Fowler. 2006. "Parties and Agenda Setting in the Senate, 1973–1998." Paper presented at the Conference on Party Effects in the U.S. Senate, University of Minnesota, September 29–30..

Krauss, Clifford. 1992. "Senate Passes Bill to Force States to Make Voter Registration Easier." *New York Times,* May 21.

Krehbiel, Keith. 1986. "Unanimous Consent Agreements: Going Along in the Senate." *Journal of Politics* 48(3): 541–64.

1991. *Information and Legislative Organization.* Ann Arbor: University of Michigan Press.

1993. "Where's the Party?" *British Journal of Political Science* 23: 235–266.

1998. *Pivotal Politics.* Chicago: University of Chicago Press.

Krutz, Glen S. 2005. "Issues and Institutions: 'Winnowing' in the U.S. Congress." *American Journal of Political Science* 49: 313–326.

Lee, Frances E. 2000. "Senate Representation and Coalition Building in Distributive Politics." *American Political Science Review* 94: 59–72.

2009. Beyond Ideology: Politics, Principles, and Partisanship in the U.S. Senate. Chicago: University of Chicago Press.

Lehnen, Robert G. 1967. "Behavior on the Senate Floor: An Analysis of Debate in the U.S. Senate." *Midwest Journal of Political Science* 11: 505–521.

Lijphart, Arend. 1971. "Comparative Politics and the Comparative Method." *American Political Science Review* 65(3): 682–693.

Linz, Juan J. 1994. "Presidential or Parliamentary Democracy: Does It Make a Difference?" In Juan J. Linz and Arturo Valenzuela, eds., *The Failure of Presidential Democracy* Baltimore: Johns Hopkins University Press, pp. 3–89.

Madonna, Anthony. 2008. "Institutions and Coalition Formation: Revisiting the Effects of Rule XXII on Winning Coalition Sizes in the U.S. Senate." Unpublished paper, University of Georgia.

2009. "The Presiding Officer and Parliamentarian: Moving Towards a Non-Partisan Interpretation of Rules and Precedent in the U.S. Senate." Unpublished paper, University of Georgia. .

Magar, Eric. 2001. "Bully Pulpits: Posturing, Bargaining, and Polarization in the Legislative Process of the Americas." Ph.D. dissertation, University of California, San Diego.

Mainwaring, Scott, and Matthew Soberg Shugart. 1997. *Presidentialism and Democracy in Latin America.* Cambridge: Cambridge University Press.

Marshall, Bryan W., Brandon C. Prins, and David W. Rohde. 1999. "Fighting Fire with Water: Partisan Procedural Strategies and the Senate Appropriations Committee." *Congress and the Presidency* 26: 114–132.

Matthews, Donald R. 1960. *US Senators and Their World*. Chapel Hill: University of North Carolina Press.

Mayhew, David R. 1974. *Congress: The Electoral Connection*. New Haven, CT: Yale University Press.

McConachie, Lauros G. 1974 [1898]. *Congressional Committees*. New York: B. Franklin [reprint].

McKelvey, Richard. 1976. "Intransitivities in Multidimensional Voting Models and Some Implications for Agenda Control." *Journal of Economic Theory* 12: 472–482.

Monroe, Nathan W., and Gregory Robinson. 2008. "Do Restrictive Rules Produce Non-Median Outcomes? Evidence from the 101st–106th Congresses." *Journal of Politics* 70: 217–231.

Moore, Michael K., and Sue Thomas. 1991. "Explaining Legislative Success in the U.S. Senate: The Role of the Majority and Minority Parties." *Western Political Quarterly* 44: 959–970.

Murray, Shailagh, and Charles Babington. 2005. "GOP Agenda Shifts as Political Trials Grow; Katrina Puts Estate Tax Repeal on Ice." *Washington Post*, September 6.

2006. "Now Playing in Senate: A GOP Double Bill." *Washington Post*, September 6.

Nather, David, and Rachel Van Dongen. 2006a. "A Well-Courted Group of Senators." *CQ Weekly Online* (August 7): 2177. http://library.cqpress.com/cqweekly/weeklyreport109–000002355223 (accessed June 26, 2009).

2006b. "Frist Loses Estate Tax Showdown." *CQ Weekly Online* (August 7):2176–2178. http://library.cqpress.com/cqweekly/weeklyreport109–000002355217 (accessed June 26, 2009).

Newmyer, Tory. 2008. "Elections Spur Upheaval on Hill; Dingell–Waxman Brouhaha Awaits." *Roll Call*, November 6.

North, Douglass C. 1981. *Structure and Change in Economic History*. New York: W. W. Norton.

Norton, Stephen J. 2005. "CAFTA Squeaks Through in House Vote." *CQ Weekly* (August 1, 2005): 2111–2113.

Oleszek, Walter J. 2001a. *Congressional Procedures and the Policy Process*, 5th ed. Washington, DC: Congressional Quarterly Press.

2001b. "Senate Amendment Process: General Conditions and Principles." *CRS Report for Congress*, Order Code 98–707 GOV.

2004. *Congressional Procedures and the Policy Process*, 6th ed. Washington, DC: Congressional Quarterly Press.

2007. *Congressional Procedures and the Policy Process*, 7th ed. Washington, DC: Congressional Quarterly Press.

2011. *Congressional Procedures and the Policy Process*, 8th ed. Washington, DC: Congressional Quarterly Press.

Oppenheimer, Bruce I. 1985. "Changing Time Constraints on Congress: Historical Perspectives on the Use of Cloture." In Lawrence C. Dodd and Bruce I.

Oppenheimer, eds., *Congress Reconsidered*, 3rd ed. Washington, DC: Congressional Quarterly Press, pp. 393–413.

Oppenheimer, Bruce I., and Mark J. Hetherington. 2008. "Catch 22: Cloture, Energy Policy, and the Limits of Conditional Party Government." In Nathan Monroe, Jason Roberts, and David Rohde, eds., *Why Not Parties? Party Effects in the United States Senate.* Chicago: University of Chicago Press, pp. 198–228.

Ornstein, Norman J., Robert L. Peabody, and David W. Rohde. 1993. "The U.S. Senate in an Era of Change." In Lawrence C. Dodd and Bruce I. Oppenheimer, eds., *Congress Reconsidered*, 5th ed. Washington, DC: Congressional Quarterly Press, pp. 13–40.

Palmer, Betsy, and Stanley Bach. 2003. "The Amending Process in the Senate." *CRS Report for Congress*, Order Code 98-853 GOV.

Patterson, Samuel C. 1989. "Party Leadership in the U. S. Senate." *Legislative Studies Quarterly* 14(3): 393–413.

Pearson, Kathryn. 2008. "Party Loyalty and Discipline in the Individualistic Senate." In Nathan Monroe, Jason Roberts, and David Rohde, eds., *Why Not Parties? Party Effects in the United States Senate.* University of Chicago Press, pp. 100–120.

Peters, Ronald M., Jr. 1990. *The American Speakership: The Office in Historical Perspective*, 2d ed. Baltimore: Johns Hopkins University Press.

Pierce, Emily. 2008. "Byrd, Lieberman Await Their Fate." *Roll Call*, October 21.
    2010. "Reid Has Killed Most Filibusters; Leader on Pace to Set Record." *Roll Call*, April 12.

Plott, Charles R., and Michael E. Levine, 1977. "Agenda Influence and Its Implications." *Virginia Law Review* 63: 561–604.

Poole, Keith T., and Howard Rosenthal. 1997. *Congress: A Political-Economic History of Roll Call Voting.* New York: Oxford University Press.

Preston, Mark. 2004. "Frist Gains Committee Appointment Power." *Roll Call*, November 18.
    2005. "Parliamentarian Takes Quiet Role in Senate Tiff." *Roll Call*, May 12.

Rae, Nicol C., and Colton C. Campbell. 2001. "Party Politics and Ideology in the Contemporary Senate." In Nicol C. Rae and Colton C. Campbell, eds., *The Contentious Senate.* Lanham, MD: Rowman & Littlefield, pp. 1–20.

Rawls, W. Lee. 2009. *In Praise of Deadlock: How Partisan Struggle Makes Better Laws.* Baltimore: Johns Hopkins University Press.

Riker, William. 1982. *Liberalism Against Populism.* San Francisco: W. H. Freeman.

Ripley, Randall B. 1969. *Power in the Senate.* New York: St. Martin's Press.

Roberts, Jason M., and Lauren Cohen Bell. 2008. "Scoring the Senate: Scorecards, Parties, and Roll-Call Votes." In Nathan W. Monroe, Jason M. Roberts, and David W. Rohde, eds., *Why Not Parties? Party Effects in the United States Senate.* Chicago: University of Chicago Press, pp. 52–72.

Robinson, William A. 1930. *Thomas B. Reed: Parliamentarian.* New York: Dodd, Mead.

Rohde, David W. 1991. *Parties and Leaders in the Postreform House.* Chicago: University of Chicago Press.

1992. "Electoral Forces, Political Agendas, and Partisanship in the House and Senate." In Roger H. Davidson, ed., *The Postreform Congress*. New York: St. Martin's Press, pp. 27–47.

Rohde, David W., and Kenneth A. Shepsle. 2007. "Advising and Consenting in the 60-Vote Senate: Strategic Appointments to the Supreme Court." *Journal of Politics* 69: 664–677.

Rosenbaum, Davis E. 2005. "True to Ritual, House Votes for Full Repeal of Estate Tax." *New York Times*, April 14.

Rubin, Alissa J. 1994. "Finance Chairman's Bill Outline Becomes Bipartisan Flash Point." *CQ Weekly Online* (June 11): 1525.

Rubinstein, Ariel. 1982. "Perfect Equilibrium in a Bargaining Model." *Econometrica* 50: 97–109.

Rundquist, Paul S. 2003. "Senate Rule XIV Procedures for Placing Measures Directly on the Senate Calendar." Congressional Research Service Report No. 98-389. Washington, DC.

Sartori, Anne E. 2003. "An Estimator for Some Binary Outcome Selection Models Without Exclusion Restrictions." *Political Analysis* 11: 111–138.

Sartori, Giovanni. 1994. "Neither Presidentialism nor Parliamentarism." In Juan J. Linz and Arturo Valenzuela, eds., *The Failure of Presidential Democracy*. Baltimore: Johns Hopkins University Press, pp. 106–118.

Saturno, James V. 2003. "How Measures Are Brought to the Senate Floor: A Brief Introduction." *CRS Report for Congress*, Order Code RS20668.

    2008. "Points of Order in the Congressional Budget Process." *CRS Report for Congress*, Order Code 97-865.

Schatz, Joseph J. 2005. "Estate Tax Battle Awaits Senate's Return." *CQ Weekly Online* (August 8): 2189. http://library.cqpress.com/cqweekly/weekly-report109-000001814757 (accessed June 26, 2009).

Schickler, Eric. 2000. "Institutional Change in the House of Representatives, 1867–1998: A Test of Partisan and Ideological Power Balance Models." *American Political Science Review* 94: 269–288.

    2001. Disjointed Pluralism: Institutional Innovation and the Development of the US Congress. Princeton, NJ: Princeton University Press.

Schickler, Eric, and Andrew Rich. 1997. "Controlling the Floor: Politics as Procedural Coalitions in the House." *American Journal of Political Science* 41: 1340–1375.

Schiller, Wendy J. 1995. "The Art of Manipulation: The Use of Senate Parliamentary Procedure to Change Policy Outcomes." Paper presented at the annual meeting of the American Political Science Association, Chicago, August 31–September 3.

    2000. "Trent Lott's New Regime: Filling the Amendment Tree to Centralize Power in the U.S. Senate." Paper presented at the annual meeting of the American Political Science Association, Washington, DC, August 31–September 3.

    2001. "Majority and Minority Rights in the Senate and the Role of Party Leaders in Internal Governance." Paper presented at the 2001 Meeting of the American Political Science Association San Francisco, August 30–September 2.

Schneider, Judy. 2003. "Committee Assignment Process in the U.S. Senate: Democratic and Republican Party Procedures." *CRS Report for Congress*, Order Code RL30743.

2005. "House and Senate Rules of Procedure: A Comparison." *CRS Report for Congress*, Order Code RL 30945.

Schofield, Norman. 1978. "Instability of Simple Dynamic Games." *Review of Economic Studies* 45: 575–594.

Shepsle, Kenneth A. 1979. "Institutional Arrangements and Equilibrium in Multidimensional Voting Models." *American Journal of Political Science* 23: 27–59.

Shepsle, Kenneth A., Robert P. Van Houweling, Samuel J. Abrams, and Peter C. Hanson. 2009. "The Senate Electoral Cycle and Bicameral Appropriations Politics." *American Journal of Political Science* 53: 343–359.

Shepsle, Kenneth A., and Barry R. Weingast. 1984. "Uncovered Sets and Sophisticated Voting Outcomes with Implications for Agenda Control." *American Journal of Political Science* 28: 49–74.

1987. "The Institutional Foundations of Committee Power." *American Political Science Review* 81: 85–104.

Shugart, Matthew Soberg, and John M. Carey. 1992. *Presidents and Assemblies.* Cambridge: Cambridge University Press.

Sinclair, Barbara. 1989. *The Transformation of the U.S. Senate*. Baltimore: Johns Hopkins University Press.

1997. *Unorthodox Lawmaking: New Legislative Processes in the U.S. Congress.* Washington, DC: Congressional Quarterly Press.

2001a. "The New World of US Senators." In Lawrence C. Dodd and Bruce I. Oppenheimer, eds., *Congress Reconsidered*, 7th ed., Washington, DC: Congressional Quarterly Press, pp. 1–20.

2001b. "The Senate Leadership Dilemma: Passing Bills and Pursuing Partisan Advantage in a Nonmajoritarian Chamber." In Nicol C. Rae and Colton C. Campbell, eds., *The Contentious Senate*. Lanham, MD: Rowman & Littlefield, pp. 65–90.

2002. "The '60-Vote Senate': Strategies, Process and Outcomes." In Bruce I. Oppenheimer, ed, *U.S. Senate Exceptionalism*. Columbus: Ohio State University Press, pp. 241–260.

2005. "The New World of U.S. Senators." In Lawrence C. Dodd and Bruce I. Oppenheimer eds., *Congress Reconsidered*, 8th ed. Washington, DC: Congressional Quarterly Press, pp. 1–22.

2007. *Unorthodox Lawmaking: New Legislative Processes in the U.S. Congress,* 3d ed. Washington, DC: Congressional Quarterly Press.

Sloan, Steven, and Joseph J. Schatz. 2010. "GOP Ends Blockade; Financial Bill Moves." *CQ Weekly Online* (May 3, 2010): 1092–1093. http://library.cqpress.com/cqweekly/weeklyreport111-000003653775 (accessed October 10, 2010).

Smith, Steven S. 1989. *Call to Order: Floor Politics in the House and Senate.* Washington, DC: Brookings Institution Press.

2005. "Parties and Leadership in the Senate." In Paul J. Quirk and Sarah A. Binder, eds., *American Institutions of Democracy: The Legislative Branch*. New York: Oxford University Press, pp. 255–278.

2007. *Party Influence in Congress.* Cambridge: Cambridge University Press.

Smith, Steven S., and Eric Lawrence. 1997. "Party Control of Committees in the Republican Congress." In Lawrence Dodd and Bruce Oppenheimer, eds., *Congress Reconsidered,* 6th ed. Washington, DC: Congressional Quarterly Press, pp. 163–192.

Smith, Steven S., and Marcus Flathman. 1989. "Managing the Senate Floor: Complex Unanimous Consent Agreements since the 1950s." *Legislative Studies Quarterly* 14: 349–374.

Smith, Steven S., Jason M. Roberts, and Ryan Vander Wielen. 2006. *The American Congress,* 4th ed. New York: Cambridge University Press.

Stepan, Alfred, and Cindy Skach. 1994. "Presidentialism and Parliamentarism Compared." In Juan J. Linz and Arturo Valenzuela, eds., *The Failure of Presidential Democracy.* Baltimore: Johns Hopkins University Press, pp. 119–136.

Stolberg, Sheryl Gay, Edmund L. Andrews, Carl Hulse, and David D. Kirkpatrick. 2005. "As August Recess Looms, Congress Finds High Gear." *New York Times,* July 27.

Strahan, Randall. 2002. "Leadership and Institutional Change in the Nineteenth-Century House." In David Brady and Mathew D. McCubbins, eds., *Party, Process, and Political Change in Congress: New Perspectives on the History of Congress.* Stanford, CA: Stanford University Press, pp. 237–269.

Swift, Elain K. 1996. *The Making of an American Senate: Reconstitutive Change in Congress, 1787–1841.* Ann Arbor: University of Michigan Press.

Tiefer, Charles. 1989. *Congressional Practice and Procedure: A Reference, Research, and Legislative Guide.* New York: Greenwood Press.

Tomz, Michael, Jason Wittenberg, and Gary King. 2001. *CLARIFY: Software for Interpreting and Presenting Statistical Results. Version 2.0.* Cambridge, MA: Harvard University, June 1, http://gking.harvard.edu.

Trochim, William M. K., and James P. Donnelly. 2007. *The Research Methods Knowledge Base,* 3d ed. Mason, OH: Atomic Dog Publishing.

Tsebelis, George. 1995. "Decision Making in Political Systems: Veto Players in Presidentialism, Parliamentarism, Multicameralism and Multipartyism." *British Journal of Political Science* 25: 289–325.

Tsebelis, George, and Jeannette Money. 1997. *Bicameralism.* Cambridge: Cambridge University Press.

Van Dongen, Rachel. 2006a. "Frist Lets Estate Tax Revision Simmer as He Looks for Support." *CQ Weekly Online* (July 10): 1876, http://library.cqpress.com/cqweekly/weeklyreport109-000002321883 (accessed June 26, 2009).

2006b. "House Backs Compromise Estate Tax Cut." *CQ Weekly Online* (June 26): 1788, http://library.cqpress.com/cqweekly/weeklyreport109-000002312127 (accessed June 26, 2009).

Van Dongen, Rachel, and Daphne Retter. 2006. "Negotiators Look at Kyl Plan to Bolster Estate Tax Overhaul." *CQ Weekly Online* (June 19): 1704, http://library.cqpress.com/cqweekly/weeklyreport109-000002305997 (accessed June 26, 2009).

Van Houweling, Robert P. 2003. "Legislators' Personal Policy Preferences and Partisan Legislative Organization." Ph.D. dissertation, Harvard University.

Walker, Jack L. 1977. "Setting the Agenda in the U.S. Senate: A Theory of Problem Selection." *British Journal of Political Science* 7: 423–445.

Wawro, Gregory J., and Eric Schickler. 2004. "Where's the Pivot? Obstruction and Lawmaking in the Pre-cloture Senate." *American Journal of Political Science* 48(4): 758–774.

    2006. *Filibuster: Obstruction and Lawmaking in the U.S. Senate*. Princeton, NJ: Princeton University Press.

Weingast, Barry R. 1992. "Fighting Fire with Fire: Amending Activity and Institutional Change in the Postreform Congress." In Roger Davidson, ed., *The Postreform Congress*. New York: St. Martin's Press, pp. 142–168.

Weingast, Barry R., and William Marshall. 1988. "The Industrial Organization of Congress." *Journal of Political Economy* 96: 132–163.

Weisman, Jonathan. 2005. "GOP Agenda in Congress May Be at Risk; Katrina's Costs, High Fuel Prices Working against More Tax Cuts." *Washington Post*, September 4.

Wilkerson, John. 1999. "Killer Amendments in Congress." *American Political Science Review* 93(3): 1–18.

Williamson, Oliver E. 1985. *The Economic Institutions of Capitalism*. New York: Free Press.

Wines, Michael. 1993a. "Senators Approve a Bill That Eases Voter Registration." *New York Times*, March 18.

    1993b. "Accord Reached on Easing Voter Registration" *New York Times*, April 29.

Yakee, Susan Webb. 2003. "Punctuating the Congressional Agenda: Strategic Scheduling by House and Senate Leaders." *Political Research Quarterly* 56: 139–149.

Index

Note: A page number followed by a t indicates a table, an f indicates a figure, and an n followed by a number indicates a footnote. In subheadings SQ means status quo, NO_L means left end of no-offer zone, and NO_R means right end of no-offer zone.